WITHOUT RESERVATION

BENJAMIN REIFEL

AND AMERICAN INDIAN ACCULTURATION

WITHOUT RESERVATION

SEAN J. FLYNN

South Dakota Historical Society Press

Pierre

Library of Congress Cataloging-in-Publication data
is available.

This publication is funded, in part, by the Great Plains
Education Foundation, Aberdeen, S.Dak.

Printed in the United States of America

The paper in this book meets the guidelines for
permanence and durability of the Committee on
Production Guidelines for Book Longevity of
the Council on Library Resources.

Please visit our website at sdhspress.com

18 19 20 21 22 1 2 3 4 5

Cover: Benjamin Reifel, congressional portrait, c. 1960.
Library of Congress

Frontispiece: Benjamin Reifel, c. 1946. *South Dakota State University Archives*

For EU customers with safety / GPSR concerns, contact:
Mare Nostrum Group B.V.
Mauritskade 21D, 1091 GC Amsterdam, The Netherlands
gpsr@mare-nostrum.co.uk

Design by Rich Hendel

To Deborah

CONTENTS

ACKNOWLEDGMENTS

Research for this book began and ended in the South Dakota State University (SDSU) Archives and Special Collections in Brookings, the repository for the Benjamin Reifel Papers. Archivist Crystal Gamradt and the staff were knowledgeable and helpful, particularly when it came time for me to select photographs that chronicled the life of Ben Reifel. It was a pleasure working with them to highlight the life of one of SDSU's most accomplished and beloved alumni.

The staffs at the following archives and libraries contributed in no small way to the completion of this book: Archives of the State Historical Society of North Dakota in Bismarck; Center for Western Studies at Augustana University in Sioux Falls, South Dakota; Karl E. Mundt Archives at Dakota State University in Madison, South Dakota; National Archives and Records Administration in Kansas City, Missouri; North Dakota State Library in Bismarck; South Dakota State Historical Society Archives in Pierre; and the University of South Dakota Archives and Special Collections in Vermillion.

The employees of the *Sisseton* (S.Dak.) *Courier* granted me access to their newspaper archive and took the time to help me analyze Roberts County election results from the 1950s and 1960s. Their hospitality was greatly appreciated.

Kevin Kenkel, director of learning resources at Dakota Wesleyan University (DWU), met my research requests and served as my principal guide on technology matters. Kevin's support for the DWU Department of History is unmatched. I also wish to thank Laurie Langland, our archivist at DWU, for her willingness to search the university's archives for materials related to the career of Ben Reifel.

I am grateful to DWU for granting me a sabbatical in the fall of 2014 to complete my research and write a large portion of the book. My colleague at DWU, Professor John Husmann, in addition to being a first-rate historian and a discerning student of American Indian history, spent many hours listening to my ruminations on the life and times of Ben Reifel.

In 2015, Ben Reifel's daughter, Loyce Anderson, invited me into her home in Delta, Colorado, where Loyce, her daughter, Laurie Elendu, and I spent a day discussing my manuscript and examining photographs of Ben's public and private lives. It was the single most rewarding day of my research journey. Laurie deserves special recognition for the time and care she took in preparing photographs for this book.

Jon K. Lauck, John E. Miller, and Donald C. Simmons Jr. chose to include my essay on Ben Reifel and South Dakota politics in the second volume of their *The Plains Political Tradition: Essays on South Dakota Political Culture*. Their interest in my topic helped launch the writing of this book.

It has been a privilege to work with the staff at the South Dakota Historical Society Press (SDHSP). Their professionalism and advice through the various stages of the publication process enhanced the quality of my work. I specifically wish to thank my chief contact at SDHSP, Jennifer McIntyre, who guided the manuscript through to publication.

Over the past seven years, Sean, William, and Cathleen routinely asked their father about the progress of his book on Ben Reifel. May they appreciate how important their love and support was to the completion of the book.

My greatest debt of gratitude is owed to my wife. Deb accompanied me on research trips, sifted through archival records, paged through old newspapers, commented on parts of my manuscript, and endured the ups and downs of the writing process. Her help in my writing of chapter 6 was critical to its completion. With love and affection, I dedicate this book to Deb; I could not have written it without her.

INTRODUCTION

An Indian American Story

In the decade after his retirement from Congress in 1971, Benjamin ("Ben") Reifel, a bilingual member of the Rosebud Sioux Tribe of South Dakota, found his loyalty being questioned by a small but media-savvy group of American Indian activists. His accusers did not dispute his love of country, for no reasonable person could impugn Reifel's patriotism or devotion to public service. As a young man, he had been inspired by the words of Benjamin Franklin and the life of Abraham Lincoln, who, like Reifel, was born in a log cabin in a remote corner of the United States. Reifel had served in World War II and, after the war, remained in the United States Army Reserve at the rank of lieutenant colonel. In addition to completing five terms in the United States House of Representatives, Reifel had enjoyed a distinguished career with the Bureau of Indian Affairs. When in 1960 he embarked on a campaign to become the first American Indian congressman from South Dakota, it was as a Republican candidate in a conservative district that numbered only forty-five hundred American Indians. During his three decades in public service, Reifel encouraged American Indians to exhibit greater initiative and self-reliance. He never tired of praising American institutions or highlighting the opportunities created by the free enterprise system. He established Boy Scout troops for reservation boys, urged Indian students to enroll in white schools, and reminded scores of Indian audiences of the rewards awaiting any citizen who was punctual, worked hard, and saved money.

In short, American Indian activists (as well as white bigots) had to concede that Ben Reifel was a loyal and enthusiastic American.

And yet it was precisely his loyalty to American values and institutions that animated activists to charge Reifel with disloyalty of another more grievous kind. According to many of the Red Power radicals who burst onto the political scene in the 1960s, any American Indian conforming to the conventions of white society betrayed his or her indigenous culture. Reifel's personal philosophy and lifestyle indicated that he had renounced his racial heritage. His repeated assertions that more Indians should move away from reservations and join mainstream society contradicted the manifesto of self-proclaimed "real Indians" who rejected middle-class aspirations, demanded the return of ancestral lands, and championed the restoration of traditional customs, economic practices, and political orders. Red militants declared their opposition to integration; instead of joining American society, they argued, Indians should withdraw from it. In their view, Reifel's decades-long crusade to depopulate Indian reservations, modernize their inhabitants, and integrate them into white society amounted to a repudiation of American Indian culture. Reifel's integrationist agenda was revealing of his underlying nature, they said. He was at times referred to as an "apple Indian"—red on the outside but white on the inside. Hence the militants ridiculed Reifel's example and swept his integrationist goals to the side.

Insinuations that he had betrayed his race wounded Reifel, who resigned himself to the likelihood that, despite his record of achievement in the white man's world, he might not be acknowledged as an American Indian role model. His success in the white man's terms had precluded him, it appeared, from being representative of the modern Indian leader. Though much better versed in his native tongue and culture than many Indian activists, Reifel was, after all, born to an Indian mother and a non-Indian father and was thus suspect in the minds of radicals (most of whom were of mixed racial descent themselves and, unlike Reifel, ignorant of their tribal languages). Reifel maintained that in the struggle to improve living standards on Indian reservations, college-educated Indians were more valuable than tribal traditionalists. And yet it was the traditionalists who were the focus of the radicals' adulation. Reifel's practical approach to Indian affairs, he suspected, had been replaced by an anti-assimilationist, separatist, and cultural-nationalist ideology that appeared to have embedded itself in the American Indian consciousness. His suspicions were probably well founded, considering that today, in his home state of South Dakota, Reifel's name may be better-recognized by non-Indians than Indians.

Despite his reputation among activists as an "apple Indian," Reifel remained unapologetic about the life he led and the integrationist philosophy he professed. His career was proof, he said, of the equality of opportunity that defined the American experience. His was an Indian version of the Horatio Alger story. The son of a Brulé Lakota mother and a German American father, Reifel had, at the age of nineteen, resigned himself to a life as an undereducated rancher on the Rosebud Sioux Indian Reservation. Everything changed when white acquaintances encouraged him to attend a vocational high school on the campus of South Dakota State College (SDSC) in Brookings. Reifel earned his high school diploma in three years and then enrolled in college, a rare occurrence for an American Indian in the 1920s. He excelled in and out of the classrooms of SDSC, and his agricultural background, academic record, leadership skills, and command of the Lakota language attracted the attention of Bureau of Indian Affairs officials seeking to place American Indians as field agents on the nation's Indian reservations.

Reifel's hiring by the bureau in 1933 coincided with revolutionary changes in Indian policy associated with Indian Commissioner John Collier, the architect of the "Indian New Deal." Because of Reifel's knowledge of the Lakota language and his close relationship with many reservation residents, he was asked to explain, and in most cases translate, the contents of the landmark Indian Reorganization Act (IRA) to Lakota audiences. Though he sometimes encountered resistance to his presentations, he succeeded in winning Lakota support for the IRA. Reifel was promoted to organizational field agent and became a pivotal figure in deliberations that culminated in the Oglala Sioux and Rosebud Sioux tribes' adoption of IRA-model constitutions and bylaws. In his travels across the Great Plains in the 1930s and early 1940s, he helped several tribes establish new governments and modernize their agricultural economies. But Reifel also observed the pitfalls of Collier's attempt to revive traditional Indian cultures, an objective that in Reifel's opinion reinforced outmoded customs and behaviors that were incompatible with private enterprise, self-reliance, and modern workplace expectations.

Following four years in the United States Army during and after World War II, Reifel was appointed superintendent of the Fort Berthold Indian Reservation in North Dakota. The assignment proved to be his most challenging and controversial, a consequence of the inundation of Fort Berthold lands by the massive Garrison Dam and Reservoir project. Reifel's tenure at Fort Berthold was temporarily interrupted by his acceptance into a graduate program in public administration at Harvard University where, from 1949 to 1952, Reifel earned a Ph.D. degree, possibly the only such degree awarded by Harvard to an American Indian at that point in history. His doctoral dissertation provided a relocation plan for the Three Affiliated Tribes, though the study also addressed universal issues affecting northern plains reservations, most notably the seemingly intractable problems associated with overpopulation, teenage pregnancies, and unemployment.

In 1954, Reifel returned to South Dakota as superintendent of the Pine Ridge Indian Reservation, widely recognized as one of the two most demanding Bureau of Indian Affairs field offices on one of the country's poorest reservations. It was the height of the Eisenhower administration's push to "terminate" the federal-tribal relationship (a policy shift opposed by Reifel) and relocate willing reservation Indians to communities with employment opportunities (a goal Reifel endorsed). At Pine Ridge Reifel began to articulate, in English and Lakota, his philosophy of Indian affairs, characterized by his advocacy of education, relocation, and integration. He fought to secure the Oglala land base yet urged individual Lakotas to adopt middle-class values and conform to Western concepts of "time, work, and saving." He enforced school attendance, harangued negligent parents, and punished law breakers. He stressed the differences between traditional culture and modern technological society while warning Pine Ridge residents that their rejection of the white man's world would resign their children to inferior schools, unemployment, and poverty. If Indians were to retain their independence and dignity, Reifel insisted, they must follow the example of other minority groups who embraced the economic values of American life yet continued to celebrate their African, Asian, European, or Latino heritages. By seizing educational opportunities provided by public and private organizations, American Indians could merge into the mainstream without sacrificing their cultural identity.

In 1955, Reifel received a capstone appointment to director of the

Aberdeen Area Bureau of Indian Affairs Office, a heavy administrative responsibility that encompassed all of the reservations, hospitals, and schools in North Dakota, South Dakota, and Nebraska. Reifel's tenure as director, besides affording him the opportunity to share his ideas with a wider audience, captured the attention of South Dakota political leaders. In early 1960, when he was only a few years removed from retirement and a comfortable government pension, Reifel was approached by local Republican leaders and asked to run for the vacant seat in South Dakota's First House District. After wavering for several weeks, he accepted the challenge. His grasp on agricultural matters, his embodiment of small town values, and his expertise in Indian affairs impressed the white voters of eastern South Dakota. In what can only be described as a historic election, Ben Reifel changed the face of South Dakota politics by winning the Republican nomination and then the general election. He became the first (and only) American Indian congressman in South Dakota history and one of only seven American Indians elected to the United States Congress.

During his ten years in the United States House of Representatives, Reifel divided his time between agriculture policy and Indian affairs. A moderate-conservative Republican, he was initially assigned to the House Agriculture Committee and then in 1963 surprised pundits by winning a seat on the powerful House Appropriations Committee. Some of his contributions to Great Plains agriculture included legislation to market surplus and nonsurplus crops, build experiment and research facilities, and establish a sugar beet industry in eastern South Dakota. Reifel obtained funding for irrigation studies and fought to divert Missouri River waters to farms, communities, and industries. Outside of agriculture, he vigorously supported the arts and humanities and took up the cause of civil rights. Reifel found little that he liked about the Great Society and War on Poverty, but he defended President Lyndon B. Johnson during the Tet Offensive and went on to support the Nixon administration's foreign policy objectives. He worked closely with Senator Karl E. Mundt and together their lobbying efforts culminated in the placement of the United States Geological Survey's Earth Resources Observation Systems (EROS) Data Center near the city of Sioux Falls.

Congressman Reifel left his mark on Indian country, specifically in the areas of health, education, and justice. He authored legislation to compensate the Crow Creek Sioux Tribe for losses stemming from the Big Bend Dam project. He procured appropriations for Indian health services and for reservation construction projects. His major floor speech on Indian affairs in 1965 secured his place as a foremost authority on reservation society, and his testimony before the House Rules Committee on the Indian Civil Rights Act of 1968 proved pivotal to the passage of that measure. Reifel's greatest political accomplishment—and one illustrative of his concern for Indian education—was his procuring of millions of dollars to finance the construction of three public schools on two South Dakota reservations. During his decade in Washington, Reifel implored his congressional colleagues to remain patient about the slow pace of change in Indian country while encouraging American Indians to cast off their victim mentality and seize educational opportunities not provided to other social groups.

After fulfilling a five-term pledge he made in 1960, Reifel retired from Congress to begin volunteer work with the National Park Service, an organization he had supported from his seat on the Appropriations Committee. He did consulting work for Indian tribes and among his numerous titles he was chairman of the National Capital Planning Board and executive officer of the American Indian National Bank. In late 1976, President Gerald R. Ford appointed Reifel—his old friend and colleague—to the post of commissioner of Indian Affairs, a position Reifel vacated shortly after Jimmy Carter's inauguration in January 1977.

Though occasionally frustrated by American Indians' resistance to change, Reifel stayed committed to integration. He looked to the day when American Indians would enjoy the fruits of full citizenship, a status within their reach if they buried their prejudices toward white society, succeeded in school, and escaped their segregated surroundings to enter off-reservation communities as contributors to the American economy. Reifel envisaged a world without reservations, or at least without the poverty-oppressed reservations that characterize Indian life on the northern plains. "A reservation is fast becoming just a place where some Indians were born," he was fond of saying. "The United States is the Indian citizen's 'reservation' today."

As previously noted, Reifel's prescription for Indian success was roundly rejected by Indian activists, whose sloganeering, flamboyant behavior, and militant theatrics attracted media attention and convinced the nation's cultural elite that if Indians were simply left to their own designs, their self-worth, economic well-being, and social welfare would undergo marked improvement. (A quick road trip through South Dakota Indian country, home to some of the worst poverty in the United States, will allow the reader to draw his or her own conclusions about the wisdom of that prophecy.) Reifel, on the other hand, predicted that conditions on reservations would remain bleak until many more of their residents were absorbed into white communities. A self-described "Indian American" who was "first and last" an American citizen, Reifel, though determined to protect the Indian land base, believed that reservations segregated their occupants in overpopulated, unhealthy socioeconomic pockets unsuited for a reasonable quality of life. The vast majority of individual Indians, if they were sincere about raising their standards of living, would not do so, Reifel submitted, by remaining on reservations.

Ben Reifel's legacy is that of an acculturated American Indian of national stature whose regard for the institutions of white society did not diminish his racial pride. As one who had successfully straddled two cultures, Reifel advised American Indians that they would enjoy economic and political equality only when they integrated and became self-reliant citizens, a transition that would not, he asserted, subvert their cultural values. An account of Reifel's life may not impact the American Indian consciousness. Reifel's example, though, suggests that there is more to American Indian history than ethnohistorical studies, Little Big Horn, Wounded Knee, the American Indian Movement, and dreary accounts of reservation life. His biography might offer an alternative to scholarly works that cast American Indians as victims of conquest or narrowly define them in terms of their eighteenth- and nineteenth-century cultures. At the very least, Reifel's story may contribute to a neglected topic in American Indian studies: the lives of twentieth-century American Indians who joined and prospered in the American mainstream without forsaking their racial identity. Ben Reifel may have been an Indian American, but that is no reason to deny him his place as an important figure of American Indian history.

1 A VERY UNUSUAL YOUNG MAN

Ben Reifel was the son of an interracial marriage that was itself the product of a reservation environment shaped by decades of government efforts to assimilate American Indians. Reifel's personal values, political outlook, and viewpoint on the American Indian condition are attributable to his upbringing in a bicultural household. But his worldview was likewise molded by his childhood experiences on the Rosebud Sioux Indian Reservation, where Reifel witnessed his Lakota friends and relatives adjusting—or failing to adjust—to modern American society. Thus an examination of the life of a principal American Indian proponent of American Indian integration begins with an overview of how the Lakota Sioux responded to efforts by federal officials, philanthropists, and white settlers to assimilate them in the decades before and after Reifel's birth in 1906. It was against the backdrop of the government's assimilation program that Ben Reifel's attitude toward Indian and non-Indian cultures began to take shape.

From the time of the administration of President Ulysses S. Grant (1869–77), the federal government's solution to the "Indian problem" had been to confine tribes to reservations where, ideally, they would be "Americanized" by their exposure to agriculture, schools, Christianity, Anglo-American political concepts, and free enterprise. Assigned in the Fort Laramie Treaty of 1868 to an agency on the Missouri River in the southeast corner of the Great Sioux Reservation, Ben Reifel's tribe, the Brulé Sioux, one of the seven divisions of the Lakota people, resisted Americanization. But the discovery of gold in the Black Hills in 1874 forced change on the Brulés and their fellow Lakotas. As whites descended on the Black Hills, officials in Washington ordered all Sioux, including the still-nomadic "hostiles" living outside the confines of the Great Sioux Reservation, to retire within reservation borders. When a large group of recalcitrant Lakotas failed to heed federal warnings, the United States Army descended upon them. Though the defiant Lakotas (and their Cheyenne allies) won a spectacular victory at the Battle of the Little Big Horn in June 1876, the scale and coordination of the army expedition eventually broke Indian resistance. In the aftermath of Little Big Horn, writes Paul L. Hedren, "Sioux Country had changed hands. . . . For both Indians and whites, a new day had arrived on the northern plains."[1] The Sioux ceded the Black Hills to the United States. They saw their material possessions destroyed. They lost access to their hunting grounds, experienced a dissolution of their military culture, and faced an acculturation policy that compelled them to adopt an agriculture-centered, individualistic, and self-supporting lifestyle that, in his teen years, Ben Reifel came to appreciate.[2]

In 1878, the Rosebud Sioux relocated to an agency west of the Missouri River and south of the White River in south-central Dakota Territory. To the west lay the Pine Ridge Agency, home to the Oglala Sioux, while further north lay the Standing Rock, Cheyenne River, Lower Brule, and Crow Creek Agencies. Together, these agencies became the scene of a grand experiment on the part of reformers and federal officials to extinguish tribalism and hasten the individualization of Indians through the introduction of private ownership, farming and husbandry, formal education, and Christianity.

Ben Reifel's Lakota ancestors were stubborn experimental subjects. Deprived of military activities, their traditional economy ruined by the destruction of the bison, the Lakota nevertheless sought to preserve the old ways. Within the confines of their agencies they retained band ties, followed the counsel of elders and spiritual leaders, and sang and danced to their music. Lakota males, determined to define their self-worth through a hunter-warrior lifestyle, gunned down government-issue steers from the backs of horses while women butchered and dried the meat.[3] On the Rosebud Agency, Chief Spotted Tail, asserting that his followers were a premodern people that could not be hurried into a self-reliant lifestyle, obstructed the introduction of agriculture, education, and

Christianity. The Brulés obeyed their leader by ignoring the government's farming program, policing themselves, and denouncing Christian schools as unsuitable for Lakota children.[4]

Though their attempts to sustain tribal communalism earned the respect of some army officers and Indian agents, the Lakota people could not (as Ben Reifel later insisted) ignore the preponderance of Euro-American culture. Military posts ringed Indian country. Land rushes, the Northern Pacific Railroad, cattle ranching, the public's impatience with frontier lawlessness, and the determination of Easterners to solve "the Sioux problem" hastened the decline of traditional culture. For architects of federal Indian policy, the reservations themselves became, in the words of Francis Paul Prucha, "an abomination, for they symbolized the great separation between the Indians and the rest of American society, a separation that precluded the absolute Americanization that was the goal of the reform organizations and their friends in the government."[5]

Americanization called for the integration of exiled Indian communities. That goal could be accomplished through, among other things, the introduction of Indians to farming and the trades, the substitution of Christian liturgy for the sun dance, the repudiation of polygamous marriages, and formal instruction in the English language and American civics. In a show of resistance to these changes, some Indians became listless and idle. They mocked and insulted the conformists among them who "scratched the ground." Their defiance, however, would not resurrect buffalo culture. Bands began breaking up. Dressed hides and buffalo robes were exchanged for woven cloth. Individual families took to living on homesteads that included a log cabin and a small patch of farmland. Some Lakota men engaged in cattle ranching, while others found work freighting annuity goods from Missouri River docks and Nebraska railheads to Indian agencies. A few worked for the Indian police force, which, in addition to paying wages of ten to fifteen dollars a month, provided each police officer with a uniform, a log house, and extra government rations.[6]

Despite the government's attempt to expand Indian agriculture on the northern plains, most Lakotas declined to participate. They remained confident that the Great White Father, having guaranteed them annual provisions in the Fort Laramie Treaty, would not let them starve. Indian agents provided government rations on a regular basis, thus removing any incentive for individuals to become self-sustaining farmers or ranchers.[7] In 1884, J. G. Wright, agent for the Rosebud Sioux, observed that many Brulé families continued their nomadic ways. "An Indian will build for himself a log house, plow and fence a small track of land," Wright wrote. "At the expiration of the season, if not before, he will . . . go to or with his relatives to another locality, and do all the work again for another season."[8] When the occasional Lakota tried farming, there were no assurances that the arid climate, severe winters, and unfavorable soil of southwestern South Dakota would support his small operation. In reports filed in 1893 and 1895, the agent at the Rosebud Reservation emphasized that much of the land was not well suited for crops. For Sioux farmers, "the results have been and are almost invariably the same, yielding no return for labor spent."[9] Nevertheless, their exposure to farming and stock raising remained, in the minds of Bureau of Indian Affairs officials, an essential means of introducing Lakotas to the Euro-American work ethic and its corresponding value of self-reliance.[10]

The transformation of Indians to fully integrated citizens—a principal object of Ben Reifel's own Bureau of Indian Affairs career—required a formal education that stressed English literacy, vocational training, Christian morality, civics, and American history. Schooling would replace the nomadic Indian's values with others that, in the words of Commissioner of Indian Affairs Thomas J. Morgan, prepared Indians "to compete successfully with the white man on his ground and with his own methods." The rewards of joining mainstream American society included a "fraternal and harmonious relationship" with white Americans, "refined homes," the benefits of commerce and trade, an opportunity to travel, and the intellectual and spiritual edification that came from one's acquaintance with literature, science, philosophy, and a "true religion." At its most fundamental level, noted Morgan, American education encouraged "self-reliance and self-respect," cardinal virtues that would bring about "the disintegration of the tribes, and not their segregation."[11]

Education became the cornerstone of the assimilation policy. Rosebud Sioux parents who accepted the importance of schools for their children's adjustment to white society chose from three types of institutions: reservation day schools, reservation boarding schools, and off-reservation boarding schools at such locations as Lawrence, Kansas, and Pierre and Flandreau, South Dakota. Despite the sometimes crude conditions of the school buildings, Brulé parents, most of whom were resistant to sending their children to distant boarding schools, resigned themselves to schools on the Rosebud Reservation, which, by 1897, included twenty-one day schools, two mission boarding schools, and a government boarding school. Some parents who sent their sons and daughters to school did so out of fear of losing their rations or in the hope that their children's attendance would result in cash payments from the government. Whatever their motivations were, all Lakota parents worried about the effects of the white man's schools on their children. They understood, observes Robert M. Utley, that the white man's education "represented the most dangerous of all attacks on basic Indian values, the one most likely to succeed . . . because it aimed at the children, who had known little of the old life."[12]

The old life, exemplified in the tribal practice of communal land ownership, was dealt a grievous blow when President Grover Cleveland signed into law the General Allotment Act, or Dawes Act, on 8 February 1887. The product of mounting impatience among budget-conscious lawmakers, Eastern "Friends of the Indian," and land-hungry whites eager to occupy "surplus" Indian lands, the Dawes Act authorized the surveying of reservations and the assignment of land allotments, ranging in size from 40 to 160 acres, to individual Indians. Allottees were granted four years to select their property sites, after which time the secretary of the Interior would assume control of the distribution process. Individual Indians whose allotments were federally approved would become United States citizens and be issued land patents held in trust by the federal government for a period of twenty-five years. At the expiration of the trust period, an Indian received his or her property in fee simple. Unallotted or "surplus" reservation lands would be purchased by the Interior Department and sold to white homesteaders, with proceeds from the sales held in a Treasury Department trust fund on behalf of the tribes.[13]

With the passage of the Dawes Act, the reformers who declared tribal communalism the chief obstacle to Indian self-reliance won their signature legislative victory. Two years later, the Sioux Act of 1889 paved the way for the reduction of the Great Sioux Reserve and the division of the Teton Sioux land base into six separate reservations. Worn down by federal negotiators and the admission of the states of North Dakota and South Dakota a foregone conclusion, the Teton Sioux ceded over 9 million acres in a massive land transfer that opened a migratory corridor from Chamberlain on the Missouri River to Rapid City in the mineral-rich Black Hills of western South Dakota.[14] Social stresses brought on by the allotment law, shrinking land holdings, reduced rations, crop failures, and disease left the Teton Sioux disposed toward a religious movement founded by Wovoka, a Paiute Indian from Nevada. Banned from holding traditional ceremonies, many Plains Indians welcomed Wovoka's teachings and began performing the Ghost Dance that distinguished his syncretic religion. The Paiute messiah announced that a new world, one without the presence of whites, awaited the Indian race. There Indians would enjoy eternal life amid relatives, friends, and great herds of buffalo.[15]

Many Lakotas, some Brulés among them, were attracted to the prophecies of Wovoka. Even those who were skeptical of his teachings (the Hunkpapa headman Sitting Bull was among the skeptics) were impressed by the rejuvenating effect they had on the people.[16] A few men, meanwhile, rejected Wovoka's pacifism and recast the Ghost Dance as an expression of hatred toward the whites. An already volatile environment was made worse by inexperienced Indian agents whose requests for a show of military force made violence all but inevitable. Groups of ghost dancers fled into the Badlands. Sitting Bull died on 15 December 1890, when an attempt by Indian police to arrest him went awry. A column of 340 Minneconjous, Brulés, and Hunkpapas, led by a Minneconjou named Big Foot, struck out for the Badlands, where, on 28 December they were intercepted by the United States Seventh Cavalry and led to a spot near Wounded Knee Creek. The following day as the soldiers prepared to disarm Big Foot's band, a few impulsive Lakota men, incited by a medicine man named Yellow Bird, discharged their carbines and set off a bloody melee that left 146 Lakota men, women, and children dead on the field. Twenty-five members of the Seventh Cavalry were also killed in the tragic Wounded Knee Massacre, the final armed confrontation between the United States and the Plains Indians.[17]

For the Lakotas, the Wounded Knee incident, which occurred when Ben Reifel's mother was eleven years old, exposed the futility of resisting the Euro-American presence among them. Whatever traditional heritage they hoped to retain must fit within a new cultural framework that rewarded individual initiative, private ownership, daily labor, and self-reliance, a complex of values that Ben Reifel adhered to in his adult life. If the Lakotas chose to defy Americanization, they would do so against the wishes of a white public determined to incorporate American Indians into the fabric of American society. In the final decade of the nineteenth century and the first decade of the twentieth century, at the height of the Progressive Era, progress in Indian affairs would be measured by the degree to which individual Indians transitioned to American institutions and self-supporting lifestyles, on and off the reservation.[18]

The effects of the transition were, at best, mixed. Plains Indians endured, in the words of Paul H. Carlson, "poverty, deprivation, shoddy housing, and poor health." And yet despite their substandard living conditions, "reservation life was not abject wretchedness." Cultural traditions survived. Others were invented. Extended family ties and some social organizations remained intact. School-age Indians "adapted quickly to altered conditions," to the degree that "some of them . . . remembered parts of their boarding school experience with fondness."[19] By 1900, school enrollment was on the rise and some progress was being made in agriculture, with some South Dakota Indian families raising livestock, crops, and vegetables, cutting hay, and selling their commodities at local markets. Cattle herds grew so steadily after 1890 that by World War I, reservation-raised beef cattle were being marketed off the reservation. Lakota men were also earning nonagricultural income in a variety of pursuits. Working as a freighter was especially popular, though other opportunities included police work, general labor, cooking, and carpentry.[20]

Still, despite signs of economic progress, there was no denying the overwhelming problems plaguing the Lakota Sioux. Possessed of a mystical attitude toward the land, perplexed by the concept of private ownership, and averse to tilling the soil, few Lakota men took to farming. As noted, some showed an interest in stock raising, and for a short time in the early 1900s, a beef cattle industry appeared on South Dakota reservations. But the division of lands by allotment and the selling of herds during the lucrative World War I years doomed the reservation cattle industry. And there remained the lack of incentive for Lakotas to derive a regular income since they could depend on government dispersals of rations (in the form of beef, bacon, flour, corn, beans, salt, coffee, sugar, baking powder, and soap), as provided for in article 5 of the Black Hills Agreement of 1877. The agreement stipulated that ration disbursements would continue only until the Indians had achieved a level of self-support and that before then, only those Indians who worked were eligible for rations. Yet in 1906, the year of Ben Reifel's birth, 5,700 of the 6,700 residents of the Pine Ridge Reservation were listed on ration rolls. The Oglalas at Pine Ridge insisted (as did the Brulés on the Rosebud Reservation) that rations were not a temporary form of assistance but a just and long-term compensation for Teton Sioux lands lost in 1877.[21]

The diminishment of the Lakota land base, of which the Black Hills Agreement was but the most dramatic example, accelerated in the two decades after the implementation of the Dawes Act. Surplus reservation lands not held by individuals fell into the hands of white buyers at an alarming rate, especially during the 1890s. Of the 91 million acres of American Indian lands lost between 1887 and 1932, two-thirds of those lands disappeared during the first decade of the allotment program.[22] Compounding the losses was a growing trend among allottees to lease or sell their property as a source of cash income or to make homestead improvements, purchase implements, or expand livestock herds.[23]

The Brulés were not exempt from additional wholesale land losses. In 1901, Indian Office Field Agent James McLaughlin negotiated an agreement with the Rosebud Sioux for the cession of 416,000 acres of unallotted lands on the eastern side of their reservation in Gregory County, South Dakota. A year later, Congressman Charles H. Burke of South Dakota introduced a bill to authorize the United States to purchase surplus properties in Gregory County and open them to white settlement. Following two years of debate, and aided by a revolutionary Supreme Court ruling empowering Congress to acquire Indian lands without obtaining a three-fourths approval vote from the Rosebud Sioux Tribe,[24] Burke's Rosebud bill became law, setting off a land rush that engulfed the 452 Indian allottees still residing in Gregory County.[25] Three years later, the occupation by white settlers of surplus lands in Tripp County reduced even further the land holdings of the Rosebud Sioux Tribe.

In 1906, another Burke-sponsored bill reverberated through Indian country. In response to the Supreme Court's ruling in *Matter of Heff* (1905), a case that legalized liquor sales to Indians holding citizenship, Burke introduced legislation that would withhold citizenship from Indian allottees until the expiration of the twenty-five-year trust period provided for in the Dawes Act. But of greater significance was a provision within the Burke Act permitting the Interior secretary, if convinced of an allottee's "competency" to manage his own affairs, to issue a fee patent before the expiration of the trust period. Though Burke may not have intended his bill to result in sweeping grants of fee simple patents, that is precisely what occurred. As Francis Paul Prucha observed, "a beginning had been made in a serious reduction of the Indian estate by premature issues of patents in fee and removal of restrictions on alienation."[26]

Thus it was that in 1906, the year of Ben Reifel's birth, the Brulé people found themselves struggling to adjust to a new language, new laws, new values, and a new economy. Their communal lifestyle, traditional practices, and cultural beliefs, it was made clear, were incompatible with Americanization. Officials and reformers pressed American Indians to become self-supportive and self-reliant within the framework of the American economy. Though still committed to their role as "guardians" of Indian tribes, federal policy makers remained confident that, through their exposure to churches, schools, and daily labor, Indians would soon be incorporated into the body politic.[27] The reduction of the Rosebud Sioux Reservation, the division of its lands into individual homesteads, the introduction of reservation agriculture, and the schooling of Brulé children were central features of the government's larger plan—the integration of all American Indians into American society as full-fledged citizens, an accomplishment that would, once and for all, resolve the nation's "Indian problem."

During this revolutionary period of Indian affairs, William M. Reifel, a German American from the state of Indiana, moved to Todd County, South Dakota, home to the largest concentration of Brulé Indians on the Rosebud Reservation. The Reifels traced their European roots to the German city of Heidelberg, situated on the Neckar River, a tributary of the Rhine in the state of Baden-Württemberg. Why the family left Germany and established in Indiana is unclear, but it is certain that sometime in the 1890s, William's older brother John and his wife Maggie moved from Terre Haute, Indiana, to South Dakota, where John became one of the first civil servants to teach in a government school on the Rosebud Reservation. William Reifel followed John to South Dakota, where he was hired by a rancher, Jack Whipple, whose spouse was a Brulé woman. It was at Whipple's Ranch within the reservation's Cut Meat District that William, better known among the people of the Rosebud by his nickname "Shorty," met Lucy Burning Breast, a Brulé woman and former student of John Reifel who worked for the Whipples. The German American ranch hand and the American Indian housekeeper were introduced, grew fond of one another, and began courting.[28]

Considering the language barrier that separated them, the courtship of William and Lucy may have been trying. William understood a few Lakota words but never became proficient in the language. For her part, Lucy, born near Cut Meat Creek in 1879, spoke little English. She learned the alphabet and some elementary English at Cut Meat Day School, but her two years of formal education concentrated primarily on the domestic arts of washing, sewing, cooking, and housekeeping. Her son Ben told a reporter that his mother was an uneducated woman who "did not go very far in the books and the 'three r's.'"[29] Much of what Lucy knew of English was picked up while working for the wives of traders and federal employees. Nonetheless, despite the language divide, Shorty and Lucy found common ground. Both were practicing Christians—Lucy had been baptized an Episcopalian and remained a devoted follower until her death—and Lucy's exposure to Euro-American institutions and values enhanced her appreciation for Shorty.[30] Over time, Lucy and Shorty fell in love, and on 1 December 1905, the two were married by an Episcopalian missionary at Whipple's Ranch.[31]

The Reifels made their home on Lucy's allotment, about two miles from Whipple's Ranch and not far from Cut Meat (now Parmelee, South Dakota). Shorty built a dirt-roof log cabin, dug a well, raised a barn, and started a small farming operation that included a few milk cows and work horses, some chickens, and a vegetable garden. It was in their log cabin that the Reifels' first child, a son, was born on 19 September 1906. They gave him the Christian name of Benjamin. Whites on the reservation called him Ben. Lucy's relatives referred to him by his Indian name, Wiyaka Wanjila, Lone Feather.[32]

Several years after Ben's birth, the Reifels moved to Rosebud Agency, about ten miles southeast of Cut Meat, where William operated a livery stable. The Reifel family grew, with Lucy eventually giving birth to four more sons: John (b. 1909), George (b. 1912), Alexander (b. 1913), and Albert (b. 1919). The five Reifel boys were raised in a rich bilingual environment. Ben, who in his youth was closer to his mother than his father, grew up speaking Lakota, which, beyond the walls of the Reifel home, remained the preferred language of the Brulé people. Yet Lucy insisted that her sons learn to read, write, and speak English in the reservation schools where teachers would instruct them in the ways of the whites. In her native tongue, Lucy counseled Ben that her people's way of life was being replaced by that of his father's people. Assimilate, she told him, if you wish to enjoy the good things made possible by the white people's culture.[33] As if to demonstrate her acceptance of that culture, Lucy became, according to her oldest son, an exceptional cook and housekeeper, "her washes on the clothesline . . . always the cleanest and whitest of any in our neighborhood, and this fact was often attested to by both our white and Indian neighbors."[34] But Ben's mother retained connections to her past. She slept on a light bedroll, wore moccasins (one pair of which was stuffed with grass for warmth in the winter months), still performed the traditional dances, and limited her diet to boiled meat, potatoes, and turnips. Lucy ensured that Ben was exposed to the old ways, which included assisting his Brulé grandmother (who ate her meals seated on the floor and rejected most white practices) in the digging of wild Indian turnips.[35]

Ben's first exposure to formal education was unintentional. One day in 1911, the Reifels left their five-year-old son at home while they attended to their shopping in Valentine, Nebraska. One of Ben's friends, a six-year-old named Robert Whipple, asked Ben if he wished to accompany him to school. "So I went to school with him," Reifel recalled. "I just stayed the rest of that year."[36] The school he attended was the Rosebud Agency Government Day School, where the teacher, Mr. Dailey, chewed tobacco during the school day. Reifel remained at the agency school until 1913, the year the Reifels returned to their Parmelee farm. To provide for the primary education of his sons and other area youth, which included some German-speaking children, Shorty Reifel helped construct a log school house at Parmelee. For a salary of twenty-five dollars per month plus room and board, the local parents hired Miss Peckham, who was proficient in German, to teach the children.[37]

Despite his parents' commitment to educate their sons through the eighth grade, Ben never experienced the stability enjoyed by white students living off the reservation, where teachers and facilities were more abundant and accessible. After the fifth grade, he rotated in and out of Todd County schools. He attended public schools, government day schools, and the Rosebud Boarding School. As he grew, he began to spend more time working beside his father on the Reifel farm. Reflecting on this period while serving in the United States House of Representatives, Reifel described long days spent on horseback, fixing fences, or "on a mowing machine cutting prairie grass."[38] By the age of fifteen, he was a sixth-grade dropout passing his free time in the Parmelee pool hall. But with the encouragement of Ms. Ethel Kraus (or Krauss), a teacher at the Cut Meat Day School, Reifel reenrolled in school and completed his seventh- and eighth-grade studies in a year's time. In 1923, at the age of sixteen, he was awarded an eighth-grade diploma, his final examination average the highest in Todd County for the 1922–23 academic year.[39]

Recognizing his aptitude for learning, Reifel's teachers and several Bureau of Indian Affairs officials approached him about furthering his education. Especially critical to Ben's decision to continue his schooling were the urgings of the Swedish American photographer John Anderson and his wife, Myrtle, who were friends of Shorty and Lucy Reifel. John, whose photographs of the Sioux from 1885 to 1925 form one of the finest collections of American Indian life for that period, owned a mercantile store at Rosebud where Ben worked on occasion. Ben looked upon the Andersons as his surrogate parents while the Andersons looked upon the half-Lakota teenager as a surrogate son who filled the void created by their own son's premature death. It was the Andersons who first recommended to Reifel that he enroll in the short-course agricultural high school on the campus of South Dakota State College in Brookings.[40]

Reifel's burgeoning interest in school contrasted with the negative attitudes of other Indian boys, few of whom valued formal education. Their indifference toward education, evidenced by their poor school attendance, puzzled Reifel. "I grew up on the reservation speaking Sioux all the time," he remarked later in life. "Why did not the other Indians respond as I did?"[41] After one of his uncles passed up an opportunity to attend boarding school in Rapid City, Reifel began to doubt his own ability to earn a high school diploma. Nevertheless, in Reifel's mind, education remained a miraculous thing, a doorway to a meaningful and satisfying life. Inspired by a Western dime novel with a fictional rancher who earned a master's degree, Reifel set his sights on becoming the first college-educated rancher on the Rosebud Reservation.[42]

It appeared that Reifel's dream might elude him. No high schools existed on the Rosebud Reservation and, even if they had, William and Lucy Reifel saw no value in their son's continued schooling. "Well, my mother didn't want me to leave," Reifel recalled. "She said, 'Nobody else is going away to school, nobody in the neighborhood is going away to school and you finished the eighth grade, why go on?'" William Reifel reminded his son that he himself had not progressed beyond the second or third grade but could still "read and write and figure a little bit."[43] Ben was a farmer now, he was told, his services needed by his father, who was working a half section of land and running cattle and horses. Ben may have pleaded with his parents to support his education, but even if they had been convinced by his arguments, they did not possess the financial means to support their oldest son's schooling. The Reifels were, according to Ben, "quite poor" at the time, and it appeared that if Ben were destined for anything, it was to be a half-educated operator of a Todd County ranch. "There just was never encouragement on the part of my parents," he told an interviewer in 1979.[44]

Reifel's fortunes changed when former teachers, a few family friends, and James McGregor, superintendent of the Rosebud Reservation, intervened on his behalf. They encouraged William and Lucy to lend moral support to their son. Financial support came in the form of small loans from the Andersons and the McGregors and a $550 "Sioux Benefit" payment awarded to tribal-enrolled eighteen-year-olds as compensation for unallotted tribal lands sold to non-Indians.[45] Emboldened by the opportunity, the nineteen-year-old Reifel followed the advice of John Anderson and applied to the secondary School of Agriculture at South Dakota State College in Brookings, some 290 miles from Parmelee. The School of Agriculture offered a four-year course of study with a five-month fall and winter calendar tailored to the schedules of working farm boys. Students who attended four consecutive terms were awarded a high school equivalency diploma, a document that might allow Ben Reifel to pursue his higher education dreams.[46]

In October 1925, Reifel, carrying a cosigned note for one hundred dollars courtesy of Superintendent McGregor, left the reservation. In the words of a former aide to Congressman Reifel, Ben "found a new and bewildering world—his longest trip away from the family farm on the Rosebud Indian Reservation in Todd County, his first train ride, his first experience with electric lights and running water."[47] A shy and naïve Reifel arrived at the Brookings train station with no knowledge of the city's taxi service. So he pushed his trunk of personal belongings end over end from the train station to the SDSC campus—a distance of seventeen city blocks.[48]

At this early stage of his adult life, Ben hoped to enhance his knowledge of agriculture so as to contribute more to the Reifel family farm. The son of hardworking parents and himself an ambitious young man, Reifel arrived in Brookings with his father's parting advice—"be on time, work hard, and save money"—foremost on his mind. Guided by the words, Reifel overloaded his academic schedule. He advanced quickly through English, math, horticulture, carpentry, and blacksmithing courses, and, in three consecutive school terms, earned his high school diploma a full year earlier than his classmates. Upon graduating, Reifel, age twenty-two, applied to SDSC, where he was admitted as a special student and became the recipient of one of the first college loans available to Indian students under a new program recommended by the groundbreaking Meriam Report of 1928.[49]

Reifel's achievements as a college student confirmed the value of his father's time, work, save formula. He excelled in the classroom and in SDSC's social environment, where his maturity, intellect, work ethic, and engaging personality made him, in the words of a Brookings reporter, "one of the outstanding students of the institution."[50] Reifel took a keen interest in the agricultural sciences, enrolling in such classes as advanced poultry culture, dairy husbandry, dairy bacteriology, advanced dairy inspection, veterinary anatomy and physiology, and soils. He won academic honors in chemistry and dairy science, and, to help finance his education, milked cows and worked part-time for the Department of Agriculture. He joined the United States Army Reserve Officers Training Corps and was quickly promoted to the rank of first sergeant in the SDSC Corps of Cadets. Reifel participated in several student organizations and won admission to academic fraternities such as the Alpha Zeta agriculture honor society. He served as a lay reader in a local Episcopal church and posted his first political victory when the student body elected him president of the student association for the 1931–32 academic year, a remarkable achievement for an American Indian student. A popular student leader who was known in the wider Brookings community as the "half breed Sioux . . . student president of South Dakota State college," he became the first American Indian to lead the college's annual homecoming festivity, the Hobo Day Parade. In 1932, the same year he was awarded a bachelor of science degree from SDSC, Reifel, age twenty-six, was commissioned as second lieutenant in the United States Army Reserve.[51]

Mindful that punctuality, dependability, and frugality were qualities not always valued by his mother's people, the bilingual Brulé boy from the Rosebud Reservation had successfully—and somewhat spectacularly—integrated into American society by adopting his father's Euro-American work ethic. Reifel would spend the remainder of his life urging his fellow American Indians to do the same.

Reifel's experiences at SDSC included falling in love with a classmate, Alice Janet Johnson, a blonde-haired, blue-eyed Norwegian American from Erwin, South Dakota, who earned a degree in home economics. Ben and Alice, who began dating during the 1929–30 academic year, graduated together in 1932. As it was the height of the Great Depression, they delayed their marriage until they could secure employment. Intent on returning to the Rosebud Reservation to work as a farm extension agent rather than a rancher, Reifel took the required civil service examination and began searching for a job. James McGregor, who had been transferred to the superintendent's post at the Pine Ridge Agency, attempted to place Reifel with the Indian Office Extension Service. McGregor appealed directly to the commissioner of Indian Affairs on behalf of Reifel, who he affectionately referred to as "a very unusual young man."[52] The superintendent's efforts proved unsuccessful, so following a summer assignment to an Army Reserve training camp, Reifel made his own inquiries with the United States Indian Field Service. When no job offer followed, Reifel approached the director of the Episcopal Hare Vocational School for Indian High School Boys near Mission on the Rosebud Reservation. Impressed by Reifel's agricultural background and his lay service with the Episcopal Church, officials at the Hare School, established to train boys for farm and ranch work, hired him as a counselor and "handy man" at a salary of fifty dollars a month.[53]

Hare School students attended traditional academic classes in the mornings and received agriculture and industrial instruction in the afternoons. Reifel lived in the boys' dormitory, where he served in the role of dorm proctor and tutor. During school hours his primary duty was to manage the school's livestock, but he also monitored study halls, cotaught agriculture classes, and supervised kitchen duties such as butchery. Alice, meanwhile, found work as a teacher at nearby Parmelee. Ben and Alice continued to search for more challenging opportunities while remaining grateful for their employment during the most trying of economic times.[54]

Reifel's term at the Hare School coincided with curricular changes implemented by W. Carson Ryan Jr., the Bureau of Indian Affairs director of Indian education from 1930 to 1935. A leader in the progressive education movement and a contributor to the Meriam Report, Ryan wanted reservation schools to serve all age groups within the Indian community. He envisioned greater state involvement in Indian education, an increase in the number of Indians enrolled in public schools, and a vocational curriculum tailored to what he believed were the needs of rural Indians. Ryan called for the elimination of what he termed "the segregated boarding school," and in a move that may have affected Reifel's assignment to the Hare School, he replaced Bureau of Indian Affairs school "disciplinarians" with advisors whose duties resembled those of a modern career counselor.[55] "Indians can not and should not forever remain the concern of the National Government," Ryan contended. "Sooner or later all Indians . . . will become participating citizens of the state and local community as well as of the United States." While submitting that their integration into public schools "might be better for Indians," Ryan confined his expectations for Indian success to a vocational model that stressed trade and industrial training for Indian boys and home economics for Indian girls.[56]

Whether at the Hare School or during his stints as a farm extension agent and organizational field agent in the 1930s, Reifel witnessed firsthand the strengths and weaknesses of reservation school systems. Throughout the decade, wrote an official on the Rosebud Reservation, Bureau of Indian Affairs personnel labored to design schools "to inspire the members of our community with the truly worth while results of an industrial rural life, to . . . improve their homes and their home life in general, to instruct them in . . . realizing the maximum benefit from their garden and farm produce." Nationally the government built over one hundred reservation day schools which, in addition to serving school-aged children, were meant to function as community centers. In smaller day schools, a single teacher might be responsible for instructing primary grade students while monitoring the school workshop, washing and laundering activities, the community garden, and canning programs. Day schools also served as centers for 4-H clubs, Boy Scout troops, and community theater productions.[57]

At the secondary level, institutions such as the Oglala Community High School at Pine Ridge focused their attention on vocational education. Oglala boys learned to care for cattle, build and repair fences, drill wells, and operate farm machinery. Girls practiced cooking, sewing, and general housekeeping. All students were introduced to money-handling and credit, as well as general health practices. The Oglala School was "an example of the Indian Service's effort to give its young people an education which will be a real preparation for life." Removed in many ways from the curriculum at non-Indian schools, where students enjoyed both academic and vocational course offerings, Indian schools were devoted to teaching their students about "the resources of their reservations and of the ways in which these resources are used in making a living." The practical, vocational approach to Indian education endeavored "to develop in children a rural, rather than a metropolitan, outlook on life; a realistic point of view on the part of students as to where their best chances lie."[58]

Reifel was not an impartial observer of the changes taking place in Indian education. He would later endorse Ryan's commitment to integrating Indians into public schools, and he likely supported the less autocratic, more nurturing school environment encouraged by the director. Based partly on his own experiences at SDSC, he would have applauded the ideal that "Indians must ultimately find their places in the economic and even the social life of the general community," an outcome at the heart of Reifel's philosophy of Indian affairs.[59]

On the other hand, Reifel was disappointed with Ryan's application of progressive pedagogy to reservation schools. Ryan championed a belief, grounded in the educational philosophy of John Dewey, that if schools were to be authentically democratic, they should provide both vocational and academic education. Legislatively, the Smith-Hughes Act (1917) had provided federal funds to high schools to promote vocational training in agriculture, trades and industries, and home economics.[60] Yet when applied to schools, particularly rural institutions like those in western South Dakota, the theories of progressive educators and legislators left much to be desired. According to Geoffrey Perrett, the consequence of progressive education theory "was a riot of well-meant scientism" for which there was "no unifying thread beyond a vague commitment to experimentation." Plans to combine academic and vocational education under one roof did not always translate into practice. "Different teachers, different school boards, meant different things when they spoke of 'progressive education,'" observes Perrett.[61]

It all added up to, from Reifel's viewpoint, a "lost" decade of education on Northern Plains Indian reservations. "There's nothing wrong with the John Dewey approach, if you had enough teachers well-trained and the equipment to follow the John Dewey method," Reifel observed during a 1967 interview. Such was not the case in Indian country in the 1930s. Having taken the position that "educated" Indians would remain on the reservation, the teachers prepared Indian students "to stay where they are," an approach that readied tribal youth for livestock care and gardening, but not "to read and to write and to figure." Reifel wanted reservation-based education to prepare Indian students for off-reservation opportunities, including attendance at colleges and universities where they could merge into white society. Better-trained teachers, reasoned Reifel, might have succeeded in reaching the lofty goals of the Dewey model. "But the teachers just weren't prepared for this. And as a consequence, I think they lost lots of time there." Reifel, who during the 1950s and 1960s was considered one of the nation's leading commentators on Indian education, judged the progressive education movement a failed experiment that did not prepare Indian youth for the challenges of modern society.[62]

When the Hare School academic year ended in May 1933, so did Ben Reifel's brief career as a secondary school educator. In June Superintendent James McGregor, in dire need of a civil servant with Lakota language skills and a willingness to work with Oglalas, offered Reifel the post of United States Farm Extension agent for the Oglala District of the Pine Ridge Reservation. It was the break Reifel had been waiting for, an opportunity to apply his farming experiences and university training to assist American Indian farmer-ranchers in the modernizing of their family operations.[63] After consulting with Alice, Reifel accepted McGregor's offer. It was the beginning of an extraordinary career in Indian affairs.

2 AGENT OF THE INDIAN NEW DEAL

Indian affairs in the 1930s were synonymous with the name of John Collier, a political activist and social reformer whose twelve-year tenure as commissioner of Indian Affairs (1933–45) altered the course of government policy. Supportive of New Deal reforms and encouraged by a national conversation about the limits of capitalism, Collier advanced an agenda that suspended the assimilation policy, reversed the dissolution of Indian lands, provided legal protection for tribes, established tribal self-governance, and initiated an American Indian cultural revival.[1] "The Indian New Deal," comments a noted authority on the subject, "marked the first time in the history of the Indians' relations with the government that a conscious attempt was made to take the Indian point of view into account and to shape a program to meet Indian needs rather than to reshape the Indians." At the end of the Collier era, Indian living standards still lagged far behind those of white Americans, an undisputed economic fact that plagued Ben Reifel throughout his civil service and political careers. On the other hand, American Indians became politically self-conscious in the 1930s and 1940s, a development that paved the way for "a new generation of leaders . . . more aware of the intricacies of white politics and legal procedures."[2]

As a young civil servant with the Bureau of Indian Affairs, Ben Reifel cut his professional teeth on the Indian New Deal and its centerpiece legislation, the Indian Reorganization Act. Following several months as a farm extension agent on the Pine Ridge Reservation, the bilingual Reifel began meeting with Lakota audiences to explain the text of the IRA, a measure designed to restore Indian self-government and tribal self-rule. He then earned a career-making promotion as a consultant to northern plains tribes who were drafting Anglo-American-style constitutions in conformity with IRA guidelines. Reifel applauded the protections for Indian lands provided by the IRA, and he welcomed the political authority it extended to the citizens of Indian country. He reasoned that modern, self-governing tribal councils could, in addition to renewing American Indians' self-respect, serve as civic laboratories for adjusting Indians to the principles and practices of American economic and political life.

On the other hand, Reifel did not share John Collier's enthusiasm for collectivism and tribal traditionalism. His upbringing in Indian country and his recent Bureau of Indian Affairs service convinced Reifel that, for rural Indians unable to make a living in agriculture, employment opportunities would remain scarce, with or without the IRA. If Indians were to break the cycles of reservation poverty and chronic unemployment, they would have to work in white communities. If Indian people were to succeed in those communities, Reifel concluded, they must learn to respect the white man's education system and the dominant society's valuing of individual initiative, self-reliance, and private enterprise. Collier's policy of preserving tribal communalism, he believed, would subvert American Indians' adoption of those values.

What became Reifel's signature message—Education is the Pathway to Indian Success—was formed in the hothouse of New Deal programs that curbed the assimilation policy. By the time World War II temporarily interrupted Reifel's career, he was beginning to question whether New Deal policies were reinvigorating Indian communities or were really segregating them further from the benefits of the economic mainstream. But until that time, he dedicated himself to those elements of the IRA that earned his unqualified support: the organization of tribal governments to underwrite Indian self-rule and the preservation of the Indian land base.

In the 1920s the federal government's Indian policy was assaulted by a former New York City social worker and California educator who, before a trip to Taos, New Mexico, at the age of thirty-six, had never met an American Indian. Filled with a lifelong aversion to free enterprise, individualism, and the pursuit of wealth for wealth's sake, John Collier concluded that tribally centered American Indians "possessed the fundamental secret of human life—the secret of building great personality through the instrumentality of social institutions."[3] Determined to reaffirm American Indian culture so as to save white America from what he viewed as the isolation and despair of industrial-age individualism, Collier committed himself to the preservation of Indian lands and the reanimation of tribal customs and institutions.[4]

Between 1922 and 1933, the year he was named commissioner of Indian Affairs, Collier led a high-profile attack on the Department of the Interior and the Indian Bureau. In his lobbying efforts, public comments, and writings, he denounced assimilation while promoting Indian civil rights, the preservation of Indian lands and religions, and tribal self-determination. Collier's assault on the Bursum Bill, a threat to Pueblo Indian land claims in New Mexico, condemned that legislation to failure. Through the vehicle of his American Indian Defense Association (an organization he ruled in an autocratic fashion), Collier defended Indian customs and religious ceremonies, and in 1926, he helped defeat the Leavitt Bill, a measure designed to extend federal law over Indians and expand the reach of Indian courts. In these and other causes, Collier struck at the heart of the assimilation policy, criticizing, for instance, the government's effort to introduce Christian values in reservation schools. He assailed the Bureau of Indian Affairs for trying to Americanize the Indian by converting him to Christianity, erasing his historical memory, and "forcing him to become a premature social half-breed."[5]

The election of Franklin Delano Roosevelt in 1932 signaled a new chapter of American history, one in which the federal government, through an array of New Deal programs, vastly expanded its obligations for Americans' well-being. Roosevelt's nominee for the post of secretary of the Interior, liberal activist and Democratic operative Harold L. Ickes, promised revolutionary changes in Indian affairs. Thus few Washington insiders were surprised when Ickes picked John Collier as Indian commissioner, a selection that guaranteed sweeping reforms under the banner of the Indian New Deal. A vocal critic of Republican Indian policy was now formulating and implementing his own policy, one that encouraged the resurrection of Indian societies, the conservation of Indian lands, the protection of Indian cultures, and the development of tribal self-government.[6]

Collier moved quickly to address reservation economic conditions. He won authority to place Indian males in the Civilian Conservation Corps, fought to make Indians eligible for relief monies from the Federal Emergency Relief Administration, and found Indians jobs with the Civil Works Administration and Public Works Administration. In the field of Indian education, Collier replaced boarding schools (such as the Rapid City Boarding School) with day schools, but, in a decision that might have troubled Ben Reifel, maintained a progressive education program that emphasized arts, crafts, and vocational training at the expense of reading and writing.[7]

The centerpiece of Collierism, and the most consequential initiative in twentieth-century Indian affairs, was the Indian Reorganization Act of 1934. Through this comprehensive piece of legislation, originally introduced as the Wheeler-Howard Bill by its two congressional sponsors, Collier hoped to institute tribal governance, prohibit further land allotments, secure the Indian land base, and stimulate reservation economic development. When implemented, the IRA, the commissioner maintained, would do nothing to inhibit the assimilation of those individuals who chose the white man's path. Yet an underlying if not paramount aim of the IRA was to support American Indian traditionalists who sought to restore tribal institutions and communal values.[8] The Indian New Deal, notes an authority on the Collier era, "was intended to enable native Americans to establish cooperative commonwealths that would serve as a model for individualistically oriented non-Indians."[9]

Collier did not conceal his preference for a restoration of tribalism. "The Indian," he asserted, "is not a 'rugged individualist'; he functions best as an integrated member of a group, clan or tribe."[10] Collier cited the Lakota as an example of a traditional community unsuited to Anglo-American property practices. "In their long, grandiose chivalric age," Collier wrote of the Lakota, "the economic ambition was not to possess wealth but to give it away. Prestige, the feeling of well-being, even the feeling of security, leaned not on the act of making oneself rich but the act of making oneself poor.

The poorest Sioux might be . . . the richest." Utterly convinced that "world-wide questions are involved in this Sioux dilemma," Collier identified the Lakota giveaway ceremony as a cultural practice that embodied man's "millennial hope of the deeper and lovelier part of the human spirit." Federal policies, Collier argued, should not thwart the Sioux people's "cooperative principle"; rather, "the way can be found—must be—to make of a dominant virtue of a people not its ruin but its way to power and to the good life."[11]

Collier's New Deal for Indians faced criticism from skeptical members of Congress, not to mention from Indians themselves. As a new Bureau of Indian Affairs employee, Ben Reifel followed closely and then witnessed firsthand the contentious debate over the dramatic changes in Indian policy. Under Commissioner Collier, Reifel recalled in a 1980 interview, the bureau halted the sale of Indian lands "with the idea of figuring out some way in which they could consolidate land holdings. And he talked about the—I'm going to use the term communalization—but the common ownership of the Indian land." The commissioner's campaign to preserve tribal holdings "was taking away some of the rights that the individual had to his land," and, as the campaign was unfolding at the very moment that President Roosevelt was establishing relations with the Soviet Union, there arose concerns "about commies involved in this thing and I think some people almost conjured up Collier as a communist and all that sort of thing." Reifel appreciated that there were well-intentioned people—both Indians and non-Indians—who opposed changes to Indian policy that might restore tribal practices inimical to mainstream economic practices. For those people, Collier's defense of tribal communalism, occurring when it did, "tended to mitigate against the Indian Reorganization Act and gave the people who were sincerely opposed to this some reason to be very skeptical about it all."[12]

Though he would play a pivotal role in the formation of IRA governments, Reifel himself grew concerned with Collier's obsession with tribal communalism. In the aftermath of World War II, as agricultural mechanization and declining farm prices squeezed reservation employment opportunities, and as northern plains Indians showed no inclination to suspend traditional practices of sharing and wealth redistribution, Reifel would adopt some of the same language favored by Collier's critics. Those critics included United States Representative Theodore Werner of South Dakota, who feared that Collier's initiatives segregated the Indian and isolated him "and made it impossible for him to ever become an assimilated part of the citizenship of our country."[13] Representative William Hastings, a Cherokee Indian from Oklahoma, echoed Werner's concerns and warned that the IRA would add another chapter to the history of federal guardianship of Indian tribes, while Representative Isabel Greenway of Arizona concluded that Collier's advocacy of collective democracy would undermine American Indians' conversion to self-reliant behavior.[14]

Collier had prepared himself for congressional opposition to his plans. He had not, however, anticipated resistance from reform groups. Matthew K. Sniffen of the Indian Rights Association declared the Wheeler-Howard Bill a reversal of policy that "perpetuates segregation under the guise of self-government" while robbing individual Indians of any incentive to own private property. The association's board of directors reminded Collier that momentum in Indian affairs dating back to the General Allotment Act had started an inexorable process that would result, despite Collier's opposition to the contrary, in "the amalgamation of the Indian with the white race."[15] Flora Warren Seymour, a member of the once influential Board of Indian Commissioners, went so far as to cast Collier's philosophy as a veiled attempt to promote communism among American Indians, a charge that would haunt the Indian Office well into the 1940s.[16]

Of greatest concern to Collier, though, was the suspicion of, if not outright hostility to, the Indian New Deal exhibited by Indians themselves. To win over Indian skeptics, he decided to speak directly to them. One of his trips took him, in December 1933, to the Pine Ridge Reservation, where Ben Reifel was destined to play a central role in the presentation of the Wheeler-Howard Bill to the Lakota people. Reifel did not yet know it, but he was about to become an indispensable agent for the Bureau of Indian Affairs in their campaign to organize and modernize South Dakota's Brulé and Oglala Sioux Tribes.

Reifel had begun his duties as a United States Farm Extension Agent for the Oglala Sioux Tribe on 1 July 1933. From his office in the town of Oglala, he managed a variety of federal programs in the Oglala Farm District at the southwest corner of the reservation, an area with a heavy concentration of traditionalists who did not speak English. Reifel stepped into the role of boss farmer, the title the Lakota gave his predecessors before reforms by the Hoover administration altered the delivery of agriculture services on Indian reservations. Much more than just extension agents, boss farmers were expected to issue rations, settle civil disputes, support school teachers, assist parents with troubled children, supervise tribal police officers, advise individuals on personal finances, purchases, land transactions, and wills, and fulfill the tasks of social workers.[17] "Promoting agriculture was secondary, he was really an assistant [agency] superintendent," said Reifel of the responsibilities of a boss farmer. Though technically Reifel was not expected to provide a range of nonagriculture services to the clients of his farm district, he elected to do so in an effort to enhance the quality of life on Pine Ridge. He became the district's unofficial education specialist, financial consultant, and social worker. "I didn't have the door closed. I let anybody come in and see me, either at the office or the house," recalled Reifel, adding that his ability to speak Lakota created a welcoming environment for his clients.[18] Superintendent McGregor placed Reifel in charge of the Federal Emergency Relief Administration's distributions of food and clothing, and, through his own initiative, Reifel assisted with New Deal programs such as the Civilian Conservation Corps Indian Department, Civil Works Administration, Public Works Administration, and Works Progress Administration.[19] He met these tasks while assisting Oglala ranchers in purchasing cattle to expand the reservation herds, though by his own admission he spent little time as an agricultural advisor in the drought-plagued years of 1933–34.[20]

On 26 December 1933, Ben and his fiancé, Alice Johnson, who had been appointed the supervisor of a Works Progress Administration quilt factory in Pine Ridge, were wed. The two made their home in Oglala, where, though their salaries were meager, they lived in relative comfort. Their house lacked electricity, but they enjoyed some amenities not always found on Indian reservations in the 1930s. The house had a water system, Alice recalled, as well as a gas stove, gas lamps, a coal furnace, and "an old fashioned ice box which necessitated two trips a week to Pine Ridge Agency for ice."[21]

As he adjusted to married life, Ben also adjusted to greater professional responsibilities. Just days before the Reifels' wedding, John Collier visited Pine Ridge to meet with tribal representatives and personnel from the Indian Field Service. In his remarks, Collier briefly explained the intent of the Indian New Deal, which included a goal to strengthen and systematize tribal governments.[22] Few in the audience grasped the changes that Collier's plan would bring to Indian country, though in his position as boss farmer, Reifel had already begun to detect a different attitude from Bureau of Indian Affairs headquarters, specifically in its policy toward American Indian ceremonies. It had been the established procedure at Pine Ridge that when residents wanted to hold traditional dances, they were required to petition the boss farmer from their district. When a man named Bert Kills Close to Lodge approached Reifel with a request for permission to organize a Saturday night dance, he was informed that the Bureau of Indian Affairs now cared little about how, when, or why the Oglalas socialized. Reifel read for Kills Close to Lodge a telegram from Collier to bureau personnel. "It said, 'If the Indian people want to have dances, dances all night, all week, that is their business.'" Kills Close to Lodge was stunned. "Bert sat there," Reifel recalled, "stroking his braids, looking off in the distance, and he said in Lakota, 'Well, I'll be damned.'"[23]

Approving powwows was one thing; making sweeping changes to tribal governments was quite another. The Wheeler-Howard Bill promised to reverse assimilation programs that had been the preoccupation of the United States government since the Gilded Age, but to do so in ways that fostered interaction between Indians and non-Indians. "There was a belief," writes S. Lyman Tyler, "that the re-establishment of Indian community and support of local Indian leadership would help prepare [Indian] communities to eventually be included in the family of local communities in the various states throughout the United States."[24] Having himself benefited from inclusion in the white community at South Dakota State College, Reifel interpreted Wheeler-Howard in the same integrative spirit.

To prepare Indian leaders for impending changes in federal-tribal relations, Collier ordered reservation superintendents to meet with tribal councils and share what Superintendent McGregor referred to as the "special" and "far-reaching" information from Washington. Additionally, the commissioner informed Bureau of Indian Affairs personnel that he would be hosting "Indian Congresses" in seven states "for the purpose of fully acquainting the Indian groups . . . with the policies and program of the present administration."[25] Regarded by Collier as a way to involve Indians in the policy-making process, the regional congresses would build communication between the tribes and the Bureau of Indian Affairs while allaying the Indian critics of reorganization. Congressional opponents of his policies drew another conclusion, however, and accused Collier of using the Indian congresses as publicity stunts to intensify his lobbying efforts for the Wheeler-Howard Bill.[26]

From 2 March to 5 March 1934, Collier, Indian Service employees, and some two hundred Indian delegates representing eighteen northern plains tribes gathered at the Rapid City Indian School to discuss the Wheeler-Howard Bill. In the weeks leading up to the Rapid City Congress, the Oglala and Rosebud Sioux tribes, uncertain of the consequences of Collier's reorganization scheme, formed factions that voiced divergent opinions about the proposed cancellation of the allotment system. Superintendents warned Collier that Lakota "full-bloods," many of whom had retained their trust properties, viewed Wheeler-Howard as an underhanded attempt to redistribute their lands to landless "mixed-bloods."[27] Reifel recalled that the bill alarmed some Oglalas who were convinced it "was going to put all this [allotted] land . . . back into tribal ownership, which really wasn't true but this was the thing that got out."[28] Just days before leaving for South Dakota, Collier found himself wiring the Oglala Sioux Tribe to assure them that no land redistribution program would be carried out on their reservation. His telegram did little to alleviate the concerns of Lakota leaders, who possessed no clear understanding of Collier's proposals.[29]

Reifel took leave to attend the Rapid City Congress, where, at the opening session, Collier was greeted by a suspicious audience. Some in attendance were convinced that the commissioner was inaugurating a "back to the blanket movement" among the northern plains tribes. In his opening remarks, Collier promised that the government would "act in partnership with the Indians and we are not going to act unless the Indians are willing to go with us." All Americans, Indians and non-Indians, were ruled by laws, but the time had come to "change the laws" and that was "the fundamental matter before the Indians and the country in Indian matters."[30] Collier asked the delegates to consider the basic thrust of Wheeler-Howard, which, before it became law, would assuredly undergo alterations in Congress. Whatever the outcome of the revision process, however, the finished bill would preserve Indian lands and organize tribes into political communities managed by Indian officials who would be empowered with an authority once reserved for white officials. Collier contended that the repeal of an old law, the Dawes Act, would end the disastrous effects of heirship land holdings that, upon the death of the allottee, were passed to numerous heirs in a practice that diluted land holdings and resulted in the "checker-boarding" of reservations. Provisions of the Wheeler-Howard Bill, the commissioner informed the delegates, called for the repudiation of the allotment policy and the restoring of inherited lands to tribal ownership, an arrangement that Collier believed would lead to more productive uses of tribal lands.[31]

Collier's lofty vision of communal ownership met resistance, with some delegates announcing their opposition to that section of Wheeler-Howard which authorized the Interior secretary to transfer land titles of deceased individuals to tribal ownership. Considering the breadth of opposition to the section, Collier had no choice but to promise to amend the bill to make all property exchanges between allottees and tribal communities purely voluntary and contingent upon the consent of allottees, most of whom would likely pass their properties on to heirs. Furthermore, the partitioning of lands among heirs was allowed to continue from generation to generation, so long as the allotment was deemed a viable economic unit.[32]

When the congress agenda turned to the topic of tribal government, the commissioner and his subordinates met with less hostility, though suspicions persisted. Collier emphasized that in the business-oriented world of the whites, "unorganized people are powerless. They are victims. Only organized groups have power in the white world."[33] An assistant to Collier, Ward Shephard, remarked that by organizing themselves, tribal leaders would be free to establish councils consistent with their political traditions. The dispersing of agency and tribal funds, currently administered by the Bureau of Indian Affairs, would become the responsibility of the tribal governments, who would inherit the authority to fill Bureau of Indian Affairs staff positions with qualified Indian applicants. Despite these assurances, some delegates were hesitant to endorse self-governance. Representatives from both the Rosebud and Oglala Sioux tribes declared that decisions about the structure and composition of governments would rest with their constituents. The chairman of the Rosebud Sioux Tribe confessed being confused by all of Collier's plan, but he was especially concerned with the provision for self-government. "I don't know whether we can look at . . . self-government at this time because we are lacking in material—good material—men as leaders," he commented. At that particular moment in history, the chairman observed, there appeared to be no individual who could "rise up to be the man of the hour" for the Rosebud Sioux Tribe.[34]

Collier had to endure strongly worded criticism from a representative of the Crow Tribe of Montana, Max Bigman, who argued that in addition to further segregating Indians from whites, the restoration of tribal communalism would shield Indians from the "competition and big knocks" that characterized the American free enterprise system. Joe Irving, a delegate from the Crow Creek Sioux Tribe of South Dakota, echoed Bigman's statement and then went so far as to call Collier a socialist. Bigman and Irving remained in the minority, however, evidenced by the thirteen tribal delegations that endorsed the Wheeler-Howard Bill. By the end of the Rapid City Congress, it was clear that most of the delegates had reversed their opinions from rejection of, to support for, Collier's plan.[35]

Having witnessed firsthand the Rapid City discussions, how did Ben Reifel react to the Wheeler-Howard proposals? As an American Indian professional who had come to enjoy the benefits of the mainstream United States, how did he respond to Collier's summons to resurrect traditions and restore prereservation communalism? Was Wheeler-Howard consistent with or contrary to the time, work, savings philosophy of Euro-Americans? Collier seemed to be promising the coexistence on Indian reservations of two conflicting world views. One view encouraged American Indians to modernize themselves through the adoption of Anglo-American constitutionalism. The other urged them to protect themselves from foreign infringements on tribal traditions. What was one to make of Collier's faith in the viability of tribal culture within a dominant society that valued Western legal principles, individual initiative, and private enterprise?

Collier's optimism was fueled in part by a self-serving ambition to show white Americans that there was an alternative to their individual-centered lives.[36] Much of his message seemed to encourage Indians to withdraw from rather than contribute to American society. But would tribal communitarianism, if practiced within insulated Indian societies, be of material benefit to individual Indians? Would it reverse the poverty that gripped their reservations?

These and other questions surfaced in Reifel's mind in the 1930s. They would ripen into a philosophy of Indian affairs that would refute some, but not all, of the assumptions of the white social worker turned-Indian commissioner who had first encountered Indians in the mountains of New Mexico in the 1920s. Reifel found much to like about the Indian Reorganization Act, and he credited John Collier with restoring tribal self-governance and preserving the Indian land base. And yet, while fiercely proud of his own Lakota heritage, Reifel never embraced the cultural revival launched by Collier. As the years passed, Reifel became increasingly impatient with crusades by Indians and non-Indians to restore premodern lifestyles and worldviews that were incompatible with modern economy, society, and technology. From his vantage point, reservation Indians had to accept the values of time, work, and financial saving or remain stranded in poverty-ridden geographical subpockets that offered no relief to residents who rejected the white man's world.

In 1934, however, Ben Reifel was busy digesting the contents of the Wheeler-Howard Bill. Parts of the legislation inspired him, none more than Title III, "Indian Lands," which called for the abolishment of the allotment system, the restoration of unallotted "surplus" reservation lands to tribal control, and the appropriation of funds for the purchase of additional tribal lands. "I was impressed with the opportunities outlined in the Wheeler-Howard bill," Reifel recalled in an interview some fifty years after the legislation became law. "I thought, 'We are going to stop the Sale and the loss of our lands.'" Reifel supported tribal efforts to purchase more land and the prospect of federal loans to Indian farmers. "All of this sounded extremely exciting to me."[37]

American Indians had no stronger advocate for education than Reifel, so it was not surprising that he praised those provisions authorizing appropriations for Indian schools. "We are going to get an educational program so kids can go to colleges and universities and trade schools" was how Reifel described his thoughts on Title II of Wheeler-Howard. Yet his philosophy of Indian education remained decidedly Anglo-American in orientation. Reifel wanted Indian schools to prepare students for the white man's world. School-based promotion of Indian arts and crafts as provided for in Title II's "Special Education for Indians" provision was not heartily endorsed by Reifel, who viewed the precious hours of the school day as the building blocks of a higher standard of living. Additionally, Reifel was disappointed that Congress failed to approve Title IV of the Wheeler-Howard Bill, "Court of Indian Affairs," which was designed to create courts of original jurisdiction for cases involving American Indians and their communities. In Reifel's estimation the establishment of an independent judiciary would have enhanced the quality of Indian judges who "are not paid anything like they should be with the tremendous decisions they have to make." Nor was Congress's rejection of Title IV helpful to the pursuit of justice in Indian country, where, because reservation courts resided outside the federal system, convicted individuals were denied the right of appeal. "There is no independent judiciary on Indian reservations," Reifel lamented in later years. "The court system is the creature of the tribal council," a weakness that, in Reifel's opinion, jeopardized the civil liberties of American Indians.[38] As a congressman, Reifel would address these and other shortcomings in the tribal justice system during his testimony on behalf of the Indian Civil Rights Act of 1968.

Reifel welcomed the Wheeler-Howard Bill as an overdue measure that would correct past injustices while it modernized Indian institutions. He was suspicious of some of the social engineering that appeared to lie at the heart of the Indian New Deal, and he was probably beginning to develop the integrationist philosophy that would define his approach to Indian affairs. Nevertheless, he was appreciative of the protections that the final version of the bill, the IRA, extended to Indian property owners. Here was a feature that might further economic acculturation. "As I look back over the fifty years," Reifel reminisced in the 1980s, "there is nothing in the Indian Reorganization Act that harms any Indian tribe or any Indian individual who has property." Reifel was convinced of the basic goodness of non-Indians, a conviction that he shared with Felix Cohen, an accomplished authority on federal Indian law, during a trip from South Dakota to Montana in the mid-1930s. "Well, American people, you know, are pretty decent people," Reifel told Cohen, who in reply noted that the United States was comprised "of wolves and sheep, and the sheep have got to be protected against the wolves." On this point the two could agree, as they did on the power of the IRA "to protect the Indians' lands, their rights, and their humaneness."[39]

Even before Congress began debating changes to the Wheeler-Howard Bill, tribal members were being asked to register their opinions of the bill through the instruments of nonbinding referenda. Reifel, technically still a farm agent, asked his superiors for permission to travel across the Pine Ridge Reservation to explain the bill's contents and to address questions from concerned Oglalas. Reifel's request was granted, and his presentations, conducted in both English and Lakota, may have proved decisive in the Oglala Sioux Tribe's approval of the legislation by a 1,542 to 953 margin. The Rosebud Sioux Tribe also endorsed Wheeler-Howard in a nonbinding poll that showed 975 in support and 399 in opposition of the legislation.[40]

Back in the nation's capital, the bill, having undergone more than thirty amendments to satisfy the criticisms expressed at the Indian congresses, faced a new level of opposition. During hearings in the spring of 1934, one of the cosponsors of the bill, Senator Burton K. Wheeler of Montana, having come to the conclusion that the bill "would be a step backward" for Indians, suddenly withdrew his support for Collier. Wheeler urged Congress to continue to assist tribes in adapting to white culture rather than segregating them into distinct political communities. Rededicating the government to an assimilation policy, Wheeler reasoned, would not only prepare

Indians for self-supporting lifestyles but would also eliminate the expense of organizing tribal governments. Senator Elmer Thomas of Oklahoma lent his voice to Wheeler's by warning that the bill, in restoring tribal communalism, would erase a century of progress among Oklahoma's tribes. If the intent of government policy was to assist Oklahoma Indians, then that policy, Thomas argued, was best served by acquiring property for landless individuals, discontinuing the issuance of fee patents, and extending the trust period on allotted lands. Representative Will Rogers, an Oklahoman and part Cherokee Indian, complained that the Wheeler-Howard Bill was too murky and complicated for any American to understand, while Representative Thomas O'Malley of Wisconsin pronounced the bill an experiment in Soviet collectivism that would never succeed as Indian policy.[41]

To counter the opposition, Collier swamped Congress with Indian Office data, pressed his case through the media, and called on political allies to lobby for Wheeler-Howard. He highlighted the broad base of Indian support for the bill, citing the results of referenda wherein fifty-four tribes endorsed it against twelve who did not. He attacked his critics, who Collier identified as cattlemen, job seekers, real estate interests, attorneys, and missionaries. In a national radio address, Collier asked the public to support the Roosevelt administration's defense of the rights and freedoms of Indian tribes. Interior Secretary Ickes leaped to the defense of the commissioner by issuing a warning to the Indian Service that any personnel attempting to obstruct Collier's plan would face the prospect of dismissal.[42]

Ultimately, it took the intervention of the president to secure passage of the Wheeler-Howard Bill. Resigned to the fact that Indian affairs ranked low on Roosevelt's agenda, Collier asked Ickes and Secretary of Agriculture Henry A. Wallace to update the president on the legislation. They did so, and in response, Roosevelt sent letters to Wheeler and Representative Edgar Howard of Nebraska in which he defended the Collier program as a means of terminating the allotment system and securing Indian lands and liberties. Succumbing to Oval Office pressure, the House and Senate redrafted the bill with enough revisions to assuage its critics and assure its passage.[43]

On 18 June 1934, President Roosevelt signed into law the Indian Reorganization Act. It was a shorter version of the Wheeler-Howard Bill that did not meet all of Collier's objectives. Nevertheless, the act, wrote one authority on the Indian New Deal, "included most of the original ideas for a reorientation of Indian policy." The IRA repealed the allotment law, permitted the transfer of surplus reservation land to tribal control, appropriated funds for purchases of additional tribal lands, and approved loans for tribal corporations and for college and vocational school students. In a major change in its hiring policy, the Bureau of Indian Affairs could now employ American Indians who lacked the appropriate civil service qualifications. Indian tribes won the right to establish self-governing tribal councils with the authority to secure legal counsel, negotiate with other governments, control the sale and leasing of tribal lands, and establish charters of tribal incorporation that would permit the tribes to manage their resources and expand their land holdings.[44]

It was the tribal self-government provision of the IRA that was of greatest importance to Ben Reifel and his Bureau of Indian Affairs colleagues, a few of whom—Reifel among them—would be assigned the task of explaining the law to the Lakotas. According to its language, the IRA would be applied only to those tribes who approved it through a binding referendum. Tribes that approved the act would then take the next step and prepare a constitution to be ratified by a majority of tribal voters. In a third step, tribal voters would elect council representatives to begin the task of governing.[45]

In the summer of 1934, the Bureau of Indian Affairs launched an educational campaign to introduce tribes to the IRA. Field agents would explain the text of the law to reservation residents and prepare them for referenda.[46] In making their presentations to tribal voters, many of whom were confused by the IRA, bureau personnel were encouraged to point out the negative consequences of rejecting the act, which, in Collier's words, would mean a tribe might "drift to the rear of the great advance open to the Indian race." A tribe excluding itself from reorganization, he stressed, "will probably continue to lose its lands while those who accept the Act . . . can preserve and increase their lands and will move forward."[47]

Whether or not Reifel used scare tactics in his presentations is uncertain. What is certain is that Reifel, who "was impressed with the opportunities outlined in the Wheeler-Howard bill," familiarized himself with the features of the IRA and then applied his language skills to explain it to the Oglalas, many of whom were not English speakers.[48] To simplify the material, Reifel located a primary school alphabet flip chart in an old commissary and wrote on the back of its pages summaries of the sixteen sections of the IRA in two separate columns, one column for Lakota, the other for English. On each page he drew or displayed symbols to help illustrate the meaning of words or concepts that might be unintelligible to Lakota audiences. His "ABC chart" in hand, Reifel traveled across his farm district introducing the IRA to the people.[49] At no time did he feel he was propagandizing his listeners. His was an educational mission. He was personally committed to the referendum process, Reifel noted in later years, but the IRA was "one of the few pieces of legislation applying to anyone in the United States that the people could accept or reject. If that is stuffing something down somebody's throat, I have got the wrong information about what it means to stuff things down people's throats."[50]

That Reifel's presentations were effective was confirmed when representatives from his farm district gathered with other Oglala Sioux leaders at a reservation-wide meeting on the IRA. Seeing that the men from Reifel's district were better versed on the law than the other delegates, Superintendent McGregor queried Reifel about his teaching methods. Intrigued by the flip chart technique, McGregor instructed Reifel to demonstrate his presentation for all who were assembled. His demonstration was a hit. "As a result of this experience," Reifel recalled in 1967, "I went with [McGregor] from one district on the reservation to another to explain the law."[51]

Reifel's translations were invaluable to McGregor, and, as became apparent, critical to the Lakotas' approval of the IRA. During his presentations, Reifel encountered opposition from tribal members who feared that the new law would result in the seizure of their allotments and the transfer of their lands to community ownership. A few Oglalas shared local missionaries' fears about the impact of the Indian New Deal on church, educational, and social services. Addressing his audiences in both Lakota and English, his improvised charts at hand, Reifel allayed the fears of most listeners, though some Indians continued to view the IRA as a "back to the blanket" policy that threatened, if not their lands, their adaptation to Anglo-American practices of private ownership.[52] In the end, so effective was Reifel in winning Oglala support for the IRA that Joe Jennings, South Dakota superintendent of Indian education and regional coordinator of tribal reorganization, asked McGregor to release Reifel to visit other reservations in North Dakota, South Dakota, and Nebraska. McGregor complied with the request and Reifel took to the road, concentrating his early efforts on South Dakota reservations, where knowledge about the IRA was uneven.[53] Alfred DuBray recalled the confusion the act produced among his Rosebud Sioux brethren. "Nobody really understood it," he noted. "They knew that they were going to have to vote on whether they wanted it or not. Of course, it was very difficult many times to get things accurately to them. It was a matter of communication—very difficult because they would interpret in many ways the minor things."[54]

In the end, it was Reifel, noted DuBray, who translated and explained the IRA in a way that the average Brulé could grasp its meaning. "Well, I would say that from my personal opinion, probably if it wasn't for [Reifel], if he didn't represent the Bureau that it would have been very unlikely that this would have been in effect. Because he could speak the language and he knew the people and had many relatives and friends on the reservation." DuBray described Reifel as "very capable" and noted that he "spent quite a lot of time" presenting the IRA to Rosebud Sioux residents.[55]

DuBray cited those features of the IRA that provided "huge amounts" of loan monies, specifically agriculture and education loans, as particularly persuasive. It is possible that Reifel, a beneficiary of a college loan and a vocal champion of higher education for Indians, highlighted the educational provisions of the law. Audiences at Reifel's presentations, noted DuBray, learned that "educational loans were beginning to be made available for the Indian youngsters who had never had an opportunity before to attend higher institutions. There was a new feeling there in education."[56]

In the fall of 1934, IRA referenda were held across the northern plains. Reifel's travels yielded mixed results, with several tribes—the Crow Creek Sioux, Sisseton-Wahpeton Sioux, Standing Rock Sioux, and Yankton Sioux among them—rejecting reorganization.

The Crow Creek Tribe, for instance, rejected the IRA by a convincing 246 to 87 margin. In a letter to John Collier, Crow Creek Superintendent James H. Hyde recalled how he, Reifel, and Jennings met with groups of tribal representatives whose opposition to the IRA "was not due to an ignorance of the bill, but rather to an early conceived determination . . . to have nothing to do with it," an attitude that Hyde attributed to "hav[ing] been fooled so many times that suspicion has taken the place of reason."[57] Yankton Sioux leaders, meanwhile, cited their fear that the legislation would lead to "the colonization of Indians on a communistic idea" with the consequences being the reduction of individual-held lands and the restriction of individual rights on the Yankton Sioux Reservation.[58]

But Reifel enjoyed his share of successes. Both the Rosebud Sioux and Oglala Sioux, along with Cheyenne River and Lower Brule Sioux, chose to establish self-governing tribal councils under IRA provisions.[59] The vote at Pine Ridge was close, with 1,169 accepting and 1,095 rejecting tribal reorganization. Voters on the Rosebud Reservation, meanwhile, approved the IRA by an 843 to 424 margin.[60] Thomas Biolsi, a leading authority on the organization of the Lakota, contends that for the Brulés and Oglalas, the referendum vote was less an endorsement of reorganization and self-governance than the anticipation among tribal members of material benefits accruing from the law's approval. Due to the complexity of the law and the difficulties (in Biolsi's opinion) of translating it into the Lakota language, Lakota voters, suggests Biolsi, "did not understand the IRA when they went to the polls in 1934 to vote on it."[61]

Though it is likely that material incentives influenced Lakota opinion of the IRA—we have already seen the attraction of agricultural and educational benefits to members of the Rosebud Sioux Tribe, for instance—there is no reason to believe that Reifel's presentations failed to convey all of the act's key provisions. As was evident to both federal officials and Indian leaders alike in the summer of 1934, the Lakota who attended Reifel's IRA sessions were better acquainted with the act's contents than those who did not. Biolsi cites Superintendent McGregor's comment to Collier "that there was 'nobody on the Reservation that believe[d] that the self-governing feature has any merit to it'" as evidence of the confusion about, or unpopularity of, the IRA among Lakota voters.[62] Yet McGregor's comments were made in April 1934, weeks before Reifel (at McGregor's behest) began his flip chart presentations in the Lakota language in the summer of 1934. Thus it could be argued that the IRA referenda results are better understood as manifestations of the division between conservative tribal elders—who feared the bypassing, through secret balloting, of the "treaty councils" they controlled—and younger Lakotas who saw in the IRA the potential for democratic and progressive forms of local government from which tribes could leverage economic and educational resources. While explaining the IRA at public forums, Reifel had witnessed the splits between "Old Dealers" who feared "losing control because of [the establishment of] an elected council pretty much patterned after our own kind of elections," and the "New Dealers" who supported the IRA and its promise of tribal self-determination and economic development. It was political division along these lines—not the Lakota voter's inability to comprehend the IRA—that, from Reifel's vantage point, fostered "a great deal of opposition and much excitement" in South Dakota Indian country.[63]

Forty-five years removed from his efforts to organize the Lakota, Reifel recalled the debates that preceded the Oglala Sioux Tribe referendum. The old dealers who dominated the treaty council "were always opposed to everything that took place" and they "never gave up" in their opposition to a new constitution that "would undermine their leadership." Old dealers defended a premodern institution that, in Reifel's judgment, was unsuited for modern representative government, inter-governmental relations, and commercial transactions. They resisted secret ballots and slates of candidates who might be representative of the popular will. From personal observation, Reifel concluded that treaty councils performed like "debating societies." "No one ever paid attention to the tribal council," he emphasized. "They had no authority, no power," and they dedicated most of their time to "talking about the Black Hills claim" or discussing the distribution of tribal funds. Furthermore, many old dealers identified with the Republican Party, and, as the IRA was a Democratic initiative, they were confident "they would get a hearing without any problem form [*sic*] the Republicans at the time." Simply put, the old dealers were losing political influence, and, accordingly, "it was a matter of survival for whatever leadership prestige they felt that they were getting out of it."[64]

Reifel contended that if Indian tribes were to "survive," they would have to reorganize their political institutions along legal lines consistent with the United States' other governing bodies. Tribes who, through the instrument of the referendum, registered support for the IRA fulfilled the first stage of reorganization.[65] The next step required them to prepare constitutions, bylaws, and articles of incorporation in accordance with sections sixteen and seventeen of the IRA. To meet those tasks, Commissioner Collier formed a new unit, the Indian Organization Division, and ordered its "organizational field agents" to work with tribal councils, agency superintendents, and other field personnel in the drafting of constitutions, bylaws, and articles of incorporation. As it was his intention to create partnerships between tribes and the federal government, Collier announced that it would be the policy of the Indian Office "to give the Indians the widest opportunity to use their own judgment, initiative, and ability in tribal organization and incorporation." He conceded that Bureau of Indian Affairs field agents would face "a most difficult task" acquainting Indians with legal documents "so that they may vote intelligently on the acceptance of those documents." To reduce confusion, tribes would be assigned organizational field agents "of the Indian race who through experience and training both in the field and the Washington Office recognize the need and value of organization and are prepared to assist the Indians in developing the kind of organization that will best meet their needs and wishes." Though the constitutions and charters would need to contain "appropriate and legally acceptable" language consistent with the nation's laws and policies, the field agents were to assist in the framing of legal instruments that embodied Indian ideas while furthering the long-standing goal of the "economic rehabilitation" of the Indian race.[66]

Having learned of Reifel's work as a translator during the recent referendum campaign, Collier ordered him to Washington in April 1935 for training as an organizational field agent. On 1 July, the commissioner assigned the twenty-eight-year-old South Dakotan to a large district encompassing the states of Kansas, Montana, Nebraska, North Dakota, South Dakota, and Wyoming. The promotion changed Reifel's life. It drew him closer to officials in the Washington office and placed him in an important advisory capacity vis-à-vis the reservation superintendents. It developed his administrative, communication, and problem-solving skills in emotionally charged environments that called for a steady personality with tireless energy, tact, and a tough exterior. As Graham D. Taylor has observed, the American Indian employees of the Indian Organization Division "included many of the Indians who were to rise to prominence in the bureau during and after the Collier era."[67] In 1935, Reifel was one of those rising stars in the Indian Bureau. His performance as a field agent accelerated his advancement in the bureau that he would one day lead.

Over the next seven years, Field Agent Reifel's consultations with Indian leaders refined his political and economic outlook. Having profited from the opportunities afforded any American Indian who was willing to be on time, work hard, and save money, Reifel came to value the culture of mainstream America. He believed that by adopting IRA governments modeled after the United States Constitution, Indian tribes would experience participatory democracy and, in time, learn to appreciate the rewards of full American citizenship. In managing their resources, formulating and balancing budgets, and investing their money, American Indians might come to accept the rewards of capitalism, which, despite being sorely tested by the Great Depression, remained woven into the fabric of American life.

During his tenure as an organizational field agent from 1935 to 1942, Reifel concluded that if American Indians adopted basic Anglo-American institutions, they would restore themselves as an autonomous and prosperous peoples, albeit within the framework of mainstream American society. With constitutions, bylaws, and corporate charters in place, Indians would practice self-governance in a civic laboratory designed to elevate them to political and economic equality with non-Indians. Consistent with James Madison's admonition that "a well-instructed people alone can be permanently a free people," and John Collier's statement (in reference to the Cheyenne River Sioux) "that the Sioux Indians are getting a fundamental political and economic education through the process of working out their constitutions," Reifel believed that American Indians would recover their material well-being by conforming to Anglo-American political institutions, the Western education system, and individual initiative.[68] This philosophical position, founded on his faith in American exceptionalism, guided Reifel through the remainder of his civil service career, during his five terms in Congress, and into retirement in the 1970s, at which time his principled opposition to American Indian radicalism was coupled with encouragement for those Indians who labored quietly to make improvements to their quality of life.

When he arrived back in South Dakota as a newly promoted field agent, Reifel was attached to the Indian Organization Division office in Pierre. There he lived for a short time with his wife Alice, who, now seven months pregnant and frequently separated from her husband during his road trips, decided to move in with her parents until the baby's birth. On 8 September 1935, in Watertown, South Dakota, Alice gave birth to the Reifels' only child, Loyce Nadine, a black-haired, brown-eyed daughter that Ben had only a short time to spend with before returning to the field.[69]

Having spent three decades straddling Indian and non-Indian cultures, Reifel found that he was uniquely qualified to perform the duties of organizational field agent. Tribes electing to establish governments under the IRA would be asked to adopt constitutions based on a United States Constitution model provided by Bureau of Indian Affairs headquarters. Such was the choice facing Indian tribes, for, as Graham D. Taylor observes, the Indian Bureau "could not simply resurrect ancient tribal institutions if the Indians were to learn to deal independently with white society." Hence, IRA-established councils "were all in some degree modeled along Anglo-American lines, with electoral districts, voting by secret ballot, tribal presidents, vice presidents, treasurers, and committees."[70] The principles embedded in the United States' founding documents posed problems for many American Indians, the Lakota Sioux among them. Their struggle with the English language, their inexperience with Western political institutions, and their slow adjustment to modern living disadvantaged the Lakotas and thus made constitutional templates and field agent consultations a necessity, if their transition to self-rule was to occur. Especially valuable in this regard were Field Agent Reifel's language skills. Reifel observed "that the Indian people were very gracious about things of this kind, a representative from Washington, and particularly someone who could speak their own language. It was not often that you had somebody coming out of Washington that could speak the [native] language."[71]

In examining Reifel's early years in the Bureau of Indian Affairs, John S. Painter writes that a field agent's responsibilities required him "to function within the contexts of both Indian and White cultures, and for this [Reifel] was exceptionally well qualified." According to Painter, Reifel possessed an invaluable skill set, one not overlooked by his supervisors. "His bicultural insight now became essential to the restoration of tribal governments that could function in agreement with Anglo-American democratic concepts."[72]

Reifel's first major field assignment was, fittingly, to the Rosebud Sioux Tribe, whose representatives began working on a constitution in June 1935. His maiden attempt at constitution-drafting once again exposed Reifel to the promises—and the snares—of tribal politics. In July, Reifel, Joe Jennings, and a second field agent assisted a special tribal committee in completing a draft of the Rosebud Sioux constitution that was forwarded to Washington for Bureau of Indian Affairs review. Reifel's translations proved critical during the drafting process, which required numerous meetings with skeptical Lakotas who wondered how tribal sovereignty would be recognized and protected by the document.[73]

When Felix Cohen, assistant solicitor for the Department of the Interior, and Bureau of Indian Affairs representative Fred H. Daiker arrived in South Dakota in July to share their recommendations with the Rosebud Sioux Tribe, Reifel found himself at the center of a debate between one faction supporting an older district system of representation and another favoring the "community plan" electoral scheme devised for the recently drafted constitution. The proponents of the community plan (which Reifel preferred) argued that the plan's smaller electoral units guaranteed a more fair and equitable representation than the larger reservation districts. Some of the council members, led by the tribe's chairman, opposed the community plan, their position being that it did not reflect the wishes of older councilmen and "full-bloods." Opponents of the community plan complained that "full-bloods" could not understand the constitution (a dubious claim, considering Reifel's bilingual explanations) and demanded a postponement of the constitutional referendum until everyone could cast an informed vote. Reifel was targeted for criticism by the tribe's chairman, who complained that it was wrong for Reifel, a member of the Rosebud Sioux Tribe, to be compensated by the government to promote a constitution he helped design.[74]

The opposition of the tribal chairman came as no surprise to Reifel, whose Brulé upbringing and recent experiences with old dealers at Pine Ridge had seasoned him to the volatile nature of tribal politics, wherein council representatives will filibuster, slander their opponents, or subvert protocol to retain their authority. As Murray Wax has observed, most tribal council members "regard election to office as a reward to be bestowed upon senior men, friends and kin rather than as a choice among competent men and competitive policies."[75] Graham D. Taylor reminds students of Indian affairs that, when it comes to the realm of tribal politics, "Indian politicians are not necessarily any more paragons of civic virtue than any other group of politicians."[76]

In the end, the dispute over Rosebud electoral districts was settled when the tribe's vice chairman, having been elevated to the presider's chair following the chairman's withdrawal from the debate, threw his support behind the community plan, "the only workable form," in the vice chairman's words, "by which the whole reservation can be represented equally in the new tribal council." Reifel was present at the meeting and reiterated his support for the community option, which was duly adopted by the Rosebud Sioux Tribal Council in a seventeen to ten vote.[77]

The constitution having been approved by the council, it now fell to the voters to accept or reject it. Bureau of Indian Affairs officials ordered the superintendent and Reifel, after first disseminating an English version of the constitution throughout the reservation, to explain its contents in both English and Lakota during a series of heavily advertised community meetings. It is probable that Reifel's translations proved critical to the average voter's comprehension of the constitution and its articles. Despite recurring objections about the alleged complexity of the document, the pace of the ratifying process, the size of representative units, and the motives of "mixed-blood" supporters of reorganization, Rosebud Sioux voters on 23 November 1935 approved their constitution by a result of 992 for to 643 against, a comfortable margin of 61 percent to 39 percent that silenced accusations that the constitution was not representative of the people's will.[78]

It was a source of pride among the Rosebud Sioux that their constitution, modeled in form and spirit on the United States Constitution, became a template for other northern plains tribes. The document's preamble expressed the people's commitment to unified government, justice, domestic tranquility, liberty, education, industry, the conservation of property, and the development of resources. Definitions of tribal membership, designations of the governing body and electoral districts, qualifications for office seekers, and provisions for elections, recalls, and the amendment process followed. A list of enumerated powers authorized the tribe to negotiate with the federal, state, and local governments, to secure legal counsel, to acquire additional lands, to conduct its economic affairs, to levy taxes, and to write and enforce ordinances. The Rosebud Sioux constitution also includes a bill of rights that recognizes many of the same rights and liberties protected by the United States Constitution.[79]

The Rosebud Sioux constitution was modeled on a template prepared by the Department of the Interior, and Reifel admitted as much when he described its similarity with other tribal constitutions as illustrative of the "blanket constitution" approach of the Indian Bureau.[80] That said, the document ratified by the citizens of the Rosebud Sioux Reservation had opened the door to tribal elections. Those elections resulted in the tribe's adoption, with the assistance of Reifel, of a charter of incorporation that empowered the tribe to manage its resources, conduct business enterprises, accept gifts and property, and hypothecate tribal property for federal loans, and to do so with a minimum of supervision from the Bureau of Indian Affairs.[81] "Reifel assisted his own tribe in writing one of the first I.R.A. charters," notes John S. Painter, "and it became a model for use by other tribes throughout the country."[82]

The forums, debates, referenda, and document-drafting meetings that distinguished the reorganization process made for, in Reifel's estimation, far-reaching "educational consequences" that introduced Indians to self-rule and the freedoms enjoyed by American citizens. By bringing them "directly into involvement with the federal law," Indians were offered the choice of "whether they wanted the law or not." Tribes that chose reorganization and experienced "the problems of setting up a constitution and by laws and . . . formulating resolutions and ordinances" benefited from the processes, but even those tribes that rejected the IRA were forced to adjust to Anglo-American political norms.[83] "I think it's one of the greatest things that ever came along for the Indian people," Reifel said of the IRA. "While some of the tribes haven't accepted the Indian Reorganization Act or set up a constitution or by-laws, they have set up governing bodies that I think begin to pattern themselves as to what organized tribes are doing."[84] Reifel believed that in adopting modern institutions to achieve local control, American Indians were "improving their knowledge of government and our society generally."[85]

Reifel's reputation as an enterprising field agent, coupled with his personal success story and professional demeanor, brought him to the attention of non-Indian audiences. A front-page story in the 26 September 1935 edition of South Dakota's *Moody County Enterprise* recounted how during a Constitution Day assembly at Flandreau Indian Vocational High School, the "well-known Sioux [Ben Reifel] urged the students to make the most of their opportunities . . . and to take advantage of the privileges that are offered them." The older generation of reservation residents, Reifel told his listeners, were unprepared for the changes wrought by tribal reorganization, changes that required the talents of educated Indians who could "shoulder the responsibility of leadership in the councils that are being organized." Sounding a theme he would repeat in dozens of high school gyms over the next four decades, Reifel, in defending the academic standards demanded by white educators, reminded the Flandreau students that it was "the duty of every boy and girl to help establish a record both here and in their own communities which will be a credit to themselves and to their people."[86]

Reifel's duties with the Indian Organization Division allowed him little time for vacationing. Nevertheless, he went to great lengths to spend time with his family. When weather permitted, Alice and daughter Loyce left their home in Pierre to travel with Ben on his assignments to the Rosebud and Pine Ridge reservations. A trip to Pine Ridge in the early spring of 1937 nearly ended in disaster. On their way to visit friends in a remote corner of the reservation, the Reifels' car became stuck in deep snow. Unable to free the vehicle and miles from any homes, the Reifels wrapped Loyce in an army blanket and set out walking toward their friends' house. "There was no road to follow," Alice recalled. "Snow had covered all tracks and . . . I had trouble following Ben. I'd step into snow up to my hips." After an exhausting and anxious six-hour walk in the dark, the family reached their destination, though they never again traveled in the winter without extra clothes, blankets, and food.[87]

It was not surprising that Ben could locate an isolated house on the snow-packed roads of the Pine Ridge Reservation in the midst of a winter's night. He knew the area well, for in addition to his time there as a farm agent in 1933–34, he had spent much of the summer and fall of 1935 crisscrossing the reservation while advising the Oglala Sioux on the drafting of their constitution. As was the case among the Rosebud Sioux, his duties as organizational field agent at Pine Ridge required him to attend tribal council meetings and district forums in order to explain reorganization as expressed in IRA-model constitutions and bylaws. His presentations sometimes lasted for hours and tested his skill at simplifying complex political concepts and technical language.[88]

In many ways, Reifel's field work on Pine Ridge proved more difficult than his assignment on the Rosebud Reservation. Though Oglala leaders relied heavily on Reifel to help them write a constitution, the opponents of reorganization characterized Reifel and other field agents as "propagandists employed by the Indian Office" and charged them with hastening the adoption of a document that was incomprehensible to Lakotas and "not representative of the general sentiments of the Pine Ridge Indians." Complicating matters at Pine Ridge was the influence of "Returned Students Organizations," composed primarily of young "mixed bloods" who resented the role played by older, "full-blood" councilmen in the drafting of the constitution.[89] Some residents of the Porcupine District voiced the concerns of IRA opponents when they informed

Reifel at an 22 October meeting that, in their opinion, Bureau of Indian Affairs officers were "trying to move too fast, that more time should be taken" in forming a new Oglala Sioux government.[90]

Though among the Oglala resistors Reifel detected "the same old excuse" made by Brulé opponents of the IRA, he was sensitive nonetheless to Oglala opposition to a community, or *tiyospae*, allocation of tribal council representatives. Reifel and other Bureau of Indian Affairs agents urged Superintendent McGregor to drop his efforts to organize the Oglalas along community lines—a system that, in Reifel's opinion, would create an unwieldy tribal council and incite tribal factionalism—and accept the existing administrative districts as the best arrangement for the Oglala Sioux.[91] Reifel approached the subject from a purely practical point of view. "The *tiyospae* itself is nothing more than just a neighborhood," Reifel reasoned, and, as an organization, it "had nothing to do with politics."[92] He emphasized to both McGregor and Commissioner Collier that the Oglalas were familiar with a representational format corresponding with reservation districts, which themselves had been established for the purposes of administering rations and maintaining records. If adopted as the official political subdivisions, the districts would send equal delegations to the tribal council, whereas a failure to adhere to the district scheme would lead to "an unmanageable number of representatives on the governing body."[93] In a letter to the commissioner, Reifel noted that "districts have functioned very much as communities for the past several years and each family in its respective district has identified itself as a member of the district rather than as a member of its particular tiyospae." It was within the district councils "that the tiyospae have found their representation" and the individual district councils in turn "acted as the political community units under the General Tribal Council." The Oglala Sioux had become, in Reifel's words, "distinctly District minded" and to alter their political organization would create unnecessary difficulties.[94]

The Bureau of Indian Affairs accepted Reifel's logic, abandoned the community plan, and adopted a district plan in accordance with the wishes of the tribal majority. In the days leading up to the constitutional referendum, Reifel, in an effort to reach as many voters as possible, chaired discussion groups at every day school on the

Pine Ridge Reservation. On 14 December 1935, Oglala Sioux voters went to the polls to decide a single question: "Shall the proposed Federal Tribal Constitution & Bylaws for this reservation be ratified?" By a 1,348-to-1,041 margin, they responded "yes" and thus approved an IRA-model constitution for their tribe.[95]

For the remainder of the 1930s, Reifel, in addition to helping other northern plains tribes develop IRA governing bodies, worked to develop the administrative skills of newly elected councilmen. He assisted tribes in Kansas, Minnesota, Montana, and North Dakota in the drafting of constitutions, bylaws, ordinances, and law and order codes. In dozens of meetings, Reifel taught tribal officials to maintain minutes and records, formulate and monitor budgets, modernize livestock and farming operations, and conduct the business of government in a manner consistent with their constitutions. He played a leading role in the staging of four-day regional conferences at Minneapolis, Minnesota; Pierre, South Dakota; Billings, Montana; and Carson City, Nevada, where, for the first time, political leaders from Midwestern and Western Indian tribes gathered to discuss mutual problems and exchange ideas. Unless requested, Reifel and the other field agents in attendance at the conferences did not join the discussions. Representative of a new generation of Bureau of Indian Affairs employees who had spearheaded the establishment of modern tribal governments, they were determined to reform the bureau into a less paternalistic institution dedicated to American Indian self-reliance.[96] As tribes assumed more responsibility, it was the duty of the field agents, Reifel believed, "to get the [Bureau of Indian Affairs] agency personnel to look upon the I.R.A . . . as being . . . a part of the procedures that govern their administration" as federal officials.[97] In short, it was time for superintendents to loosen their hold on the day-to-day operations of tribal government. The new attitude was reflected in the field agents' refusal to interfere in tribal council meetings. The agent's task was, in Reifel's words, "to [get] the constitution approved and [get] the tribal council set up and the election laws and all that. Then you would move to another place."[98]

Reifel's professional maturation and interest in the thornier issues affecting Indian affairs were evident in a 1939 article he wrote for *Indians at Work*, a journal published by the Department of the

Interior for Bureau of Indian Affairs employees, American Indians, and the general public. In "Organizing the Sioux," Reifel lamented the factionalism that kept the Lakotas "separated within themselves." Opponents of IRA constitutions, working through loosely organized "treaty councils," grossly misrepresented the spirit of the governing documents and worked to undermine the authority of popularly elected leaders. Partisan rancor was inherent to all democracies, Reifel conceded, but constitutionally mandated tribal elections assured that there would be regular opportunities for the loyal opposition to legitimately seize power and pursue their preferred agenda in a formal fashion. Regardless of their differences, citizens in a "democratic method of constitutional government . . . are together as a group on one thing—in this country, at least—and that is a cooperative democratic form of government as the best way of life." Reifel cited the long distances between reservation communities, the shortage of reservation transportation, and the dearth of radio and newspapers as "spatial factor[s]" that contributed to the Sioux Indians' "internal dissension" and the unfounded fear among some Lakotas that the IRA would dispossess them of their land.[99]

Despite these obstacles to effective governance, the constitutionally elected Lakota leaders, Reifel continued, performed admirably. Inexperienced councils committed honest mistakes and were sometimes guilty of occasional "irregularities," to include transacting meetings without a quorum and failing to submit minutes and reports. Nevertheless, as a self-governing people, the Lakota were coming to appreciate the potential of their governing documents. Considering the great distances many of them traveled to attend council meetings, not to mention the difficulties of finding places to eat and sleep once they arrived, elected Lakota officials had "responded in a most patriotic fashion to keep the wheels of their respective tribal governments moving. . . . Few public servants serve as unselfishly."[100]

The title of unselfish servant might have been applied to Reifel, who, by the end of the 1930s, had accepted and performed admirably in every task assigned him. From his duties as an entry-level farm agent, to his volunteering to translate the Wheeler-Howard Bill to Lakota audiences, to his taking on the heavy responsibilities of organizational field agent, Reifel had contributed mightily to the implementation of the IRA on the northern plains. It is not an exaggeration to assert that Ben Reifel was at the forefront of a revolution in tribal self-government, especially as that revolution affected the Indians of the northern plains, and, more specifically, the Oglala Sioux and Rosebud Sioux tribes of South Dakota.

And yet, ironically, by 1940, the revolution had run its course. Insomuch as it stood for a renaissance of tribal communalism and indigenous culture, the Indian New Deal as a foundation for Indian policy was faltering, due in large measure to the intransigence of its founder but also as a consequence of Congress's skepticism about the effects of John Collier's policies on Indian modernization. It was a skepticism that, in the coming years, Reifel would grow to share. When the United States entered World War II, federal Indian policy was undergoing a transformation that would be accelerated by the demands of a global conflagration that Reifel participated in. The romantic spirit of the Collier era was being replaced by a national impatience with American Indians' isolation from mainstream society. After the war, Ben Reifel would find himself at the forefront of another policy sea change, and, in his attitude toward Indian affairs, growing nearer in philosophical outlook to the non-Indians who urged Indians to move beyond their premodern customs and down the path of modern American life.

3 RESPONSIBILITIES OF WEIGHT AND IMPORTANCE

With the dawn of a new decade, Ben Reifel's civil service duties expanded to include strategic planning for Indian communities in Iowa, Kansas, Montana, Nebraska, North Dakota, and South Dakota. A sampling of his work as an organizational field agent in 1940 finds Reifel assisting staff at the Sac and Fox Reservation, speaking at the Rosebud Sioux Tribal Fair, discussing tribal reorganization with the chairman of the Winnebago Council, assessing soil samples from the Lower Brule Sioux Reservation, and working with the Flandreau Santee Sioux General Business Council on land-related matters. At the Fort Belknap Agency in Montana, Reifel helped the tribal council devise a rehabilitation plan to better utilize their irrigated and grazing lands. During his Montana swing, Reifel discovered that he did not require an interpreter to communicate with Assiniboine speakers and that the leader of the Gros Ventre found him a sincere man who would assist the Gros Ventre people on their "hunting trip for a better life."[1]

In late 1939, Reifel had been appointed secretary of the Dakotas-Nebraska Superintendents' Council (later renamed the Northern Plains Superintendents' Council), a position that required him to organize quarterly conferences at which reservation superintendents, national and state officials, educators, farm extension agents, and law enforcement officers tackled problems in Indian country. In 1940 and 1941, conference panelists addressed such topics as tribal reorganization, land use, reservation policing, tribal courts, and education.[2] Reifel's selection as council secretary indicated that his superiors in the Bureau of Indian Affairs were grooming him for a superintendent's post. That he was later assigned to two of the bureau's most demanding posts was evidence of their confidence in the thirty-three-year-old South Dakotan.

Ironically, Reifel's professional ascent was occurring at the very moment that Commissioner John Collier's influence was waning. As early as 1937 it had become apparent that the philosophical tenets of Collierism were losing support in Congress, if not among some Indians themselves. Collier bore much of the blame for his deteriorating relationship with Congress. His use of the bureau's *Indians at Work* journal to endorse President Roosevelt's Supreme Court–packing scheme, for instance, drew the ire of Senator Burton K. Wheeler, cosponsor of the Wheeler-Howard Bill. Additionally, Collier's comments that United States Indian policy should serve as a model for other nations ran counter to the isolationist sentiments of Wheeler and many of his congressional colleagues. Having grown exasperated with Collier's attitude that the Indian commissioner alone knew what was best for Indians, Wheeler was, within four years of introducing his signature legislation, calling for its repeal, his faith in Collier diminished.[3] Other politicians charged Collier with attempting to achieve through bureaucratic conniving what was denied him by Congress, and some said that Congress's commitment to Indian self-reliance was being undercut by Collier's promotion of traditionalism, tribalism, and racial segregation. Collier abused his powers, charged his critics, and the legacy of his leadership was, in their opinion, a bureau committed to an anti-Christian if not communist agenda.[4]

Collier's opponents included American Indians. Objections to the IRA from the Navajos and from tribes in New York and Oklahoma gained traction in the press and distracted the commissioner, who found himself spending an increasing amount of time refuting critics. An attack on Collier by the American Indian Federation (AIF), headed by activists of the Creek and Seneca tribes, expressed that group's opposition to special status for Indians and highlighted their demands for repeal of the IRA, termination of federal services to tribes, and the resignation of Collier, who the AIF branded as an atheist and a communist. Despite Collier's insistence that AIF "extremists" represented only a segment of the nation's Indian population, the organization's charges were taken seriously in Congress, where investigations into the costs and conduct of the Indian Office were already underway. Ben Reifel alluded to the scrutiny of the bureau in a letter to a South Dakota legislator who had called for an Oglala Sioux delegation to visit Washington to learn more about the benefits of tribal charters. While acknowledging the legislator's good intentions, Reifel questioned the timing of the trip. "As you know," he wrote, "the Indian Office is following very closely all the bills introduced in Washington that would affect the Indian Reorganization Act and it might be that right now may not be the best time for tribal representatives to go to Washington."[5]

Congress's opinion of the Bureau of Indian Affairs hardened even more after 1941, when the national unity demanded by war with the Axis powers made voters unsympathetic to policies that appeared to promote ethnic and racial differences. Confronted with an international crisis that required drastic reapportionments of economic resources, politicians from both parties registered their impatience with the Indian Office. Most of the investigations and reports from the period drew the same conclusion, namely, that under Collier's leadership, Indians appeared to be reverting to tribalism and that programs designed to assimilate them were being replaced by policies that retained them as federal wards outside the political mainstream. What had happened, congressmen wished to know, to the goals of encouraging individual initiative and self-sufficiency? What had become of the decades-long efforts to merge Indians into the mainstream, efforts that, at least at the time of its passage in 1934, seemed to lay at the heart of the Indian Reorganization Act? Had the Indian Bureau grown more concerned with preserving Indian traditions—and its own survival—than in freeing American Indians from their special status as segregated, reservation-bound wards of the state?[6]

An investigation of Indian affairs by a special House committee chaired by Karl E. Mundt of South Dakota, while acknowledging that a sudden dissolution of the trustee-ward relationship would be a mistake, declared that the government should prepare the Indian "to take his place in the white man's community on the white man's level and with the white man's opportunity and security status." Tribes, stressed the Mundt Report, should not resign themselves to dependency on Washington, nor should the goal of

Indian education be "perpetuating the Indian as a special-status individual." Instead, assimilation should remain the government's bedrock policy. "The goal of our whole Indian program should be, in the opinion of [the] committee, to develop better Indian Americans rather than to perpetuate and develop better American Indians."[7] Fifteen years later, Ben Reifel would use similar language when expressing his desire to become the first "Indian American" from South Dakota to serve in the United States Congress.

During World War II, Congress revealed its opposition to the classification of Indians as special citizens. Deep cuts in domestic spending reduced Bureau of Indian Affairs appropriations from $46 million in 1939 to $28 million by 1944, a period in which many of the most-experienced bureau personnel—Ben Reifel among them—entered the United States Armed Forces. The temporary relocation of the Bureau of Indian Affairs main office from Washington to Chicago to create space for wartime enterprises symbolized the decline of John Collier's Indian program.[8]

The deprioritizing of Indian affairs during World War II must be examined alongside the improvements the war made in the lives of individual American Indians, sixty-five thousand of whom left reservations to join the Armed Forces or seek employment in defense plants or wartime activities. The war had a profound impact on Indian life. Twenty-five thousand Indians served in the military, most of them in integrated units. Few encountered the discrimination endured by African-American servicemen, and many, in the words of historian Gerald D. Nash, "found their war service enlightening." American Indians adjusted quickly to military life. They enjoyed their travels and developed a self-confidence and healthy lifestyle that impressed their loved ones back home. Many of the forty thousand reservation Indians who worked in wartime industries were transformed by their experiences. No longer isolated from mainstream society, they were exposed to other subcultures and introduced to dozens of employment opportunities in a variety of industrial, service, and technical fields. "The war demonstrated," Nash writes, "that Indians were willing to leave their reservations to learn skills and were able to make adjustments to varied lifestyles in American communities."[9]

Higher incomes for American Indians were but one manifestation of their migration to cities during the war years. Other manifestations included a newfound respect for formal education and political involvement. Whether employed in a factory or serving in uniform, American Indians received training that, when coupled with their exposure to different peoples and places, stimulated their intellectual curiosity and changed their attitudes toward schooling. Uncomfortable with their educational deficiencies, they vowed to do more to raise the academic standards of their tribes. Some veterans took advantage of the G.I. Bill to further their education, but even those who did not were an ambitious group from which much of the tribal leadership of the 1950s, 1960s, and 1970s was drawn. Having observed tribal self-government at work before the war, Indian veterans who returned to the reservations—and two-thirds of them did—intended to leverage their governments in ways that would accelerate economic and social modernization. A dramatic example of the war's impact on the American Indian political consciousness was the founding in 1944 of the National Congress of American Indians, a pan-Indian group dedicated to lobbying for Indian interests at the highest levels of government.[10]

Despite John Collier's wish to dismantle the assimilation policy, the immersion of tens of thousands of Indians into white society during the war, observes Francis Paul Prucha, "greatly accelerated the movement toward assimilation. The orderly adjustment of 'the ancient social forms and archaic cultures of primitive Indian groups to the demands being made upon them by modern society,' which was Collier's goal, was upset by the rapidity of change brought about by war." Whether clad in olive drab fatigues or industrial plant overalls, transplanted American Indians experienced a higher standard of living than was possible on their home reservations. Improvements in their economic condition "meant that a return to old reservation ways would not satisfy many of the veterans and war industry workers."[11] Their exposure to urban lifestyles and employment opportunities meant that, if they returned home, their presence on reservations would reopen, if not widen, the divisions between assimilationists and traditionalists that surfaced on reservations during the heady days of the Indian New Deal.[12]

Since his late teen years, Ben Reifel had benefited from integration into mainstream American society. His military service from

1942 to 1946, then, did not affect him in the same way it did those who were leaving Indian country for the first time. Of his experiences in World War II, Reifel spoke little. Interviews and photographs provide only cursory information about his duties and assignments. Few records relating to his military career are included in his personal papers, and they reveal nothing of his memories of wartime service in the United States and Europe. What is certain is that First Lieutenant Reifel, a member of the United States Army Reserve since his commissioning at SDSC in 1932, was called to active duty in March 1942 and ordered to Fort Leavenworth, Kansas, to undergo training as a military police officer. His departure from the Bureau of Indian Affairs in his ninth year of service was felt keenly by his colleagues, whose sentiments were expressed in the pages of *Indians at Work*. Ben Reifel's "intense interest in the region and the people with whom he worked and his sincere desire to be of service to them, combined with his superior mentality, unusual ability and likeable personality, have made him one of the most widely and favorably known members of the Indian Service field personnel." Of the many attributes of this "Outstanding Sioux Indian," Reifel's cultural knowledge and problem-solving skills were most sorely missed. "He had the faculty of seeing the pertinent problems in a given situation and usually gave some interesting comment or suggestions as to the solution," remarked the editors.[13]

Why the army assigned Reifel to the military police is unknown. What is certain is that he joined a police corps that had achieved permanent status just six months before his activation. Before World War II, the selection of army police personnel had been a haphazard process. During and after World War I, military policing was typically performed by soldiers who lacked law enforcement training and learned on the job. It took the outbreak of World War II and the nation's fear of espionage and subversion to move Congress on 26 September 1941 to create the military police corps. From a small force of two thousand men in 1941, the corps grew to more than two hundred thousand during the course of the war.[14]

On 8 December 1941, the same day Congress declared war on Japan, the military police corps announced its mission, which consisted of operating prisoner-of-war camps, investigating crimes committed by soldiers, protecting public buildings and works from sabotage, and controlling traffic on bases and in battle zones. The army established the Military Police Service School at Fort Myer, Virginia, and it is possible that Reifel attended that facility in 1942.[15] After a short tour at Fort Leavenworth, he was assigned to Fort Bliss in El Paso, Texas. He later served at Camp Chaffee, Arkansas, a post that detained German prisoners of war, and at Fort Custer, Michigan, where he attended the Provost Marshal General's advanced course for military policemen. For nearly two years during World War II, Reifel, accompanied by Alice and Loyce, lived in Dallas, Texas, where he was assigned to Eighth Army Headquarters in downtown Dallas.[16]

Shortly before the Japanese surrender in August 1945, Reifel, now a major, was transferred to Europe to serve in France and then in occupied Germany, where he was assigned the unenviable task of retraining combat soldiers as military policemen.[17] His command of combat veterans may explain his reservations about discussing the war with friends and reporters. Battle hardened and anxious to return home, Reifel's students were probably disinterested in (if not defiant about) their stint in a retraining regimen conducted by a bespectacled officer who passed his wartime duty in the comfortable confines of the United States. It is possible that Reifel's reticence about the war was his way of playing down his noncombat role out of respect for those who faced far worse conditions in the European and Pacific theaters.

In April 1946, Reifel, having recently been promoted to lieutenant colonel, returned to the United States, where he was released from active duty and assigned to the inactive reserve. He arrived in South Dakota in May to be reunited with his family and to recover from a serious ear infection. To restore his health, Reifel vacationed with Alice and Loyce until returning to his position with the Bureau of Indian Affairs in July. The Reifels moved to Billings, Montana, where Ben was appointed district tribal relations officer for the northern Great Plains, a job that required him to perform duties similar to those that he had performed as an organizational field agent. It was a brief assignment, for by the fall of 1946, the forty-year-old was familiarizing himself with the agency superintendent's desk at the Fort Berthold Indian Reservation in North

Dakota, home to the Arikaras, the Hidatsas, and the Mandans, the Three Affiliated Tribes.[18]

Reifel's two separate appointments to Fort Berthold, divided by a leave of absence to pursue a Ph.D. degree at Harvard University from 1949 to 1952, proved to be the most difficult and controversial of his twenty-two-year Bureau of Indian Affairs career. Yet his five years in North Dakota were critical to the development of the integrationist philosophy that defined his public service. As he guided the Three Affiliated Tribes through the traumatic events visited upon them after World War II, Reifel gained the confidence to articulate and broadcast his vision for a fuller assimilation of American Indians into modern life.

Reifel's posting in North Dakota involved him in one of the more unfortunate chapters in recent American Indian history, the inundation of the Fort Berthold Reservation by the Garrison Dam and Reservoir project. Located in the Upper Missouri Valley between Bismarck and Williston, the Fort Berthold Reservation consisted of, in the year of Reifel's arrival, 2,034 enrolled members of the Arikara, Hidatsa, and Mandan tribes. Their reservation was (and remains) divided by the Missouri River. It supported an economy that, while unfavorable in comparison to neighboring white communities, was in some ways an improvement over the economies on other northern plains reservations. Cultural traditions persisted, however, and were evident in "an economy of abundance" that was characterized by spending rather than investing and by a sharing of wealth that stood in contrast to the individualistic, market-oriented practices of neighboring white communities. Though a majority (64 percent) of reservation families owned cattle, only 2 percent of those families were agriculturally self-sufficient. The rest lived on an income procured from a few cattle, temporary work, leased lands, hunting and gardening, or, at times, from supplemental incomes provided by the Bureau of Indian Affairs or Christian missions. A majority of Fort Berthold Indians endured poverty, but many possessed land holdings from which they could generate some income.[19]

Some signs of a developing economy suggested that the Three Affiliated Tribes were adjusting to modern living. There were, after all, elements of the mainstream United States evident on the reservation. Christianity (in superficial form) was practiced by many residents. High school students played football and basketball, led cheers, attended dances and proms, and participated in rodeo and 4-H clubs. Members of the three tribes had ratified an IRA constitution, and there was some evidence in the 1940s that traditional practices of communal land ownership were competing with private ownership and individual initiative. Younger, educated Arikaras, Hidatsas, and Mandans, some of whom had distanced themselves from ancestral traditions, were acquiring skills to compete in the off-reservation job market. War veterans, many of whom had anglicized their names to fit into white society, showed a readiness to leave the reservation and settle among non-Indians so that their children could be exposed to better teachers in academically rigorous schools.[20]

And yet despite some evidence of economic modernization, a majority of Fort Berthold Indians sought to preserve the reservation community and the security it provided. While working as a social economist at Fort Berthold in the postwar years, Gordon McGregor observed that "remaining on the reservation . . . and continuing under the Indian agency administration is a behavior pattern which the Indians will follow as long as conditions make it possible." Members of the Three Affiliated Tribes showed little inclination to acquire the status of other American citizens, despite the fact that staying on the reservation left them dependent upon the very government "they criticize . . . bitterly in detail and in general." Special health and education benefits, combined with tax exemptions and a general relief at not having to "make one's way in white life," appealed to even the most educated Fort Berthold Indians. High school graduates were acquiring skills to live independently off the reservation, "but at the same time, not even all of these are willing to forego the practical advantages or abandon the protection of government supervision."[21]

Nor could the residents' ties to their ancestral homelands be underestimated as an explanation for their preference for the reservation. As is the case with Americans of all races who feel an emotional and spiritual attachment to the communities of their birth, for the people of the Three Affiliated Tribes, their reservation was a homeland, a place where, if they encountered obstacles in the white man's world, they could return.[22]

Hence the shock and trauma visited upon the Fort Berthold people when they learned during World War II that their family dwellings and a significant portion of their homeland would be swallowed up by Missouri River waters, the consequence of the giant Garrison Dam that was to be built downriver from their reservation.

Garrison was one of five Missouri River dams in North Dakota and South Dakota provided for in the Pick-Sloan Plan, a joint Army Corps of Engineers–Bureau of Reclamation project authorized as part of the Flood Control Act of 1944. Destructive flooding in the Midwest in 1943 and 1944 led to calls from Missouri Basin residents and their congressmen to tame the river. Federal officials acted. The monstrous Pick-Sloan engineering project made possible the construction of five Corps of Engineer dams—Garrison in North Dakota, and Oahe, Big Bend, Fort Randall, and Gavins Point in South Dakota—that when completed, would eliminate flooding on the Missouri River and its tributaries. Hydroelectric power would be generated by the project, and programs for irrigation, public recreation, and water development would extend the scope of the Pick-Sloan project beyond basin relief.[23]

All of the North Dakota and South Dakota Indian reservations bordering the Missouri River were impacted by Pick-Sloan (a circumstance that assured Ben Reifel's involvement with the project well into the 1960s), but the Three Affiliated Tribes were the first and in many ways the most adversely affected by the corps's construction plans. As early as 1943, engineers were surveying the area around Garrison, North Dakota, and further upstream, an activity that did not go unnoticed by the Fort Berthold Indians, whose tribal business council registered their opposition to any dam project that would cause damage to the lands and economy of the Three Affiliated Tribes. Following the passage of the Flood Control Act, the Fort Berthold Indians appealed to Congress and to William A. Brophy, John Collier's successor as commissioner of Indian Affairs.[24] Though handpicked by Collier as his replacement, Brophy shared little of the crusading zeal exhibited by his predecessor. Brophy's duty, as he saw it, was to repair relations between

Congress and the Bureau of Indian Affairs and to work with rather than against congressional "terminationists" who aimed to fully assimilate American Indians so that Congress could terminate its responsibility to tribes. To achieve termination, the federal government would commit itself to repealing laws that, in the minds of the terminationists, encouraged the "segregation" of reservation Indians from the mainstream United States. Bureau of Indian Affairs services that could be performed by other federal agencies or by state or local agencies would be transferred to those agencies. Congressmen would devote themselves to "liberating" individual Indians from Bureau of Indian Affairs supervision and terminating federal responsibility for tribes judged acculturated enough to thrive without government support.[25]

Despite his commitment to improving Congress–Bureau of Indian Affairs relations, Commissioner Brophy functioned as a moderate terminationist. He pursued termination as a long-term goal while remaining sensitive to the deplorable conditions faced by Indians whose circumstances required the continuation of Bureau of Indian Affairs services. Brophy likewise fought for the protection of Indian lands and Indian property rights.[26] But when it came to supporting the Three Affiliated Tribes in their opposition to the Garrison Dam, Brophy balked. He declined an invitation to meet with the Fort Berthold Tribal Business Council in April 1945, informing the council via a letter that it was too late to halt construction of the dam. The focus of Congress, the Bureau of Indian Affairs, and the tribal council, Brophy argued, should be on ensuring fair compensation for losses resulting from flooding and on acquiring lieu lands for the tribes if the residual reservation proved inadequate for the population. Members of the Three Affiliated Tribes refused to accept the inevitability of the dam and criticized the bureau for not halting its construction. But Brophy understood, rightly, that neither he nor the Fort Berthold Indians were going to prevent the building of the country's fifth largest dam. The Bureau of Indian Affairs possessed neither the resources nor the political influence to resist the inexorable momentum created by Pick-Sloan. The issue was settled. In the words of Roy W. Meyer, a foremost authority on the history of the Three Affiliated

Tribes, "the Bureau had accepted the Garrison Dam as inevitable and could offer only token opposition at this stage."[27]

In May 1946, just five months before Ben Reifel arrived at Fort Berthold, an ill-advised presentation to members of the Three Affiliated Tribes by General Lewis A. Pick, coauthor of the Pick-Sloan Plan, poisoned an already deteriorating relationship between the Indians and the Corps of Engineers. Before Pick's address, Congress disclosed that no appropriations for dam construction would be expended until the Interior and War Departments had identified compensation lands "comparable in quality and sufficient in area" to those lost to inundation. The deadline for a lieu lands agreement was set for 1 January 1947, at which time construction on the Garrison Dam would commence. Speaking to an audience at Elbowoods High School, General Pick, in a poor choice of words, encouraged the reservation residents "to cooperate . . . in carrying out the law as now written" and then bluntly announced, "I want to show you where we will place you people." Pick's insensitive remarks led to several volatile exchanges, the meeting climaxing in an arms-length verbal attack on Pick by a member of a reservation faction opposed to negotiating with federal officials.[28]

Such was the emotionally charged environment Ben Reifel inherited when he became superintendent of the Fort Berthold Agency on 12 November 1946.[29] By that date, preliminary construction projects were underway. Studies were being conducted to determine how best to relocate the agency administrative plant, its hospital and boarding school, and the hundreds of families whose homes would be lost to the Garrison Reservoir. Looming over these events was the deadline given the War Department to identify substitute lands for the condemned reservation property.[30]

Reifel's tenure at Fort Berthold would be consumed by the Garrison Dam project, and, by most accounts, he performed well under strains that few twentieth-century superintendents had to bear. In addition to preparing the Three Affiliated Tribes for relocation, there were other matters to attend to, all defined by the Interior Department in Reifel's Position Description. Reifel was expected to develop plans to meet the economic, social, health, and educational needs of reservation residents. He was to foster relationships with tribal councilmen and individual Indians in an effort "to learn their opinions and to understand their attitudes." He was to encourage "independent thinking" among tribal officials. Of special significance for the Interior Department were Reifel's public relations duties, which included the requirement that he acquaint, through speaking engagements and press releases, non-Indians with the Bureau of Indian Affairs and the Indian people it served.[31] It was in his role as bureau spokesman that Reifel honed his public speaking skills, insuring that by the time he returned to South Dakota in 1954, he had become a compelling orator.

But of all the duties specified in Reifel's job description, none compared in difficulty to that requiring Reifel "to assume additional responsibilities of considerable weight and importance, growing out of the construction of the Garrison Dam by the United States Corps of Engineers." Of 357 resident families, 305 would be displaced by flooding, a movement of men, women, and children which assured "a period of extreme uncertainty, economic instability, and emotional upset for the Indians." Reifel would be called upon to design and implement relocation programs while making recommendations to improve the general condition of the Fort Berthold Indians. His superiors cautioned Reifel that, in executing his charge, he would have to reckon with the tribal business council's staunch opposition to the Garrison Project.[32] Fortunately for Reifel, his labors were supported by the Missouri River Basin Investigations (MRBI) group, a team of specialists that assisted Bureau of Indian Affairs personnel on problems related to the Garrison Dam. Working in coordination with MRBI staff, Reifel and his coworkers devised strategies to humanely relocate the Three Affiliated Tribes and rebuild their economic foundations.[33]

Before tackling problems associated with the Garrison Dam, Reifel had to establish himself as agency head. From his headquarters at Elbowoods, a town destined to be submerged by the reservoir, Reifel familiarized himself with the administrative functions of a superintendent. He inherited a staff of seven division heads charged with safeguarding Indian properties, improving tribal welfare through agricultural, educational, and health care services, and administering funds appropriated for the Indians or derived from their trust lands. None of these tasks was performed without the input and oversight of the ten-member Fort Berthold Tribal Business Council, an IRA-constituted body that administered tribal property, income, and general affairs under the supervision of the Bureau of Indian Affairs superintendent.[34]

Reifel worked closely with his division heads to assure that their offices were executing plans and maintaining accurate records. He monitored staff morale and encouraged interagency communication. His working relationship with the tribal council was shaped by a conviction that he was preparing them for a day when the bureau's authority would be reduced and the powers of the council expanded so that they might conduct their affairs with a minimum of supervision. Those affairs would include administering tribal property, a weighty responsibility that required meticulous record-keeping, the management of rent collection and land distribution systems, and the issuance and monitoring of tribal grazing permits.[35]

Having spent eight years assisting northern plains tribes in the writing of constitutions and bylaws, Reifel harbored no illusions about the difficulties facing the Fort Berthold Indians as they adjusted to Anglo-American institutions. Nor did he underestimate deeply rooted habits that led Indians to look to the Bureau of Indian Affairs, instead of themselves, to solve their problems. Reifel understood that, for the moment, the Fort Berthold Tribal Council would function as an advisory body with few substantive powers. Hence he worked to provide "sympathetic and patient guidance" to council members while mollifying the "dissident elements . . . who were disaffected by the actions of the Tribal Business Council." But he remained committed to tribal self-governance as expressed in the tribal constitution. "The Tribal Business Council," he asserted, "can become the most important element in the relocation program and the future rehabilitation of the Fort Berthold people."[36]

A considerable amount of Reifel's time at Fort Berthold (and at the Pine Ridge Indian Reservation in 1954–55) was spent in meetings with individual tribal members. Gordon McGregor observed that the "informal relationship" that existed between the superintendent and the individual "can be one of [the superintendent's] greatest time-consuming problems and must be handled delicately." Because of his or her feelings of dependence on federal services, the individual viewed the superintendent as "official father" or "Chief." The expectation that there be personal connections between agency head and individual tribal members resulted in Reifel's being sought out for "the most trivial of decisions in personal and family affairs and for guidance in every group activity or progressive step."[37]

Reifel accepted the role of personal advisor as a necessary though not unwelcome part of his job. In 1952, he wrote that he possessed the staff, equipment, and funds "to assist Indians in the most personal kinds of situations. For example, a widowed mother may telephone in from one of the schools on the reservation and complain that the welfare worker has denied her further assistance from A.D.C. The Superintendent is in a position where he can then and there direct a member of his staff to go out and investigate the case, or go himself." Reifel believed that the "informal link" between superintendent and individual provided the superintendent with teaching moments to introduce tribal members to the "highly impersonal society" that existed off the reservation. Since some Fort Berthold Indians would leave the reservation and fall under the umbrella of state services, Reifel could, through his associations with individuals, prepare them for immersion. As such, the practice of one-on-one meetings was "probably the most important integrative pattern in the reservation social system."[38]

At Fort Berthold Reifel confronted social problems that would absorb his thoughts for the next four decades. Outside of dam-related business, the reservation education system was of greatest concern to Reifel. A 1948 analysis of schools on the Fort Berthold Reservation found that educational levels were "low" and that the "great majority" of Indian students were dropping out of high school to work or to marry, despite "a great belief in education as a means to success and better jobs in the whiteman's world." Simply put, the people's faith in education did not translate into action. Most disturbing was the attitude displayed by parents. They did not require their teenagers to attend high school and appeared to lack the initiative and "continual and persistent work" necessary to educate their children.[39]

Reifel faced the tall task of developing among the Fort Berthold Indians a greater respect for formal education.[40] Toward that end, he personally monitored attendance at the eight reservation schools.[41] He invited specialists to reorganize the schools' curricula.[42] He strived to improve school-based agriculture programs, and in November 1948, brought together twenty-three government and tribal officials to discuss educational challenges facing the Three Affiliated Tribes.[43] As a way of addressing the high dropout and unemployment rates among young males, Reifel served as the United States Army's Auxiliary Recruiting Officer for Fort Berthold, a position that gave him the opportunity to work with veterans from the local Joseph Young Hawk American Legion Post.[44]

Reifel believed that the poor academic performance of Fort Berthold students was a symptom of their parents' failure to adjust to modern American life. In more ways than not, conditions at Fort Berthold were comparable to those observed by Reifel at Pine Ridge, Rosebud, or any of the other northern plains reservations he served at in the 1930s and 1940s. Though exposed to the formalities of the private sector, the Three Affiliated Tribes still continued to practice an economy of abundance wherein they spent or consumed all they had in flush times, only to suffer privation when their food and money were gone. They failed to save or invest their income. They sold their cows rather than sustaining herds to provide a permanent source of income. They enforced a spread-the-wealth attitude to insure that "accumulations of wealth were siphoned off into a general distribution for the benefit of all," a practice that blunted their "full adoption of the modern accumulative economy."[45]

Reifel, whose personal time, work, save philosophy had begun to develop into a public manifesto, used his office to help Fort Berthold residents adapt to modern economic and societal expectations. He did so during meetings with individuals whose spending habits left them reliant upon the government in the person of the agency "chief." Reifel found himself assisting in "the most trivial of decisions in personal and family matters" and providing financial guidance to persons whose relationship with the Bureau of Indian Affairs was, because of their adherence to indigenous economic practices, characterized by "dependency and subordination." Nevertheless, despite his being "swamped" by residents' personal problems, Reifel maintained close relationships with dozens of

Fort Berthold Indians who regarded their superintendent "as the fountainhead of all local authority and the traditional person to whom the Indian turns when in need."[46]

Reifel's ties to individual tribal members bolstered his relationship with the tribal council, whose agenda was limited almost exclusively to issues surrounding the Garrison Dam.[47] The council's first dam-related dilemma confronted them with the choice of accepting or rejecting a lieu lands proposal made by the secretary of War on 21 November 1946, just nine days after Reifel assumed his post. For the next three weeks, Reifel attended community meetings at which he assisted tribal leaders in explaining the government offer. He kept local newspapers abreast of the tribe's deliberations and reported regularly to the Commissioner of Indian Affairs. He facilitated a dialogue between tribal leaders and non-Indians affected by the Garrison Dam and opened communications between the tribal council and North Dakota elected officials.[48]

According to the language authorizing the proposed land swap, the tribe's new properties were to be "comparable in quality and sufficient in area to compensate" for the lands submerged by the Garrison Reservoir. An acquisition of 145,000 acres in Mercer and Oliver counties and 14,570 acres of alienated lands restored to tribal ownership would satisfy Congress's "sufficient in area" requirement. Less certain was whether the new lands were "comparable in quality" to current tribal holdings. Eager to gauge the people's opinion of the proposal, the tribal council decided to delay their decision until after a series of public meetings held at reservation community centers between 4 December and 10 December 1946. Reifel and two representatives from the tribal council attended each of the seven district meetings to explain the lieu lands proposal. The public responses, recorded by Reifel for Bureau of Indian Affairs review, were overwhelmingly against the government offer. The most common objections emphasized the lesser quality of the top lands, the loss of bottomland resources such as coal and timber, the social disruption caused by the breaking-up of the reservation into five districts, and, not insignificantly, the sanctity of treaty provisions that guaranteed the tribes' possession of the current reservation space. Several residents noted the irony of an army project that would take "away from our young men the very thing that they fought for in the war just ended." An individual from the Shell Creek District commented that "the Army's job is to fight wars, not build dams to flood out people like us." And at least one member of the Mandan Tribe gave Reifel a history lesson, noting that "the Superintendent's tribe (the Sioux) fought the whites, but we Mandans did not. Why don't they remember? It seems that the Army Engineers have not upheld treaties."[49]

Making manifest the people's emotional opposition to the War Department offer, the Fort Berthold Tribal Business Council on 11 December unanimously rejected the government's lieu lands proposal, the council having concluded that the offer was "generally inadequate" and the lands themselves "not 'comparable in quality and sufficient in area' to compensate the Tribes for the lands to be inundated by the Garrison Project and Reservoir Area." Significantly, Reifel and his Bureau of Indian Affairs superiors defended the tribal council's decision, insisting, among their other objections, that the Mercer-Oliver tracts were not comparable in quality to current tribal holdings.[50]

Roy W. Meyer has noted that, from the Indians' perspective, the rejection of the government land offer was an expression of their disapproval of the Garrison Dam and their high degree of confidence that they could prevent its construction.[51] A more specific explanation of the tribes' strategy comes from Ben Reifel, who engaged in the negotiations and wrote in his 1952 Ph.D. dissertation that the Three Affiliated Tribes rejected the land swap because they intended to invoke a treaty provision requiring tribal consent for the release of any tribal lands to the United States. The Bureau of Indian Affairs, Reifel emphasized, concurred with the tribal council in their interpretation of the Fort Laramie Treaty of 1851 and joined them in opposition to the War Department's offer.[52]

Despite the Fort Berthold Indians' rejection of the land offer, neither the Corps of Engineers nor Congress would tolerate the derailing of the Garrison Dam project. Seeing that a lieu lands option was not an acceptable form of compensation, Congress, without consulting with the tribes, went forward with a bill to provide a cash settlement for tribal losses. Public Law (PL) 296, passed by Congress on 31 July 1947, authorized a payment of $5,105,625 to the Fort Berthold Indians, the settlement contingent upon the government and the tribal council approving a contract by 1 June 1948. The tribal council accused Congress of forcing the legislation on them, with councilman Carl Whitman Jr. testifying that the Three Affiliated Tribes "did not willingly agree to it." Nevertheless, in the fall of 1947, the council resigned itself to the inevitability of the Garrison Dam and agreed to a cash settlement for forfeited lands. Reifel and the council, though they continued to protest the project, turned their attention to monetary compensation levels. They traveled to Washington in January 1948 to lobby for a higher dollar figure but their initial effort was unsuccessful. After Fort Berthold voters approved the government's cash offer in a tribal referendum, Reifel and fourteen representatives of the Three Affiliated Tribes went to Washington, D.C., where, on 20 May 1948, in an emotional ceremony held in the office of Secretary of the Interior Julius A. Krug, the Indians signed over 155,000 acres of their lands to the federal government.[53]

The Three Affiliated Tribes received some consolation in the form of PL 437, signed by President Harry S. Truman on 29 October 1949. Reifel and tribal officials had lobbied for additional compensations, arguing that monetary remuneration for damages to tribal life and other intangibles brought about by the dam was fair and just. Their cause was taken up in a joint resolution introduced by Representative William F. Lemke of North Dakota, which increased compensations to the tribe in the amount of $7.5 million. House Joint Resolution 33 became PL 437, which was in March 1950 approved in a tribal-wide vote of 525 for and 466 against. For $12,605,625, the Three Affiliated Tribes had released 155,000 acres to the United States. Their 430,000 remaining acres were separated into five segments by the advance of the Garrison Reservoir. It was on the treeless prairies of the Missouri River bluffs that three hundred displaced families resettled and attempted to restore their lives.[54]

Writing in 1952, Reifel contemplated whether the government's lieu lands offer—rejected by the tribes with Reifel's support—"would have been a much better settlement than the cash settlement ultimately accepted." Had the tribal council accepted the initial government offer, Reifel noted, the reservation land base would have been diminished by only ten thousand acres, and the new lands in Mercer and Oliver counties would have provided irrigation opportunities. Farm and ranch units existed on the lieu lands, as did a road network and access to various public facilities. "Relocation now under the cash settlement," Reifel confessed, "must take place on undeveloped prairie land without as yet any system of roads or public buildings."[55]

What should be made of Reifel's complicity in the rejection of a land offer that might have been of greater benefit to the tribe than the cash settlement they ultimately accepted? Tribal leaders may have looked to Reifel for his appraisal of the War Department proposal. As a former rancher and farm extension agent, Reifel might have made an argument for the future potential of the top lands offered to the Three Affiliated Tribes. Had Reifel done more to convince the tribal council of the potential value of the lieu lands—inferior in quality to the bottomlands though they were—the council may have reconsidered its position toward the government offer.

On the other hand, and in Reifel's defense, the Fort Berthold Indians did not believe that the Mercer and Oliver county lands were anywhere near equal in value to their current holdings. For them to have accepted the land deal would have been, in their view, to trade superior lands in the Missouri Valley—holdings protected under the Fort Laramie Treaty of 1851—for inferior top lands they did not covet. It was their principled legal stand that explains the Fort Berthold Indians' rejection of the lieu lands settlement in the referendum of December 1946. And it should be added that although tribal leaders may have sought Reifel's input, they likely trusted their own judgment about land matters, a judgment that preceded the Lakota superintendent's arrival at Fort Berthold in November 1946.

Second-guessing aside, the Three Affiliated Tribes dismissed the government's land offer, accepted a cash settlement, and, in the words of Roy W. Meyer, "the long struggle between the Fort Berthold Indians and the United States government over the Garrison Dam project came to an end. The Tribes had recognized that the dam was going to force them to move, and they set about making the best of their misfortune."[56]

The tribes now turned to the monumental problem of relocating more than 80 percent of the households on the reservation while Bureau of Indian Affairs officials designed plans to move those households and the facilities, cemeteries, and materials threatened by inundation.[57] As early as 1948, Reifel was coordinating relocation plans with the MRBI team. The task of formulating a relocation strategy would consume Reifel until the moment in the spring of 1949 that he learned of his admittance to graduate school at Harvard University.[58]

In the 1980s and 1990s, four Fort Berthold residents who lived through the Garrison Dam negotiations and their aftermath evaluated Reifel's performance during those difficult months. Allen Cross and former tribal chairman Martin Cross questioned whether the Bureau of Indian Affairs adequately expressed the people's opposition to the dam. Though he provided no evidence to support his suspicions, Allen Cross considered it a possibility that Reifel, described by Cross as a "hard-liner" and "company man," colluded with the Bureau of Indian Affairs to use "pressure and coercion and intimidation" to get the tribes to consent to the dam. According to Cross, Reifel "engineered" the tribes' approval of the Garrison Dam project, and in return, he might have received a "pay-off" in the form of a congressional seat in his home state of South Dakota.[59]

Aside from the fact that the 126,000 South Dakota voters who elected Ben Reifel to Congress would had to have been part of the payoff that Cross alluded to, and aside from the fact that a mid-level civil servant like Reifel could not have halted the construction of the Garrison Dam, Cross would have to explain Reifel's opposition to the government's unpopular lieu lands proposal, his defense of the Fort Laramie Treaty, and his efforts to boost the value of the final cash settlement, actions that were fully supportive of the tribal council and do not appear to be those of a hard-liner or company man in collusion with federal officials. Other assessments of Reifel's role in the Garrison Dam ordeal are provided by former tribal councilman Carl Whitman Jr. and Marilyn Hudson, a teenager at the time of her family's relocation from Elbowoods to Parshall, North Dakota. Bureau of Indian Affairs officials worked for the government, noted Whitman, who could not recall Reifel doing anything to prevent the building of the dam. Reifel and his staff "had particular responsibilities" and were "rather perfunctory" and "indifferent" in carrying out those responsibilities.[60] For her part, Hudson, whose father served on the tribal council in the 1940s, concluded that the Bureau of Indian Affairs "had no choice" in the Garrison Dam matter. As an agency of the federal government, the Bureau of Indian Affairs, which was "working against the clock," was "mandated" to carry out the laws of Congress, after which the bureau, as "trustee for the Indian people," fulfilled its responsibility to "carry out the relocation plan." Throughout the negotiation and the relocation processes, Hudson contends, "the BIA and the tribal government worked very well together," the council conducting tribal business in tandem with bureau officials. Hudson bore no ill will toward the Bureau of Indian Affairs. Both the bureau and the council made the best of a bad situation. In Hudson's estimation, Fort Berthold representatives and Bureau of Indian Affairs officials "worked together as a team."[61]

Having supported the Fort Berthold Indians during the difficult Garrison Dam negotiations, and having laid the groundwork for the relocation of families and facilities, Reifel applied for a leave of absence to pursue an opportunity that promised to benefit him both personally and professionally. In March 1949 Reifel, desirous to "improve my future services in the Bureau," sought admittance to the selective Littauer School of Public Administration at Harvard University.[62] One of his references was Allan G. Harper, director of the Billings Area Bureau of Indian Affairs Office, who provided a revealing description of Reifel's character. "He possesses an exceptional combination of personal charm, emotional stability, high intelligence, and capacity for sustained intellectual effort," Harper said of Reifel. The director found Reifel's "constructive attitude" toward reservation problems "refreshing," and he specifically praised Reifel's administrative leadership at Fort Berthold, "where the situation is charged with explosive potentialities." As superintendent, Reifel "demonstrated firm mastery of his job and also skill in handling human relations. In the long drawn-out contract negotiations which we had with the Army Corps of Engineers over the Garrison land taking, he showed noteworthy diplomacy and resourcefulness." In Harper's estimation, only three Bureau of Indian Affairs officials of American Indian descent were worthy of appointment to the top position of Indian Commissioner. Reifel was one of those men. If Reifel were to leave the Indian Service, Harper was "certain that he would quickly achieve a prominent place in the public life of South Dakota."[63]

On April 30, Reifel learned of his acceptance to the Littauer School as a graduate student in a nine-month public administration program designed for federal, state, and county agricultural extension officers or, as in Reifel's case, administrators with extension responsibilities. At the completion of their studies, the members of Reifel's cohort would be awarded master's degrees and given the option of pursuing doctoral studies in public administration. Harvard awarded Reifel a grant and a faculty scholarship for the 1949–50 academic year, providing him with the financial support to move his family to Cambridge, Massachusetts, so that he could pursue a Ph.D. in public administration.[64]

North Dakotans with a concern for Indian affairs regretted Reifel's departure. Speaking on their behalf, United States Senator Milton R. Young thanked Reifel for the ability, forthrightness, and pleasant attitude he brought to his position at Fort Berthold. "For my own part, Ben," wrote Young, "I only wish we had a superintendent of your capacity and type on all our reservations. My problem here would surely be far less if that were true."[65]

In June, just two months before the start of his classes, Reifel suffered a tragic personal loss. While in Cuzco, Peru, as a member of a North American delegation to an inter-American Indian congress, Reifel learned of his mother's death in a house fire. Compounding his shock and grief was his inability to be in South Dakota for her funeral. "We could not get word to Ben," Alice told an interviewer, "so Loyce and I joined Ben's four brothers and their families for the Sioux service in the Episcopal church at Parmalee, South Dakota. The saddened people of the community came to pay their respects to one of their loved and admired members."[66]

Still grieving his mother's death, Reifel arrived at Harvard, where he transitioned from an administrator to a full-time student whose thoughts were never far from Fort Berthold. Reifel's studies focused on agricultural economics, economic analysis, and public administration, though he audited or enrolled in cultural anthropology, rural sociology, and social psychology courses to sharpen his understanding of cultural differences between American Indians and European Americans.[67] "I wanted to know why the Indians did not respond to advantages made available to them through churches, schools, and so on," he recalled.[68] Reifel found particular value in a guest lecture by anthropologist Alfred L. Kroeber, who shared his theories on cultural misunderstandings between future-minded Europeans and present-minded Indians that stemmed from their conflicting attitudes toward time. At Harvard, Reifel, in his words, "came to the conclusion that what you had was a question of two life styles. The Indians were a people who were oriented to the present whereas the North American whites were oriented to the future."[69] Reifel received solid marks in his courses and in June 1950 was awarded a master's degree in public administration. He immediately began doctoral studies, for which he was given one academic year to take additional courses and conduct research in preparation for his final examinations and the writing of his dissertation. The Reifel family's finances received a welcome boost in April 1951 when Ben received a prestigious John Hay Whitney Fellowship, awarded to deserving minority or financially disadvantaged students who displayed extraordinary academic ability.[70]

Reifel's research was decidedly practical and tailored to the issues confronting the Three Affiliated Tribes. In an article on the effects of the Garrison Dam in the November 1950 issue of the *Journal of Farm Economics*, Reifel acquainted readers with the material benefits to the "American community" furnished by the development of the Missouri River basin. To create these benefits "some few must be called upon to sacrifice for the good of the many." For most of the Indians of the Dakotas, Reifel noted, the benefits of the Missouri River dams would eventually outweigh the damages wrought by the loss of their bottomlands. The balance sheet for the Fort Berthold Indians, however, might prove to be less favorable. As compensation for land takings and human and material relocations, every member of the Three Affiliated Tribes stood to receive a payment of six thousand dollars. These one-time disbursements would, in the Indians' consumption-minded economy of abundance, "evaporate" before being put to productive use. Hence Fort Berthold residents faced "devastating effects" from the Garrison Reservoir's inundation of their "material core" and from their relocation to other reservation areas. It would be a tall order for the

Bureau of Indian Affairs, Reifel concluded, to ensure that "a sound process of reintegration is . . . carried out; a program that will restore a balanced way of life capable of meeting the demands of our time."[71]

Before beginning his dissertation, Reifel returned to Fort Berthold to consult with agency officials and tribal leaders and advise them on relocating families and facilities to five designated sites on the reservation. True to his promise of composing a dissertation with "practical meaning for other tribes of Indians that are imminently facing similar relocation problems," Reifel traveled to South Dakota to meet with representatives of the Crow Creek Sioux and Lower Brule Sioux, two tribes impacted by the Fort Randall and Big Bend dam projects. MRBI director J. M. Cooper and the staff of the Aberdeen Area Bureau of Indian Affairs Office relied on Reifel to assess conditions on the two reservations and make recommendations to the appropriate directors. "It has occurred to me," Cooper wrote to Reifel, "that with your intimate knowledge of the Sioux peoples, along with your recent training in rural sociology, an examination of social differences between the two groups . . . will be extremely valuable."[72]

Reifel's field work in South Dakota in July and August 1951 resulted in socioeconomic surveys of the Crow Creek and Lower Brule reservations that documented the tribes' economic conditions, reported on their governing bodies, and gauged the residents' degree of self-reliance. He met with tribal councilmen and collected information about family incomes and property holdings. He shared his opinions on relocation issues confronting the tribes and kept the Bureau of Indian Affairs abreast of problems plaguing residents in the affected areas.[73] While it provided the Bureau of Indian Affairs and MRBI with valuable information on the effects of dam construction in South Dakota, his field work was also of professional benefit to Reifel, who now possessed a region-wide view of challenges Indians faced in the Missouri Basin.

Back in Cambridge for the fall of 1951, Reifel set to work writing his dissertation, which he titled "Relocation on the Fort Berthold Indian Reservation: Problems and Programs." Though it can be appreciated as a broad study of American Indian adaptation to modern society, three specific investigations or discussions dominate the work.[74] First, Reifel adopts an expansive definition of "relocation," referring specifically to the Fort Berthold Indians' impending removal, but also taking into consideration the voluntary migration of other northern plains Indians to non-Indian communities. A second research thread, closely related to the first, is a candid analysis of the corrosive effects of overpopulation on the Fort Berthold Reservation, while the third discussion introduces Reifel's lofty vision for Indian quality of life. Throughout the work, Reifel, in a thoughtful tone that showcased his grasp on rural economics, Indian education, and traditional Indian cultures, offers practical proposals for the rehabilitation of the Three Affiliated Tribes. The result is a culturally sensitive yet future-oriented action plan that encompasses reservation demographics, Indian acculturation, and economic development.

From Reifel's perspective, the primary problem on the Fort Berthold Reservation was overpopulation. Even before the Corps of Engineers had selected sites for Missouri River dams, reservation landholdings were, Reifel argued, too small to support the local population. Land reductions brought about by the Garrison Dam meant that, even if remaining lands were put to productive use—and Reifel was not confident that they would be—the reservation could support only one-half of its current population. Compounding the imbalance between resources and people was the alarmingly high reservation birth rate. Fort Berthold's population increased 40 percent between 1930 and 1946, the product of a reservation birth rate that exceeded that of Puerto Rico, which in 1952 had one of the most rapidly growing populations in the world. Ironically, the Fort Berthold population boom occurred at the very moment that North Dakota's rural population was declining at a higher rate than the population in the state as a whole.[75]

Cultural norms, Reifel conceded, helped explain the birth rate. In premodern times, the high mortality rate suffered by the Arikara, Hidatsa, and Mandan tribes demanded a high birth rate to assure their survival. The people's current marital and sexual norms were rooted in a premodern past, but that past, wrote Reifel, did "not fit present conditions." The high pregnancy rate among young, unmarried Fort Berthold females indicated a "break down in social controls" that prevented "any early reduction in . . . overpopulation." Reservation residents needed to abandon old attitudes about sexuality, population, and tribal survival and adapt to new socioeconomic realities. Cultural practices that once saved the tribes from extinction now stood "in the way of economic adjustment necessary for the profitable use of the land."[76]

Addressing the reservation birth rate was but one side of the equation of Fort Berthold's population stress. The other was the integration of educated, technically skilled tribal members into white communities. Reifel urged bureau and tribal officials to establish more families off the reservation so as to enhance their quality of life while bringing about a healthier people-to-land ratio on the reservation. The alternative to depopulation, Reifel warned, was an increased tribal dependency on the federal government. "Unless many leave the farms each year there will be too many people to share too little and public funds will be required in increasing amounts merely to keep families from starving."[77]

Those who remained behind on the reservation must commit themselves to modern agriculture, Reifel argued. Farmers and ranchers would be moving from the well-protected river valley to barren, undeveloped uplands, where blistering summers, harsh winters, and unfamiliar soil required heightened levels of planning and physical effort. Livestock on the open prairies would not be protected against destructive blizzards, so additional care of cattle would be required. By moving against their will to this "strange land," would tribal ranchers, most of whom lacked managerial skills, "be pioneers without the prerequisite spirit" to profit from agriculture?[78] Reifel was uncertain of their future.

Ultimately, the future of the Three Affiliated Tribes hinged on formal education. Any opportunity or experience that exposed Indian youth to the white man's world would benefit them. But encouragement to explore that world would not necessarily come from their families, since the parents' level of acculturation was still at that of "the hoe culture age of the original village life." It was in schools, Reifel insisted, that students learned about career opportunities and developed the social and technical skills to achieve in white communities. Bureau of Indian Affairs and tribal officials should focus their energies on "intelligent planning of educational programs and the successful placement of Indian families in off-reservation opportunities to meet . . . overpopulation at Fort Berthold."[79]

Reifel viewed public schools as doorways to equality. Such a notion was gaining traction and in 1954 would be reinforced in the Supreme Court's historic ruling in *Brown v. Board of Education of Topeka*. Speaking in the spring of 1953, Bert Johnson, director of Indian education for the state of Wisconsin, observed that in the northern part of his state, racial prejudices were declining as the result of a program that integrated Indian students into local public schools. "Integration of Indians and whites in youth is a good prelude to assimilation of many problems that may arise later," Johnson declared. "We feel that the program is opening up the gates to citizenship for many Indians." While some reservation schools might provide an "adequate" education, their weakness derived from their segregating of Indian children from their white peers. Segregation reinforced prejudices among whites, whereas integration, Johnson posited, disarmed the white attitude "that the Indian is a somewhat different type of being than we are."[80]

Reifel rejected the idea that the American Indian experience was so unique that it precluded comparisons with other racial groups. European immigrants had once faced the daunting task of acculturation but came to realize that they must conform if they wished to prosper. They adjusted to American society while still retaining their ethnic identities, a transition, Reifel argued, that American Indians could emulate. Reifel was sensitive to the "disparity in the degree of acculturation amongst Fort Berthold families," a circumstance that complicated efforts to relocate and integrate. Further complicating the integration process were traditions that discouraged men from performing agricultural labor or any other form of "women's work." And yet the private sector had no place for hunter-warriors. Nor did the modern economy reward the "attitude of generosity" and the giveaways practiced by American Indian cultures. Anglo-American culture encouraged the individual's accumulation of capital and it valued "women's work." Resistance to modern culture was futile. Fort Berthold Indians needed to adjust their social behavior to meet new economic conditions, though Reifel conceded that the adjustment would take time. "The resistances created by [their] cultural lag make the habilitation process an uphill struggle," he acknowledged. "They remain to plague, in some measure, every effort to improvement."[81]

Reifel believed that whites were anxious to accept American Indians as full-fledged citizens with complete participatory rights. Discriminatory attitudes were in decline, evidenced by Fort Berthold women's teaching in public schools, by Indian membership in the Masons, Knights of Columbus, parent-teacher associations, veterans groups, 4-H, and the Girl Scouts, and by Indians' involvement in churches and political parties. In none of these circles did Indians risk a loss of racial identity. Indeed, their acculturation paved the way for what Reifel characterized as the "overall objective" of relocation and self-rule: "self-supporting families at a decent level of living with no more governmental assistance than that provided for the general public." If the cultural obstacles preventing Indians from living off the reservation were removed, the economic position of all Fort Berthold Indians would be advanced and "the Fort Berthold case . . . could be presented to Congress as one way to get the Government out of this Indian business humanely."[82]

Reifel concluded his study with a presentation of proposals and program ideas. He recommended that, on a reimbursable basis, Fort Berthold students enroll in the public school being built at New Town, a new, predominantly white community formed from two towns that faced inundation by the Garrison Reservoir. Reifel's recommendation accounted for bussing reservation students to New Town. He emphasized the greater variety of coursework awaiting Indian students who attended New Town School and predicted that, since the school was new, it was less likely that established social cliques would discriminate against Indian teens. To meet the post-secondary needs of Fort Berthold youth, the tribal council, suggested Reifel, should earmark funds for financing the education of college and trade school students. Tribal loans and grants would make students and parents more post-secondary-minded and expose more Fort Berthold residents to off-reservation living. Reifel specifically recommended that $1 million in tribal funds be designated for post-secondary support.[83]

Reifel's most original proposal was for the tribal financing of placement programs for those seeking off-reservation employment. As a means of assisting relocated families, Reifel suggested that the tribal business council rent apartment properties in North Dakota cities with fertile job markets. The apartments would provide relocated families with a place to establish themselves before seeking permanent living arrangements. Another feature of the placement proposal involved an arrangement with a North Dakota university wherein a small group of families could be trained in the ways of municipal living. The tribal council would install trailer houses near the campus for a half dozen families who could develop their shopping skills, learn to manage their finances, enroll their children in local schools, and utilize health clinics and social service agencies. These and other "real life" programs would advance the rehabilitation forced upon the Fort Berthold Indians by the construction of the Garrison Dam.[84]

On 19 May 1952, Harvard's Graduate School of Public Administration approved Reifel's dissertation. Ten days later he passed his doctoral exam in agricultural economics. As a teenager, Reifel had dreamed of earning a graduate degree. He was now probably the only American Indian to have received a doctorate from Harvard University.[85] Congratulations poured in from various sources, but Reifel would have been most grateful for the words of Harvard professor John M. Gaus, who, in a letter to Indian Commissioner Dillon S. Myer, wrote that he was "tremendously impressed with the maturity, even temper and wisdom" of Reifel's research. Gaus informed Myer "of the outstanding work which has been done here by this former officer of the Indian Service. It makes me feel good for our country when I see such a resource."[86]

Gaus incorrectly identified Reifel as a "former officer of the Indian Service." Within a few months of earning his Ph.D., Reifel was back at the superintendent's desk in Elbowoods and beginning a new phase of his civil service career. Great professional challenges would emerge over the next few years, but so would the voice of Ben Reifel.

4 THIS IS THE WHITE MAN'S WORLD

The 1950s witnessed the emergence of Ben Reifel as a leading voice in Indian affairs. After a three-year leave of absence, during which time he produced a Fort Berthold rehabilitation plan suitable for other northern plains tribes, Reifel returned to work with an ambition to share his ideas with a wide audience. With one or two notable exceptions, his ideas accorded with the assimilationist goals of the Truman and Eisenhower administrations. During an eight-year period in which he filled two demanding superintendent posts, was a leading candidate for Indian commissioner, and received a promotion to director of the Aberdeen Area Bureau of Indian Affairs Office, Reifel rose to prominence in his home state, where he was recognized by both Indians and non-Indians alike as an effective administrator with oratory skills that rivaled any South Dakota politician. By 1960, Ben Reifel, already one of the nation's most-recognizable American Indians, had become a dynamic public figure that South Dakota party leaders—despite their reservations about an American Indian candidate—could not ignore.

During a temporary assignment to the Bureau of Indian Affairs Washington office following the completion of his doctorate, Reifel received word of his reappointment to the superintendent's chair at Fort Berthold, effective 31 October 1952. In Reifel's absence, Reginald ("Rex") W. Quinn had continued the task of preparing the Three Affiliated Tribes for the inundation of 150,000 acres of their lands by the Garrison Reservoir. The Fort Berthold Reservation straddled both sides of the Missouri River, the Four Bears Bridge at Elbowoods connecting the two halves and providing access to agency facilities and services. But the Garrison Dam would dramatically change this physical setting. Henceforth, due to the removal of the bridge and the swelling of the Little Missouri River and the Shell and Lucky Mounds creeks, the reservation would be sliced into five separate units, a radical alteration that created numerous infrastructure problems and threatened to undermine community cohesion. Agency offices, the reservation hospital, schools, employees' quarters, warehouses, garages, and shops would be lost, as would utilities and telephone poles and over two hundred miles of roads. Compounding the challenge of relocating the agency's physical plant and infrastructure was the emotionally charged task of relocating the people themselves.[1]

Quinn faced, in his words, the "negative attitude" of Fort Berthold residents who complained bitterly about their forced relocation. Their new upland destination was "foreign" land for which they showed no enthusiasm. Rather than studying relocation plans or arranging for the investment of settlement monies, the Indians used public meetings to criticize the federal government, a pattern that complicated Quinn's responsibilities.[2]

Reifel returned to a demoralized reservation. Due to the impending damming of the river in the summer of 1953, the bureau and tribal council could no longer delay the removal of people and facilities from the taking area.[3] Reifel had hoped to implement the education and relocation programs outlined in his doctoral dissertation, and, to a degree, he did so. But he spent the majority of his fifteen-month tenure at Fort Berthold supervising the removal of people and material and, when not performing that task, mediating a rancorous intertribal debate over the disbursement of government compensation funds. Reifel served the Fort Berthold Indians during the most difficult chapter of their recent history and did so while gently encouraging them to face the reality that overpopulation, unemployment, and educational underperformance threatened their quality of life.

Upon his arrival at Elbowoods in late October, Reifel had little time to reorient himself. Having decided it was too expensive to construct a new agency town, the Bureau of Indian Affairs made plans to move its offices to a predominantly white but easily accessible community. Faced with the loss of their communities to flooding, the citizens of Sanish and Van Hook selected a site on the reservation's northern periphery for the construction of the joint community of New Town. It was here that Fort Berthold Agency offices were relocated in the summer of 1953. Reifel helped secure housing for bureau employees and arranged for the renting of temporary office space in New Town until permanent bureau offices were completed in 1954. He devised a plan to close the hospital at Elbowoods and replace its services with local clinics staffed by Bureau of Indian Affairs–contracted doctors and with contracting hospitals in Minot, Bismarck, and elsewhere.[4] While some Fort Berthold residents lamented the loss of their hospital, others looked forward to the prospect of superior health care off the reservation.[5]

Little could be done to alleviate the hardship caused by the closing of the Four Bears Bridge on 16 June 1953. Described by Reifel as a "big jolt to accustomed ways," the bridge closure separated residents living south and west of the Missouri River from families, friends, offices, churches, and cemeteries on the other side. Long drives to Elbowoods and limited telephone service on parts of the reservation compounded residents' frustration. Reifel attempted to provide a service for ferrying residents across the river, but it was an undependable operation and eventually cancelled.[6]

In May 1953 in the midst of solving the host of problems associated with Garrison Dam, Reifel learned that he was one of nine men under consideration for the top Bureau of Indian Affairs post of commissioner of Indian Affairs. The forty-six-year-old was undeniably qualified for the position and enjoyed the support of prominent Midwesterners and national groups who favored the appointment of an American Indian. The appointment, however, went to Glenn L. Emmons, a Gallup, New Mexico, banker who enjoyed the support of the large and influential Navajo Tribe.[7] Flattered by having been considered for the promotion, Reifel was brought back to earth by pressing issues, of which the schooling of Fort Berthold students displaced by the Garrison Dam proved to be the most immediate.

Reifel's preoccupation with Indian education, articulated in his doctoral dissertation and elsewhere, corresponded in some ways with post–World War II assimilation programs that fell under the heading of "termination." A policy objective that defined Indian affairs in the 1950s, termination spurned the cultural preservationist goals of the Indian New Deal, an unfortunate experiment, argued terminationists, which delayed Indians' integration into American society. Termination's proponents called for the repeal of laws that set apart or "discriminated" against Indians. They urged the transfer of existing Bureau of Indian Affairs services to other federal agencies, to state and local governments, or to the tribes themselves. Terminationists sought to "emancipate" individual Indians from federal guardianship, and, in what proved to be their most controversial aim, advocated the withdrawal and termination of federal responsibility for tribes deemed capable of thriving without bureau supervision. Convinced that reservation residents would never assimilate while walled off from the institutions of American life, terminationists imagined a day when Indians' relationships to national, state, and local governments would be equivalent to that of other Americans.[8]

For a moment, it appeared that the Three Affiliated Tribes were among the groups that, in the minds of Washington officials, had reached a level of acculturation suitable for the suspension of federal supervision. Dillon S. Myer, commissioner of Indian Affairs from 1950 to 1953, requested the drafting of a termination bill for the Fort Berthold Indians, despite comments by his predecessor, William Zimmerman Jr., that they should remain under federal guardianship. At a meeting between federal officials and American Indians at the Interior Department in June 1952, Carl Whitman Jr., representing the Fort Berthold Indians, listened to Commissioner Myer outline the bureau's agenda for the withdrawal of its programming, the transferring of Indian students to public schools, changes to reservation law enforcement, and relocation. Myer submitted that if the Three Affiliated Tribes were capable of managing millions of dollars without federal oversight, they might qualify for termination. But neither Whitman nor the other Indian representatives were impressed with Myer's presentation, and they, along with the Fort Berthold Tribal Business Council, registered their opposition to tribal termination.[9]

During conferences with various tribes in the fall of 1953, Myer's successor, Glenn L. Emmons, offered his own definition of termination: "What we are trying to achieve essentially, as I see it, is a condition of parity or equality for the Indian people as compared with the rest of the population." While not suggesting that Indians should sacrifice their cultural heritage, the Bureau of Indian Affairs did want "to give the Indians the same opportunities for advancement—the same freedom and responsibility in the management of their properties—as other American citizens." Commissioner Emmons admitted that while some tribes were "ready and anxious to take over full responsibility for their affairs," others were in "a real need for a continuation of the trusteeship and will be for several years." He promised to consult with every tribe recommended for termination, but added that the bureau would continue to explore means by which federal health, education, and welfare services could be transferred to state and local agencies. Emmons was "greatly encouraged" by programs that placed Indian children in public schools and he shared his hope that the Bureau of Indian Affairs might "speed up and broaden our efforts in this direction." Like his predecessor, Emmons anticipated the day "when the Indian people will be able to move forward without further restrictions or special services from the Federal Government."[10]

For his part, Ben Reifel regretted the pace of the termination policy, and in later years, he specifically opposed state government efforts to assume law enforcement responsibilities on reservations in South Dakota and elsewhere. In Reifel's view, it was "the responsibility of the Federal Government to get the Indian people up to an economic level of their non-Indian neighbors before steps are taken to leave their future economic development entirely with the states." After all, he reminded his Bureau of Indian Affairs colleagues, it was the federal government, not the states, that forcibly removed Indians to reservations.[11]

On the other hand, Reifel was deeply troubled by American Indians' dependence on government assistance, a destructive dependency, he argued, that sapped a once vigorous people of agency and vitality. Federal supervision acted as a "supporting crutch" for traditional cultures, and removing that crutch, Reifel confessed, would result in a "disequilibrium" that would disrupt social patterns. And yet, if it was the case that "the policy of segregation and the present pattern of reservation administration seems to leave the Indians clutched in the dead hand of the past[,] it is possible now to turn to other policies and other means." Reifel was not opposed to the Bureau of Indian Affairs exploring the effects of termination on the Three Affiliated Tribes. Due to the redistribution of the reservation population among five North Dakota counties and the availability of new services off the reservation, Fort Berthold might serve as a "laboratory" to test the transfer of federal services to state, local, and private institutions. If—and only if—the Fort Berthold Indians decided their new services were adequate, then their reservation might be a place to give the termination policy "a fair trial." Their withdrawal from federal services and their access to services used by non-Indians might be "politically, sociologically and psychologically advantageous" to the Three Affiliated Tribes, Reifel reasoned.[12]

Reifel acknowledged that the termination policy was an expression of Washington's goal "to get out of the Indian business," and, in the long run, he approved of that goal. Their reliance on the Bureau of Indian Affairs had relegated American Indians to second-class citizenship. "If the Fort Berthold people are to one day be 'full-fledged' citizens of the community, taking on the responsibilities as well as the privileges of citizenship, then that citizenship must develop in an environment of equality. Such equality does not exist so long as an Indian Bureau must fill in the gaps." The gaps would be closed, Reifel submitted, only when Indians availed themselves of state and local services that leveled the playing field with white Americans.[13]

To "close the gap" at Fort Berthold, Reifel hoped to integrate reservation students into the North Dakota public school system. Though the tribal council wanted to rebuild the Elbowoods boarding school and high school at a new reservation location, the bureau opposed a return to the status quo. With the backing of the North Dakota Commission on Indian Affairs, the Bureau of Indian Affairs proposed that Fort Berthold students enroll in public schools off the reservation. The tribal council initially rejected the proposal. But then, in what was later described as a compromise settlement, tribal representatives approved a site in the Eastern Segment of the reservation for the building of a high school open to both Indian and non-Indian students.[14]

Architectural planning for new elementary schools and a high school had commenced a few months before Reifel returned to Elbowoods. As families relocated and school construction went forward, Reifel hurried to provide temporary school facilities, transportation services, and dormitories for students of the Charging Eagle Day School, where the failure of a well created unsanitary conditions.[15] In preparation for the closing of Elbowoods High School in the spring of 1953, Reifel assisted in the recruitment of teachers and consulted with more than thirty state and county officials on how best to place students in off-reservation schools.[16] He made sure that parents of elementary-age children were afforded the opportunity to board their sons and daughters at a temporary school that remained open until April 1954. During this trying period for the Fort Berthold Indians, Reifel, whose commitment to school attendance remained undiminished, praised parents for getting their children to school: "For the sake of the children and our own future, we need to keep after our children to go to school every day and to study hard to learn all they can."[17]

Reifel's efforts did not go unnoticed. At the completion of her eleven-day inspection of Fort Berthold schools, Rose Ellen Doyle, a specialist with the Aberdeen Area Bureau of Indian Affairs Office, apparently displeased with the performance of Reifel's predecessor, informed Reifel that "it was most pleasing to see the genuine interest, in our school problems and policies, as was displayed by the new superintendent. . . . It is very evident that any problem that may arise will now receive immediate attention."[18]

A less immediate problem, but one that from Reifel's perspective could no longer be ignored, was reservation overpopulation, an issue that received special attention in Reifel's dissertation and perplexed him for the remainder of his life. The influx of returning World War II and Korean War veterans and alarmingly high birth rates complicated life in Indian country, where income-producing lands and employment opportunities were limited. Without a constant supply of federal services and support, reservations could not sustain their populations. Education and relocation, Reifel asserted, provided the only way out of the dilemma of too few resources for too many people.[19]

Reifel's personal relocation journey was not unknown to the residents of Fort Berthold. Nor was he the only bureau official promoting the voluntary relocation of reservation Indians. Robert L. Bennett, an Aberdeen area placement officer of Oneida Indian ancestry (and who, when named Indian commissioner in 1966, became the first American Indian to hold the post in nearly a century), visited Fort Berthold in 1950 to assist residents seeking off-reservation employment.[20] The following year, Indian Commissioner Myer, in an address to the National Council of Churches of Christ, shared his ideas for reducing reservation poverty and ending government paternalism. Congress, Myer recommended, should approve a program to resettle Indians in urban areas, a move that would encourage Indians to live without federal support, reduce the resource strain on reservations, and create space in overcrowded reservation boarding schools. Invoking the philanthropic spirit of a previous era of Indian affairs, Myer urged churches to involve themselves in relocation activities in cities where Indians' exposure to mainstream culture might raise their living standards and engender self-reliance.[21]

To abet relocation, Myer opened employment centers in Chicago, Los Angeles, Salt Lake City, and elsewhere. He established a relocation branch at the bureau's Washington office and lobbied Congress to fund relocation programs. Intrigued by the possibilities of city life, veterans, former defense plant workers, landless Indians, and young families took advantage of the relocation program. "Relocation," writes Kenneth R. Philp, "offered these people an alternative to Indian Bureau paternalism, economic insecurity, and second-class citizenship." As the decade progressed, the Bureau of Indian Affairs, witnessing a rise in Indian population and a corresponding reduction in uninhabited Indian lands, became more intentional in its crusade to relocate volunteers. In 1956, PL 959 provided vocational counseling, training, apprenticeships, and on-the-job training for adult American Indians. The expansion of relocation centers encouraged thousands to relocate. The fact that in the 1950s the Bureau of Indian Affairs received more relocation applications than it could process was evidence of the program's popularity.[22]

Reifel endorsed the relocation program. Among his fellow American Indians, he was not alone in his enthusiasm, for many tribal leaders asked families to consider migrating to cities of opportunity.[23] If Fort Berthold Indians were to enjoy off-reservation success, however, they had to become acquainted with the careers available in white America. The responsibility of acquainting young people with careers rested with high school guidance counselors. Working with agency staff and an official from the North Dakota Employment Service, Reifel reformed school guidance programs along lines that prepared students for off-reservation jobs. Henceforth, counselors were to introduce students to jobs that would do more than just "satisfy immediate need." Reservation farm-hand jobs with "marginal cattle and farm operators" would not provide long-term employment. Fort Berthold students had to look beyond the confines of the reservation and explore "the vast range of . . . jobs and careers in our modern industrial civilization." It was the responsibility of school staff to "raise [student] conception above limited reservation opportunities," and, once a student had selected a career path, "to provide follow-up counseling."[24]

School-based counseling reinforced the value of formal education. Reifel hoped that through career planning, Indian students might come to appreciate the importance of schools in preparing them for life. Their respect for education would then be passed on to their children. An effective career planning program would help Fort Berthold students in "overcoming any tendency to look upon schooling as something in which others are requiring that they participate." Coordination between agency officials and the state employment office, the state college at Fargo, and the University of North Dakota would better address unemployment problems particular to Fort Berthold and encourage state officials to accept more responsibility for the relocation of reservation families and educated Indian youth.[25]

Reifel never tired of telling American Indians about the benefits of the white man's world. He urged the leaders of the Three Affiliated Tribes to promote relocation, pointing out that, according to Bureau of Indian Affairs studies, only 175 families could sustain a satisfactory living on the Fort Berthold Indian Reservation. Economic conditions, tenuous before the execution of the Pick-Sloan Plan, had deteriorated since Reifel's arrival in 1946 due to losses associated with Garrison Dam. The population could not sustain itself at a pre-1946 standard of living. Reifel did not deny cases of failed relocations, of individuals falling into urban poverty or returning to the reservation to rejoin the ranks of the unemployed.

Nor was unemployment a peculiarly "Indian problem"; white North Dakotans were leaving the state to search for work elsewhere. Nevertheless, in the case of the Fort Berthold Reservation, a voluntary relocation program to reduce overpopulation was a sensible and humane option. "Whatever the shortcomings of the relocation program as applied nationally," observed historian Roy W. Meyer, "given the situation at Fort Berthold, there was emphatically a need for part of the population to leave the reservation if they were even to continue to live at the standard of living they had enjoyed before the Garrison Dam crisis."[26]

Reifel's was a relocation philosophy writ large. Unlike other Bureau of Indian Affairs officials who lacked firsthand knowledge of agriculture, Reifel understood clearly the socioeconomic realities facing rural communities—Indian and non-Indian—on the northern plains. The declining rural population in states like North Dakota confirmed the need for an Indian exodus to cities. Few white counties on the northern plains, after all, could accommodate the population growth occurring at Fort Berthold and other reservations. It was a matter of numbers, of the number of people in a community relative to the quantity of material resources for that community. If northern plains Indians resisted the relocation policy while multiplying their populations, their economic livelihoods would remain dependent on the services and support of the federal government. If that were the case, then their status as independent, self-determining peoples would—and should—be called into question.

Reifel hoped to witness a steady migration of Fort Berthold high school graduates to white communities. In a statement that was probably more wishful thinking than reasoned analysis, he predicted that twenty members of the Elbowoods High School Class of 1953 would relocate to other parts of the country. Wishful or otherwise, such thinking characterized Reifel's vision of relocation as the closing of an era of segregated reservation life and the opening of an era of Indian mobility and economic advancement. "A reservation is fast becoming just a place where some Indians were born," Reifel mused. "The United States is the Indian citizen's 'reservation' today."[27]

Unfortunately for Reifel, the time he had hoped to dedicate to relocation programs was limited by his involvement in a rancorous debate over the distribution of compensation funds appropriated for the tribes by Congress in 1949. At the heart of the dispute was whether the $7.5 million would be applied to reservation programs or distributed in per-capita payments to individual members of the Three Affiliated Tribes. Members of a tribal programs faction envisaged the settlement money being allocated for a credit program, a land consolidation fund, a housing finance program, and well-drilling projects. In contrast, leaders of the rival faction urged a per-capita distribution of the entire amount. The dispute played out in the 1950 elections for tribal chairman when the candidate of the per capita faction defeated the leader of the tribal programs faction in a special runoff election. For the next two years, Fort Berthold politicians bickered over whether compensations should be divided between tribal programs and individuals or simply allocated in their entirety to individuals. In the meantime, per-capita distributions went forward. The Bureau of Indian Affairs opposed the mass dispersal of remaining funds and warned tribal representatives that if they were willing to manage their economic affairs without bureau advice, termination might be the consequence.[28]

In 1953, as increasing numbers of Fort Berthold residents clamored for a per-capita distribution of the remaining settlement money, Reifel inserted himself into the debate. "This is something that should not be taken lightly," he wrote in the *Fort Berthold Agency News Bulletin*.[29] "My own feeling," he later wrote, "is that the Tribal Council is going to have to sit down and work out a plan that puts . . . tribal funds into use in a way that gets the Three Affiliated Tribes on the road to self support." Reifel reminded readers of the disparity that existed between reservation land owners and job holders on the one hand and the "large number" of irresponsible spenders on the other. The latter "get a big bunch of money, run right through it and are back on the Federal government or the county for help." He warned that a decision to exhaust the appropriation in a mass distribution would undermine students' education, then cited the disappearance of nearly all of the twelve-hundred-dollar per-capita payments made to that time. "We have boys and girls in high school right now who need clothes and other things so they will be happy in school. But they don't have a penny left. Their folks used it up."[30]

Reifel suggested that financing schools might reduce the reservation's high dropout rate while "protect[ing] the children against those parents who just don't seem to care." Per-capita payments amounted to handouts, and what was needed was "a plan—not handouts." The reckless spending that occurred after per-capita payments meant that when the children grew up, they "will have no per capita payments. They will be on their own and the thing we can do is to help them get the best education possible."[31]

Reifel's pleas had little impact on the opinions of the Fort Berthold Indians. The per-capita momentum rolled on after Reifel departed the reservation in early 1954, and by 1957 all of the money appropriated by Congress for the Three Affiliated Tribes had been distributed to individual tribal members.[32]

In the midst of the compensation debate, Reifel learned that he had been offered the option of filling one of two key Bureau of Indian Affairs posts: assistant area director for the Gallup, New Mexico, office or superintendent of the Pine Ridge Reservation in South Dakota. Confident that he "could be of some help at Pine Ridge," he decided to return to South Dakota.[33] In January 1954, Ben Reifel bid farewell to Fort Berthold, where he had served for nearly four and a half years. He expressed his gratitude to the tribal business council and to tribal members, agency staff, and state and county officials who had worked with him to address the monumental challenges facing the tribes. Reifel referred to his North Dakota assignment as "a most pleasant experience" and the friendships he formed as "the greatest treasure" he would take from his years on the Fort Berthold Indian Reservation.[34] A Garrison businessman assured Reifel that both "the folks at Ft. Berthold" and those "on the outside" would miss his presence.[35]

The Reifels packed their belongings and moved to the town of Pine Ridge, where they arrived on 17 January. In addition to bringing them a little closer to their daughter Loyce, a student at South Dakota State University, their return to Pine Ridge made for a homecoming of sorts. The reservation was the site of Ben's first Bureau of Indian Affairs posting and where, as an organizational field agent, he helped the Oglala Sioux Tribe write its constitution. The assignment was also historic, for Reifel became the first American Indian superintendent of the Pine Ridge Indian Reservation, a post that, with the possible exception of the Navajo Reservation, was considered the most demanding Bureau of Indian Affairs assignment in the country.[36]

Though its population had grown considerably since the 1930s, little else had changed at Pine Ridge. The reservation, the most populous in the state, remained one of the poorest places in the United States. Most of its eleven thousand residents lived in scattered rural communities and hamlets. Many Oglalas lived in log homes or frame shacks, though there were some living in tents, tipis, or abandoned cars. The majority lacked electricity and running water. Reservation residents hauled water from wells or creeks, cooked on bottle-gas stoves, and heated their homes with wood stoves. The nine hundred or so "town Indians" of Pine Ridge, the site of the agency headquarters, schools, and hospital, occupied makeshift houses in conditions well below the living standards of white South Dakotans.[37]

The reservation's land holdings (46,522 acres of which had been declared submarginal during the 1930s) could not support a population that was too dense for the available resources. While some Oglalas owned land and leased it for income, many more depended on food commodities for at least a portion of their dietary needs. The Interior Department's relaxation of a New Deal–era moratorium on the sale of trust-allotted lands had resulted in land alienation. Some town-based Oglalas could derive cash income from steady employment, but job opportunities were scarce and unemployment levels high. At the time of Reifel's return to Pine Ridge in 1954, only 200 of 1,700 families were earning a living on a reservation capable of supporting only 600 families. Oglalas could find day work off the reservation, or they could relocate. If they resisted those options, they would likely remain dependent on the federal government.[38]

Having confronted these conditions as a boss farmer and field agent, Reifel now faced them as a superintendent. The Oglala Sioux's heavy dependence on federal aid made them a unique administrative challenge. Compounding the challenge was the inflammatory nature of Oglala politics, wherein tribal factionalism, noisy agitators, and what Reifel referred to as "government by personalities rather than government by principles" made the Pine Ridge superintendent's job as difficult as any in Indian country.[39]

Some of Reifel's day-to-day duties were of a routine nature. He worked with specialists on water, predator, livestock management, wind erosion, and trespassing problems. He met regularly with hospital and school staffs and updated reservation residents on health care and education programs. Frequent visits to reservation districts allowed Reifel to ascertain the people's opinions and their immediate needs. He kept state officials abreast of reservation affairs and coordinated his efforts with theirs to provide Oglalas with child welfare, sanitation, and health services. As an army reserve officer with a military police background, Reifel provided guidance to tribal law enforcement officers who were combating high reservation crime rates. When not performing these tasks, Reifel attended tribal council meetings and school events and spoke to college students, business and civic groups, women's clubs, and farm and ranch organizations in towns in western South Dakota and northwestern Nebraska.[40]

Exhibiting a confidence that came from his command of the Lakota language and his sixteen years of field experience, Reifel called on the Oglala to be engaged, responsible, and law-abiding citizens. In the pages of the superintendent's *Daily News Sheet* or in the *Pine Ridge*, the reservation news bulletin, he kept readers abreast of school and community activities, tribal council agendas, and bureau programs. His tone was, for the most part, upbeat and optimistic. He praised students' achievements and lauded parents who involved themselves in their children's education. He highlighted notable individual and group accomplishments and called attention to examples of good financial decision making. Though Reifel encouraged the Oglala to be forward-thinking, he was not at all averse to ceremonials and cultural events, where he was nearly always in attendance and conversing in English and Lakota. Despite all of the professional burdens he shouldered at Pine Ridge, Reifel genuinely enjoyed his assignment, which he would refer to in July 1955 as "the happiest period of my years in the Bureau of Indian Affairs."[41]

And yet despite his cheery disposition, Reifel was quick to denounce lawlessness, destructive behavior, irresponsible parenting, reckless financial decision making, and undependable employees. Those guilty of disorderly conduct, assault and battery, resisting arrest, or a failure to fulfill court orders found their names listed in the *Daily News Sheet*. He shamed parents for not enforcing their children's school attendance and directed special criticism at those parents who fell back on "the same old excuses we have listened to year after year while watching . . . their children become so retarded that they finally become discouraged and drop out of school before entering high school. The future for this group of students is not bright." Reifel grew impatient with cynical and sarcastic reservation residents who ridiculed the more civic-minded Oglalas living among them. Wasn't it odd, he mused, that descendants of Crazy Horse and Red Cloud were publicly drunk on trash-strewn streets and playgrounds? That a once proud and spiritual people seemed to have lost "a faith to love by and die for"? Oglala heroes were no longer respected. Nor, ironically, were those Oglalas working to improve life on the Pine Ridge Reservation.[42] What would Crazy Horse and Red Cloud say, asked Reifel, if they returned to live among the modern Sioux? "They would see that there are Indians at Pine Ridge who seek to destroy the good name of the Sioux nation. They would cry, 'Shame,' and their hearts would be saddened by the degree of depravity that has besmirched Sioux pride and honor." Reifel, forever mistrustful of anthropologists and sociologists "who sought to retain Indian glory" while doing nothing to elevate Indian livelihood, swore "to defend the Sioux glory as long as there is breath in me."[43]

In an essay that, had it been published fifteen years later, would have been thundered against by Red Power radicals, Reifel encouraged Lakotas to emulate Christian saints and non-Indian heroes if they could find no role models among themselves. After returning from a meeting of the American Public Welfare Association in Salt Lake City in April 1955, he described how Mormons, a people "willing to die for the way they believed," were products of their faith. Reifel, a lay leader in the Episcopal Church, suggested that a closer connection between Lakotas and their respective churches "would help us as a Sioux people to *work by ourselves* and to *work together*."

Christian saints were worthy role models, as were heroic white Americans. Reifel, a longtime admirer of Benjamin Franklin and Abraham Lincoln, told Lakotas that if there were no heroes in their midst then they should "follow in the path of the Saints" or the great Americans "who helped build this wonderful land in which we live." Seek inspiration in saints and American heroes, Reifel told his audiences, and not in misguided notions that repaired treaties or large cash settlements would magically improve reservation life.[44]

Fundamentally, Pine Ridge residents could choose between destructive or productive lifestyles. To make his point, Reifel recalled the story of an Oglala Sioux couple who in 1953 received over eighteen thousand in government monies but squandered it all in less than two years. The attitude of entitlement exhibited by many Lakotas masked moral problems that money could not repair. Residents of the Pine Ridge Reservation should engage in soul-searching. "It is something deeper than money that we as Sioux people need," Reifel observed. Money was "not enough."[45]

Reifel's frank appraisal of reservation life was not limited to news bulletins; he was equally candid with representatives of the Oglala Sioux Tribal Council. Reifel's comments at council meetings resembled "State of the Reservation" addresses in which he evaluated policies and programs, examined ongoing problems, and offered constructive solutions. Speaking alternately in Lakota and English, he urged tribal leaders to confront crime, poor school attendance, land alienation, and the deplorable work ethic of many of the reservation's residents. Law enforcement was typically the first order of business. "We have a state of low-down gangsterism of the most sickening type," Reifel announced at a tribal meeting in July 1954. Vandalism and gang activities spread fear and despair among law-abiding families, who, ironically, were better-protected off the reservation than in their own communities. Reifel's remarks on crime raised the ire of his critics. "It may be that one of these times I may get beaten up," he announced. But he was not intimidated. "I feel courageous about maintaining law and order in the community," he told the council.[46]

As he had done at Fort Berthold, Reifel pressed Pine Ridge parents to get their children to school. He took pride in having increased school attendance to nearly 100 percent by January

1955. "It's amazing how excellent the school attendance has been throughout the reservation since Reifel became superintendent," a local principal commented.[47] Reifel helped organize a Boy Scout troop, 4-H clubs, and other youth groups that extended the tribe's educational reach and provided recreational outlets "to eliminate our boys getting into troubles, such as the 6 boys now held in jail here."[48] Respect for education and law went hand in hand. "Without law and order we cannot have education and without education we cannot have law and order," he reasoned.[49] It might be the case, Reifel reflected, that the Oglala leadership pyramid was becoming inverted. Educated youth were now in a position to set an example for the older generations. "The hope of the Sioux people does not rest in treaties and handouts from the government, but in the education of our boys and girls," he declared.[50]

While continuing to insist that eleven thousand people was too large a population to sustain on the Pine Ridge Reservation, Reifel was also concerned about the alarming rate of Oglala land losses. At one point he claimed that trust-allotted lands were being sold to non-Indians at a rate of 100 to 320 acres per day. Should that pace continue, he predicted, the Oglalas would lose their trust-allotted lands within fifteen years. But alongside these warnings Reifel promoted the voluntary relocation of reservation dwellers to communities where they could secure gainful employment.[51] At Pine Ridge (as at most reservations on the northern plains), opportunities for individual self-support were wanting, land resources insufficient, and the local economy stagnant or nonexistent. Reservation residents faced the alternatives of leaving Indian country to make a living or staying behind to live in privation on the public dole.[52]

By 1954, the Bureau of Indian Affairs Branch of Relocation had assisted nearly a thousand North Dakota, South Dakota, and Nebraska Indians in moving to cities, adjusting to their surroundings, and securing employment. Los Angeles, Denver, Chicago, San Francisco, and Oakland were common relocation destinations, although for many Lakotas, moving to nearby Rapid City was their first preference. Reifel welcomed a Lakota relocation program and remained one of its principal champions. He did not pressure individuals to migrate, but he promoted the program and worked with relocation officers to assist single men and family heads in applying for off-reservation jobs. Oglalas were informed about job placement services, financial assistance packages, and urban support offices. At the same time, they were cautioned that Bureau of Indian Affairs hospitals, schools, and social services would not be available at their destinations. Since migrants would have to buy insurance, enroll their children in public schools, and apply their income to rent, clothing, and food, Reifel went to great lengths to prepare them for the transition to independent living.[53]

Relocation was a step on American Indians' path to full citizenship, the results of which, Reifel believed, would profit all Americans. The large number of Oglala men submitting relocation applications heartened Reifel, who, due to the glut of applications, prioritized the enrollment of heads of households. Their adjustment to urban life would not be easy, he told them. Relocated families had to be thrifty and resilient. Too many recipients of relocation funds drank away their cash or failed to budget for monthly expenses. Declaring that "relocation is the only thing for many of us," Reifel hoped to prepare potential migrants for the challenges that lay before them. He wanted applicants to be certain about their decision and, once decided, to ready their families for the transition.[54]

Overall, the results of the relocation program were mixed. If measured by the number of Indians who relocated, the program was popular. For instance, between 1952 and 1956, some sixty-five hundred American Indians relocated to Los Angeles alone, where, if they so requested, they were provided up to four weeks of subsistence money while searching for housing and employment. Relocatees found work in more than five hundred Los Angeles firms, landing jobs in the aircraft and electronics industry, textile manufacturing, retail sales, public schools, and county and municipal offices. They lived in efficiency apartments and homes with electric ranges, running water, and modern plumbing, and purchased radios and televisions, luxuries that were rare on Indian reservations. The children of relocated adults enjoyed school and their classmates. Indian students won academic and athletic awards, and their parents were active in PTA, with one relocated Pueblo woman serving as PTA president in an Inglewood school district.[55]

In his study of the termination and relocation policies of the 1940s and 1950s, Donald L. Fixico recounts the many social, economic, and psychological struggles of relocated Indians. Yet Fixico points out that Indians who remained on reservations also "experienced considerable economic difficulty" and "often paid a high price for staying on their reservation homelands." At the Pine Ridge and Rosebud reservations, where unemployment runs much higher than in American cities, Indians suffered from "economic and social malaise." Some of the best minds in Indian country merged into the American mainstream and chose not to return home, contributing to the reservation talent drought which negatively impacted rural Indian life. Although some city Indians "traded rural poverty on the reservation for urban slums," their children benefited from immersion into white society. "Indian youths growing up in an urban environment often became teachers, lawyers, doctors, and other professionals," writes Fixico.[56]

The number of reservation Indians participating in the relocation program from 1953 to 1960—a total of 33,466—was small in comparison to the roughly 166,000 Indians residing in American cities in 1960. In Boston, New York City, and elsewhere, Indian families had already settled in ethnic pockets without the assistance of federal officials. Indians relocated under Bureau of Indian Affairs supervision, however, faced unique challenges. Assimilating to urban life proved difficult. Locating an apartment, selecting a doctor and dentist, enrolling their children in schools, shopping for food and clothing, and paying utility bills demoralized the least resilient migrants. One-third of relocated families returned to their respective reservations. Many of the returnees chose not to shed their old lifestyles and never viewed their city dwellings as anything but temporary lodging. Some had never seen a watch or a clock or adhered to a work schedule. The Bureau of Indian Affairs bore much of the blame for relocation failures, an unfortunate truth that Ben Reifel, a proponent of relocation, often alluded to. From firsthand observation, he discovered that transplanted Indians overspent their incomes and landed in debt. Bureau officials had not established criteria for relocation candidate selection and, more importantly, they had not taken into account the educational preparation necessary for an individual's transition to white society.[57]

A 1952 study of Indian residents of Rapid City, the majority of whom were born on the Pine Ridge and Rosebud reservations, revealed that most of the transplanted individuals were poorly educated, unskilled, and resistant to steady work. A majority had not graduated from high school and many felt entitled to a life provided for them at the expense of the government that seized their lands. Many Rapid City Lakotas lived for the present and planned little for the future, an outlook that began to manifest itself in lethargy, alcoholism, and abnormally high incarceration rates. Unemployed Lakotas disavowed any employed Lakotas who did not share their money or possessions, a pattern that destroyed the ambition of "energetic" Indians. Educated Indians interviewed for the Rapid City study blamed their fellow Indians for the city's "Indian problem." Poorly educated Lakotas, they said, were fixated on the past and placed more faith in tribal elders than in the working Indians living among them.[58]

The animosity, malaise, and lack of resiliency exhibited by many Lakotas did not surprise Reifel, who attributed the behaviors to a combination of inadequate education and obsolete cultural values. Reifel routinely enlightened white audiences about the average Lakota's ignorance of time, a word that did not exist in the Lakota language. A present-minded people, the Lakotas were not concerned with calendars, clocks, and schedules. But until they adopted Western notions of time and economy, Reifel explained, the Lakotas would remain destitute.[59] "Three things are important in the white man's world, and in fact the entire economy is built upon them: Time, Work and Saving." He described how the rhythms and practices of premodern buffalo culture conflicted with Euro-American conceptualizations of time, work, and saving. Time had not been important to nineteenth-century Lakotas, who enjoyed an unlimited supply of bison to meet their needs. The storing of possessions was unnecessary and even discouraged, as it might attract enemies or delay the movement of the band. Lakota men fought, hunted, stole horses, and protected the camp; they scoffed at "women's work." Generosity was expected, so Lakotas shared their belongings with extended families and the larger community. Yet generosity, however admirable, was not institutionalized in white culture, where acquisitiveness, individualism, and the needs of the nuclear family took precedence. When extended family members moved in with an Indian family playing by the rules of white society, friction was inevitable. "It's great to keep these values—especially those traits of generosity and caring for others," remarked Reifel. "But the old values can also hold you back. You can't continue to hold the same values as when we had the buffalo."[60] Customs associated with their ancestors' culture would retard Lakotas, for "the idyllic life of nomads who eschewed wealth, work and individual ambition" was incompatible with modern capitalist society.[61]

An iconic symbol of capitalist society was the clock. Reifel's recurring message to Oglalas was that they would continue to suffer the effects of poverty "until they develop[ed] a consciousness of time."[62] To promote time management, Reifel ordered teachers to hang clocks in classrooms and enforce the school day schedule. Clergymen were encouraged to begin Mass and worship services on time. Tribal council meetings started on time. Punctuality was expected on the reservation because it was demanded off the reservation. "This is 1954 and the white man's world," Reifel told a reporter. It may not be the world they preferred to live in, but the Lakotas needed to "learn to live in it—they must."[63]

Schools introduced young Indians to the white man's world, and few twentieth-century Indians lent a stronger voice to the cause of Indian education than Ben Reifel. His was a hard-nosed approach not appreciated by some Oglala parents. But Reifel remained undeterred in his mission of raising academic standards on the Pine Ridge Reservation. "It takes courage to do what is right," he stated.[64] Pine Ridge parents who failed to enforce school attendance were publicly shamed and faced the prospect of arrest. Reifel challenged high school students to become better role models for their younger brothers and sisters. Tribal councilmen were urged to promote the work ethic and punctuality. "Ben Reifel has the right idea," observed a local Jesuit priest, who was impressed by the superintendent's success at indoctrinating the Oglala to school expectations. "That educational whip of his will speed the day of complete adjustment in the white man's world. The residue of the white man's culture is beginning to wear off on the Sioux. The parents are getting tougher, thanks to Ben, with their children."[65]

At a 1955 meeting of the South Dakota chapter of the White House Conference on Education, Reifel reported that possibly half of the Indian families in the state had adjusted to "the social, economic, and spiritual design that is America." But these successes could not conceal the monumental problems plaguing South Dakota tribes. American Indians made up 34.3 percent of the inmate population of the South Dakota State Penitentiary. Twenty-five percent of the boys and 50 percent of the girls committed to the State Training School were American Indians, and 38.6 percent of South Dakota families receiving Aid to Families with Dependent Children assistance were American Indian. "These unfortunates," observed Reifel, "are not coming from the Indian homes that have made adjustment."[66]

After acquainting his audiences with the stark realities of Indian country, Reifel would sometimes discuss the Indian relocation program. The movement of reservation residents into white communities meant that *all* Indians must adjust to white culture, even those who "still listen to a voice of the past. . . ." The task of educators, Reifel declared, was to assist unadjusted individuals in "find[ing] their way to a meaningful place in our way of life." No barriers need stand in the way of Indian students inculcated to the values of time, work, and saving. For the acculturated student, "the road to economic and social success . . . is wide open. The American dream may still become a reality for the person who will work hard, save, become a slave to time, get an education and do difficult and distasteful but honorable tasks when necessary to achieve his goal."[67]

Education was the essential ingredient for American Indian success, and success, as Reifel defined it, meant American Indians' integration into the economic mainstream. American Indians were not the only Americans to have endured a difficult transition to a foreign culture. While acknowledging that the assimilation of the Indian formed a unique chapter in American history—What other group was forcibly removed to reservations? he asked—Reifel refused to excuse his people's resistance to a new economic order. He pointed out that Asian Americans and other immigrants with no formal education or English language skills had moved away from their homelands and native cultures, joined a new and dominant culture, strived to succeed in that culture, and did so.[68] Many Lakota Sioux, on the other hand, turned their backs on American culture. They decided that if the institutions and values of their nomadic buffalo culture were to survive, they must remain segregated in a geographical subculture protected by reservation boundary lines. Such thinking, Reifel asserted, conveniently dismissed the presence of European American subcultures in South Dakota that had embraced the values of the American mainstream yet energetically maintained their cultural heritages. "Just as the Norwegians and South Dakota's other ethnic groups have continued to practice their crafts and preserve the foods, the American Indians should continue their dances and arts . . . but anyone who wants to get into the mainstream is going to have to learn the Work-Time-Save elements."[69]

The government itself, admitted Reifel, bore some responsibility for Indians' social and economic condition. The IRA, for all of its emphasis on tribal self-determination, had not inspired individual initiative. Tribal governments routinely failed at economic development, a fact evidenced, for instance, by the failure of a Pine Ridge tent-making industry that closed its doors because of an embezzlement scandal. In July 1955, during Reifel's final month as Pine Ridge superintendent, a panel of experts concluded that the IRA was not helping Indians adjust to modern living. Indians remained dependent on the federal government, and tribal councils, tribal enterprises, and tribal courts had failed to improve the living standards of reservation residents in the twenty years since the Wheeler-Howard Bill was signed into law.[70]

According to Reifel, Indians had only themselves to blame if, from 1955 forward, they remained dependent and destitute. The time for blame and self-pity, for playing the victim and not the agent, had passed. Unlike other ethnic groups, American Indians had been provided numerous educational and economic opportunities by the federal government and the private sector. Since the colonial period, Indians had access to higher education, with Dartmouth College, for example, waiving tuition costs for American Indians. Instead of seizing the opportunity to enjoy the rewards of full citizenship, Indians remained on reservations where they held fast to unreasonable prejudices toward whites. In a candid speech to the delegates of the National Congress of American Indians in Omaha in November 1954, Reifel accused members of his own race of practicing racism. "We've got to get this nonsense about racial prejudice out of our systems," he exclaimed. "And I'm not talking about white man's prejudice against the Indian, but about the prejudice of the Indians against the white man. We've got to get it out of our heads that we are a different kind of American citizen." A speaker of Choctaw descent, Peru Farver, spoke after Reifel and echoed his remarks. "We cry our heads off about being discriminated against. I think a lot of the time it's our own fault."[71]

Reifel proudly noted that, historically, the Lakota Sioux were an adaptable people with a record of environmental and economic accommodations. Once a forest people, they had migrated to the Great Plains, developed an equestrian culture, built an economy around the bison herds, and became a regional military superpower. But that age had passed. The demands of twentieth-century living required a new adaptation to a modern economy. Indians must henceforth conform to the rhythms of the workday, earn a regular paycheck, and manage their personal finances. "Change," Reifel told the Oglala Sioux, "is the order of the day." The ways of the old days would not suffice. "In these changing times what fit the need yesterday may be no good today," he cautioned. "It will do no good to sit around and kid ourselves about the good old days, Like the buffalo they are gone forever and gone for good. Ours is to figure out what is upon us and ahead of us, not only for ourselves but our children and our people, and to work out an answer with the tools of today." Change was inevitable. If they wished to thrive as they once had, the Lakotas must meet change head-on, and "the place to get ready to meet it is in our schools and colleges."[72]

Reifel shared his formula for Lakota success with dozens of white audiences. Having perfected his oratory skills during sixteen years of public functions, Reifel was in 1954–55 enjoying a reputation as one of western South Dakota's most dynamic speakers. Newspaper reporters interviewed him. High schools and colleges invited him to address student assemblies and graduating classes. At five feet, nine inches in height and 175 pounds, he was not an imposing figure, but his sonorous, slightly raspy baritone voice and remarkable vocabulary mesmerized members of chambers of commerce and Rotary, Lions, and Kiwanis clubs. Agriculture organizations respected his understanding of the rural economy, while church and women's groups valued his presentations on the conditions facing reservation Indians. In the summer of 1955, Reifel shared his expertise with twenty-six public school administrators as the instructor for a graduate course entitled "Cultural Impact on Human Adjustment." These and other engagements led a Rapid City journalist to describe Reifel as "one of the ablest orators ever to bless this section of the country" and "one of the best known figures in the state today."[73]

Reifel urged white audiences not to succumb to stereotypes. Technically, American Indians were not wards of the government but United States citizens with the same rights as other Americans. In explaining the challenges facing South Dakota Indians, Reifel adopted the theme "Education is the last and only hope for our Sioux people." He touted his efforts to improve school attendance and highlighted the connection between educational achievement and off-reservation success. He shared how frustrated he had become with backward-looking Lakotas who stereotyped whites as unfriendly and mean-spirited. Reifel delivered a balanced message, and the impression he left behind was of a man patient enough to accept the cultural lag affecting Indians without offering excuses for the members of his race who failed to "pitch in with the rest of the 162 million Americans." His words and the sincerity with which he uttered them made an impact on journalists like Will Spindler of the *Rapid City Daily Journal*, who praised Reifel for "valiantly making that last-ditch stand for his people to bring them, through education and enlightenment, out of the dire poverty, confusion, insecurity, exploitation, and chaos that has been their unhappy lot [and toward] a new era of independence, pride, higher living standards, and consequent fuller lives."[74]

Considering the leadership positions he had held in North Dakota and South Dakota, it probably came as no surprise to Reifel when, on 6 July 1955, he was named director of the Bureau of Indian Affairs Aberdeen Area Office. It was a capstone appointment, but one that came with great responsibilities and expectations. As a line officer, he would report directly to Commissioner Emmons, who placed Reifel in charge of all Bureau of Indian Affairs programs in the states of North Dakota, South Dakota, and Nebraska. The Aberdeen office was "a Government in miniature and encompasses the highly complex mission of providing services to Indians that are normally provided to the general public by local, state, and highly specialized individual federal government bodies." As a former superintendent on two reservations, Reifel understood better than most bureau officials what those services entailed. He now faced the task of administering education, health, welfare, law enforcement, relocation, and resource development services at twelve reservations, three schools, and several hospitals, and to do so in a budget-cutting environment that placed heavy strains on area directors. His administration would be carried out under the umbrella of a termination policy that, because of its speed of implementation, was not welcomed by Reifel. He did not oppose a long-range goal of termination, defined in his official duties as "the eventual assimilation of the Indians within the Area into society as co-equals of other citizens"; Reifel could not have better articulated his own philosophy of Indian affairs. But he insisted that the federal government fulfill its promise to equip Indians for independent living before it discontinued its historic relationship with the tribes.[75]

Reifel's new post, which he held from 1955 to 1960, required him to liaise with state officers and congressmen. He would also be expected to institute public relations and information programs, an assignment that permitted him to continue his public appearances on a scale that elevated his name recognition on the northern plains.[76]

And whereas his recent speaking engagements had been limited to West River South Dakota, Reifel would now appear before business, church, civic, and education groups in the more populous eastern half of the state. By the end of the decade, with critical elections looming in the fall of 1960, Ben Reifel had become an intriguing prospect for political office, presenting the accomplished civil servant with an opportunity to participate in an historic campaign that would, quite literally, change the face of South Dakota politics.

5 THEY'LL NEVER VOTE FOR AN INDIAN

The appointment of Ben Reifel as director of the Aberdeen Area Office, effective 1 August 1955, was applauded by other area directors and by superintendents, attorneys, college professors, congressmen, and the president of the Association on American Indian Affairs.[1] Robert L. Bennett, superintendent of the Ute Agency in Utah and himself of Indian descent, praised Reifel's leadership and looked forward to a time when "Indian voices will be heard in some more of the Bureau's administration."[2] Ralph Hoyt Case, a South Dakota native and respected attorney with a history of representing tribes in Indian claims cases, considered Reifel the best official in the Bureau of Indian Affairs. He had worked with Reifel while negotiating the Garrison Dam settlement and commended the new Aberdeen director for his moderate approach to termination. Reifel was not "the extremist type, either for or against the present movement." Case predicted that Reifel would succeed at every level of the Bureau of Indian Affairs. "You are still my candidate for Commissioner of Indian Affairs," Case wrote to Reifel.[3]

Indian residents in the Aberdeen Area discovered that Reifel was a different kind of director. Early in his tenure, he made a lasting impression on elders from the Standing Rock Sioux Tribe in attendance at a House Subcommittee on Indian Affairs forum at Fort Yates, North Dakota. A man named Station Many Deeds asked to speak in his native tongue. Reifel granted his request and then translated Many Deeds's remarks for the members of Congress. Following the translation, surprised tribal members noted with pleasure that this was the first time a high-ranking Bureau of Indian Affairs official had spoken for them in their native language.[4]

Reifel took charge of an office established in Aberdeen just five years before his promotion. He assumed responsibility for over 1,200 Bureau of Indian Affairs employees in three states; about 135 of them worked out of the Aberdeen office. Reifel's new post required him to direct all bureau activities on the northern plains. He would serve as consultant and coordinator for superintendents and field employees under his charge and act as liaison to governors, state legislatures, and members of Congress. He exercised an authority second only to that of the Indian commissioner and yet confronted the day-to-day challenges faced by agency superintendents, albeit on a wider geographical scale.[5]

The Aberdeen Area Office impacted nearly every feature of life on reservations in North Dakota, South Dakota, and Nebraska. Reifel and his staff attended to the people's immediate health and welfare needs, which were increasing daily due to rising populations in Indian country. To meet the demands, Reifel expanded area welfare services, doubled the number of social workers at the Aberdeen office, and made improvements to adoption and foster care programs. Continuing an effort he had begun in 1946, Reifel extended social services to families displaced by dam construction on the Missouri River. He traveled frequently to reservations within his jurisdiction to speak with residents about the social welfare issues affecting them. Meanwhile, he and his staff attended to reservation health care systems. To introduce tribal leaders in the three-state area to the range of health care services for American Indians, Reifel invited them to Aberdeen to meet directly with officials of the Indian Public Health Service. In an effort to foster more state involvement in reservation health and welfare programs, he chaired the Indian Affairs Committee of the South Dakota Social Welfare and Public Health Conference and was active in the South Dakota Tuberculosis and Health Association.[6]

The education of tribal youth remained of paramount importance to Reifel. As area director he possessed a bully pulpit to address dropout rates while urging boys and girls to immerse themselves in white society. During regional youth conferences at Crow Creek, Flandreau, and elsewhere, he encouraged high school students to stay in school, involve themselves in church activities, abide by the clock, adopt a work ethic, and save their money. Reifel did not ask Indian students "to change from Indians to something else—you are just being asked to change your methods of living." American Indian youth, he explained, occupied a space "between two worlds—the American way and the Indian way." Their situation did not require them to reject the "good things about the Indian way of life," but as students they must come to accept that "times have changed and as a result the Indian way of life is going to have to change to the American way."[7]

The "American way" was a principal theme of an adult education program launched by Reifel in 1957. On five reservations in the Dakotas and at the Sioux Sanatorium in Rapid City, adult learners were taught to live within a budget and make sound personal finance decisions. The program attracted recent high school dropouts, who, along with their adult peers, were invited to enroll in reading classes, sewing and craft classes, or correspondence courses offered by North Dakota and South Dakota colleges and universities.[8] In 1957, Reifel's own educational journey attracted some attention when it was announced that he had been awarded a Fulbright scholarship to study in India. Reifel turned down the offer, explaining that "the work of the Bureau of Indian Affairs in this country is more important from my point of view than participating in a project of that kind in India."[9]

American Indian education and relocation were intimately linked, and from Reifel's perspective they remained cardinal objectives of the office of area director. Agency relocation officers supervised the adult education programs on their respective reservations, from which residents might relocate to Denver, Los Angeles, San Jose, Oakland, Chicago, or Saint Louis, or closer to home in cities like Rapid City or Minneapolis–Saint Paul. Reifel's office provided support for relocation officers who, in addition to preparing families for their moves, arranged for grants and subsistence payments and connected the families with relocation officials at their destinations. In the first four years of relocation operations, Bureau of Indian Affairs officials assisted in the relocation of over 1900 South Dakota Indians, though the number of successful relocatees continued to be an area of concern. A 1955 study by the Association of American Indian Affairs found that at three South Dakota Indian reservations, the number of migrants that had successfully transitioned to their new communities varied from 53 to 70 percent.[10] There were also complaints from Rapid City relocatees that they were being "picked on," though longtime Indian residents of Rapid City insisted that recently arrived Indians were "the same as everybody else."[11]

Reifel remained unapologetically committed to relocation. Having done more than most officials in establishing a dialogue about the effects of reservation overpopulation, he repeated his warning that northern plains Indians were subject to a "rapidly increasing population without adequate social programs . . . to live meaningful lives in our time."[12] He refused to entertain pessimistic claims by members of his own race that the white man would never accept the red man as his equal. "There'll be a lot of sweat and tears before we can have a triumph that is sweet for many of our people," Reifel told a reporter. But he remained adamant that "there's no place in America that any Indian boy or girl can't go if you respect those three things: time, work, saving."[13]

Reifel's responsibilities thrust him into the arena of South Dakota politics. Of significance to South Dakota Indians was his rapid response to legislation involving the expansion of state jurisdiction on tribal lands, a leading goal of the federal government's termination policy. In January 1957, the Aberdeen Bureau of Indian Affairs Office received a request from the Lower Brule Sioux to approve state assumption of criminal jurisdiction on their reservation. The following month the tribe confirmed their decision by passing a resolution requesting that the South Dakota Legislature enact a law empowering the state to assume criminal jurisdiction on Lower Brule lands. A measure along these lines, House Bill (HB) No. 892, was drafted and submitted to the House Indian Affairs Committee, before which Reifel testified on 25 February. Reifel was not necessarily convinced that Indians would receive unfair treatment under state law or in the state courts, nor did he think that white prejudice against Indians was as flagrant as some tribal leaders were claiming. Instead, his chief concern was that, as drafted, HB 892 would immediately grant the State of South Dakota jurisdiction on *all* Indian reservations, and do so without the concurrence of the other tribes. The bill was seriously flawed, Reifel argued, and it required amending before it fulfilled its intent, which was the limiting of the state's criminal jurisdiction to only the Lower Brule Sioux Reservation.[14]

Following his testimony, Reifel met with Attorney General Phil Saunders to discuss amendments to HB 892. During the meeting, Reifel recalled the efforts of United States Senator Francis Case of South Dakota to amend PL 280, the termination bill of 1953 that transferred to five states civil and criminal jurisdiction over reservation Indians. In an attempt to revise Section 7 of PL 280, which allowed for additional states to assume reservation jurisdiction, Case introduced an amendment requiring the consent of every affected tribe before a state assumed jurisdiction on tribal lands within its borders. Case's amendment failed. (It was not until 1968 that Congress, with Reifel once again at the center of the debate, passed an Indian Civil Rights Act that required tribal consent before states assumed civil and criminal jurisdiction on reservations.) Though futile, Case's struggle had inspired Reifel, who shared his opinions on termination with Saunders. The attorney general took Reifel's comments into account, the result being a new section in HB 892 that required a tribal referendum to precede any plan to expand state jurisdiction on a South Dakota Indian reservation.[15] "The democratic principle of 'consent of the governed' was retained in this legislation," Reifel wrote in 1957.[16] He had played a critical role in checking the reach of termination in his home state, in the process demonstrating a grasp on tribal rights and legislative procedures that was not overlooked by the state's leading politicians.

In addition to termination policy, the Corps of Engineers Pick-Sloan Project continued to demand the attention of the Bureau of Indian Affairs. On this subject, Reifel was unusually experienced and thus a welcome asset to the Aberdeen Area Office. He assisted in the relocation of the Cheyenne River Sioux Agency to the town of Eagle Butte, a move necessitated by the inundation of reservation lands by the Oahe Reservoir. On the Standing Rock Reservation, 174 families displaced by the taking area of the Oahe Dam were relocated in 1959, a process supervised by Reifel, who also took part in meetings between the Crow Creek and Lower Brule Sioux tribes and the House Indian Affairs Committee, at which tribal members testified about compensation for lands, water damage, and rehabilitation. On another occasion, members of the Missouri River Basin Interagency Group listened to Reifel lecture on "The Indian Today in the Missouri River Basin—A Cultural Analysis." And not surprisingly, Reifel continued to play a part in the Garrison Dam and Reservoir project. In June 1956, Congress authorized a final payment to the Three Affiliated Tribes to be dispersed through a per-capita distribution that awarded about twelve hundred dollars to each tribal member. In his capacity as area director, Reifel and his staff reviewed plans submitted by each compensation recipient explaining his or her intentions for the application of payments.[17]

Affairs at Pine Ridge were never far from Reifel's mind. A careless, poorly researched article on conditions at Pine Ridge published in the 18 March 1956 issue of the *Minneapolis Sunday Tribune* left readers with the impression that Bureau of Indian Affairs officials at Pine Ridge were at best disinterested or at worst hungover on the job.[18] Reifel found no evidence that bureau employees arrived at work under the influence of alcohol, and he criticized the reporter for failing to highlight bureau efforts to improve life at Pine Ridge. The *Sunday Tribune* might have done better to report on a conference held at Pine Ridge in January 1957, organized and chaired by Reifel, under the name "Pine Ridge Conference on Community Organization and Development." The event brought together dozens of tribal councilmen, Bureau of Indian Affairs officials, social scientists, lobbyists, agricultural and industrial specialists, public health officials, and church leaders to generate "an exchange of experiences and ideas in community development through the community organization process." Though Reifel continued to urge Indians to pursue off-reservation opportunities, he acknowledged the fact that most Pine Ridge residents were staying home, a circumstance that called for imaginative thinking about local economic development. Not all the Oglalas at the conference, however, shared Reifel's enthusiasm. After listening to some caustic remarks during one of the panel discussions, Reifel concluded that, at least among Oglala activists, "there seems to be a feeling that there isn't much to be done in the community because we [Indians] are different and sometimes we are made so because of discouraging comments and observations."[19] Such race-based, victim-centered outlooks reinforced Reifel's belief that American Indians spent too much time blaming whites for their condition and too little time working to change it.

His grueling travel schedule to Indian reservations and beyond made Reifel one of Aberdeen's most traveled men, prompting the *Aberdeen American-News* to designate him the "Sioux Version of [Secretary of State] John Foster Dulles." Reifel estimated that as area director he traveled nearly fifty thousand miles per year, half of that amount occurring in his car, the rest on commercial airlines, chartered aircraft, or by rail. A typical automobile trip might take him to the Indian Bureau Relocation Office in Denver, on to an Indian student seminar in Colorado Springs, to Fort Meade for a lecture before the staff of the Veterans Administration hospital, and back to the area office in Aberdeen, a distance of 1,600 miles in one work week. His lectures and presentations drove home the themes developed during his posting at Pine Ridge: the need for American Indians to become time-aware and future-oriented and to habituate themselves to hard work and fiscal responsibility.[20]

Reifel's effectiveness as an area director and the respect accorded him by the American Indians within his jurisdiction explain Commissioner Glenn L. Emmons's landmark decision in the spring of 1958 to delegate his authority to approve tribal ordinances, resolutions, and budgets to Reifel, the first such delegation of its kind in Bureau of Indian Affairs history.[21] For Reifel, Emmons's announcement was not as gratifying as the one he had received two years earlier, when his professional accomplishments, his reputation as an orator, and his involvement in civic, church, and professional organizations had so impressed a panel of judges that they named him the Outstanding American Indian of 1956. Reifel accepted the prestigious award at the All-American Indian Days, a gathering of representatives from forty-seven tribes held in Sheridan, Wyoming, in August 1956. Reifel was one of several nominees, placed in nomination by tribal councils, whose lives were devoted to improvements in Indian country.[22] On behalf of the citizens of South Dakota, Senator Francis Case inserted into the Congressional Record a letter of congratulations. "Not only the Sioux Indian, but all Indians," the letter read, "can take pride in the honor that has come to one of them and is so well deserved."[23]

The year 1960 brought more national awards. Reifel's support for the Boy Scouts and his place on the Scouts' National Interracial Service Committee earned him the prestigious Silver Antelope Award.[24] He was also the recipient of the Indian Council Fire's Indian Achievement Award for 1960. In presenting the achievement award on behalf of the council, Indian Commissioner Emmons described Reifel as one of the "top lieutenants carrying major responsibilities" for the bureau. Emmons praised Reifel for his compassion, his wisdom, "and his truly formidable managerial capabilities," though his most enduring contribution, noted the commissioner, was his strengthening of relations between Indians and non-Indians.[25]

By 1960, Ben Reifel, if not quite a household name in South Dakota, was a known quantity in the state's business, civic, and education circles. His associations with the state's leading politicians, his speaking engagements, and his membership in organizations such as the American Legion, Elks, and Rotary Club showcased his talents and magnified his record as a civil servant. Reifel was a member of the South Dakota Advisory Committee of the United States Commission on Civil Rights, and he sat on the boards of directors of the South Dakota Parent Teachers Association and the South Dakota Tuberculosis and Health Association. He was a lay leader in the Episcopal Church, where he served on the Committee on Racial Minorities of the Home Department of the National Council of the Episcopal Church.[26] In a state where agricultural credentials mattered, Reifel could reference his ranching experience, his degree from SDSC, and his work as a farm extension agent. He had a winning personality but was described as a selfless man. He was a magnetic speaker who proposed down-to-earth, common sense solutions to reservation problems. His government service spoke for itself, though masters of ceremonies took joy in highlighting his long list of personal and professional accomplishments.

Whether he acknowledged it or not, Ben Reifel had become an intriguing candidate for public office. Accordingly, in early 1960 the South Dakota Republican Party, uncertain of his party affiliation but aching for a victory after a poor showing in the latest election, approached Reifel to gauge his interest in a run for the United States House of Representatives.

Republicans dominated South Dakota politics in the 1940s and early 1950s. But results from the 1956 elections revealed some disturbing numbers. Unpopular agriculture programs of the Eisenhower administration, embodied in the person of Agriculture Secretary Ezra Taft Benson, eroded Republican support among farmers. Though President Eisenhower carried South Dakota by a fairly comfortable margin in 1956, his vote tally dropped over twelve percentage points from 1952. Senator Francis Case defeated his Democratic challenger by only 4,620 votes, and Democratic newcomer George S. McGovern upset Harold O. Lovre, the four-term United States Representative for the First District. At the state level, Republican Governor Joe Foss was reelected, but Republican margins in the legislature were shrinking.[27]

South Dakota Republicans fared even worse in 1958, a disastrous year for the GOP. For the first time since 1934, voters elected a Democratic governor, Ralph E. Herseth. McGovern beat back a challenge from Governor Foss, and Democrats took control of the South Dakota Senate and most of the state's administrative posts.[28] Nationally, the Republicans suffered a humiliating defeat. In an impressive show of strength, the Democrats, tapping into voters' dissatisfaction with the economy, added to their congressional majorities by gaining forty-eight seats in the House and thirteen in the Senate. Votes for Democratic congressmen had increased nearly four million since 1956, and Democrats controlled thirty-four of forty-eight governorships. Stephen E. Ambrose describes the election as "a massive defeat, unprecedented, and decisive. The '58 election gave the Democrats control of the government so completely that they held it for the next decade."[29]

Stung by the results, South Dakota Republicans committed themselves to fielding a formidable candidate for the 1960 race in the First House District, where the seat was vacated after Congressman McGovern decided to challenge Senator Karl Mundt. (Republicans maintained comfortable control of western South Dakota's Second District, where the popular Ellis Y. ["E.Y."] Berry held the seat from 1951 to 1971.) Though he had expressed no interest in running for elected office, Reifel, sometime in February 1960, was approached by several Brown County Republicans representing a larger group of 25–30 Aberdeen businessmen, all confident that Reifel could win the First District seat. It is not certain whether the Republicans knew of Reifel's party preference, for during scores of public appearances he had avoided references to party affiliation. As a civil servant, Reifel was bound by civil service regulations and the Hatch Act, which restricted partisan political activity by federal workers.[30]

Privately, Reifel identified with the Republican Party. In 1924, when Reifel was seventeen years old, President Calvin Coolidge signed the Indian Citizenship Act, which granted citizenship to United States-born Indians and relaxed restrictions on Indian voting rights.[31] Rollyn ("Rolly") Samp, an aide to Congressman Reifel, recalled his former boss's pride in the Republican commitment to civil rights as expressed in the Indian Citizenship Act. "He would talk about what a great thing it was when Native Americans got the chance to go and cast their vote," Samp told a reporter in 2011, adding that Reifel's GOP affiliation made him an anomaly among the state's American Indians, who were, in response to the Eisenhower administration's unpopular Indian policies, distancing themselves from the Republican Party.[32]

A decade after Aberdeen Republicans urged him to run for Congress, Reifel described his reaction to their appeal: "I told them that it was a compliment but that I didn't have the money and questioned whether it could be raised." When the group promised to raise $8,000, Reifel agreed to run for the House seat if the party continued to help him finance the campaign.[33] Reifel's wife and daughter, on the other hand, opposed his candidacy. Reifel had become a grandfather, his daughter Loyce and son-in-law Emery Anderson the parents of two daughters, Lisa and Laurie. Furthermore, if he chose to run, Reifel would have to resign from the Bureau of Indian Affairs, forego the security of his $12,000 annual salary (which, when adjusted for inflation, would be equivalent to approximately $96,000 in 2015), and sacrifice a federal pension that would leave him comfortable in retirement. To allay his family's concerns, Reifel assured them that, if defeated in the primary or general elections, he would secure a university teaching post. Nevertheless, his family's reservations planted doubts in Reifel's mind about the wisdom of leaving a stable position with the Bureau of Indian Affairs to embark on a risky and uncertain political quest.[34]

Having caught wind that he was considering a run for Congress, the *Aberdeen American-News* queried Reifel about his intentions.

Reifel responded that while he was gratified by "the confidence my friends have in me," he remained undecided about the campaign and was allowing himself ten days to make a decision.[35] After the interview, Reifel, suddenly apprehensive about the prospect of fundraising, decided against running. He attempted to place telephone calls with local Republicans to announce his rejection of their offer, only to be confronted with a succession of busy signals. The party leaders, Reifel later learned, were on the phones raising money. When they informed him that they had secured sufficient resources, Reifel changed his mind for the last time, and on 16 March, he announced publicly that he was resigning from the Bureau of Indian Affairs to become a candidate for the United States House of Representatives.[36]

In a press release, the candidate made plain that he was offering his services to repay South Dakota for the many opportunities the state had provided him. "South Dakota has been good to me and my family," he told a reporter. The education he received at a state university gave him, an American Indian, the chance to serve fellow American Indians for over twenty years. "In deep appreciation," Reifel emphasized, "this is now a way to offer myself for public service to the state and the nation."[37] In 1964, Reifel confessed that his decision to run was also motivated by a desire to prove a point to the members of his race. In running for Congress, he said, he could "demonstrate to the Indian people what can be accomplished with hard work."[38]

Reifel was leaving behind an illustrious career with the Bureau of Indian Affairs. The editors of the *Aberdeen American-News* observed that voters "were amazed that he would end a successful career in the Bureau of Indian Affairs administration and risk election to public office."[39] Area directors were first in line for the top post of Indian commissioner, and there was ample reason to believe that Reifel, a finalist for the position in 1953, would have been a leading candidate in the future. It is conceivable, if not likely, that Ben Reifel would have been named commissioner of Indian Affairs in 1961 had he not run for Congress.

Commissioner Emmons was profuse in his praise for the outgoing area director, who was honored at a farewell party in Aberdeen a month after he announced his candidacy. The "great and enduring contributions" Reifel made to bureau administration, Emmons wrote in a letter read at the party, were matched by his dedication "to the cause of better mutual understanding between Indians and their fellow citizens of other races." Reifel's presence would be missed. "He has been an exemplary public servant and has carved out a record of accomplishment that will be remembered far into the future."[40] A year later Secretary of the Interior Stewart L. Udall presented Congressman Reifel with the Distinguished Service Award, the Interior Department's highest honor. The citation recognized the recipient's "personal interest" in the condition of the nation's Indian people and his "never-ending efforts" to educate the non-Indian public about the American Indian condition. "No problem was too small or too great," especially in the area of education, where Reifel's concern for young Indians "never ceased." Udall praised many of Reifel's contributions, none more than his "dedicated purpose to achieve better social standing for his people," an effort that was "a source of inspiration to all whom he came in contact."[41] Reifel's former Aberdeen colleagues added their congratulations and ensured their former boss that his "impact . . . on the Aberdeen Area and its Indian people . . . will long be remembered."[42]

Having made his decision to run for Congress, Reifel had little time to reflect on past accomplishments. In the primary election he would face Ray Dana, a Sioux Falls attorney and state representative, and Dan Stuelpnagel, a businessman and civic leader who served two terms as Yankton mayor. Neither man could match him in name recognition, but Reifel took nothing for granted. "He campaigns the way he fishes," his wife Alice told a reporter, adding that her husband was reluctant to waste time eating, did not take coffee breaks, and did not quit working at dark. With Alice driving the family car while Ben wrote speeches or scribbled thank-you letters to donors and volunteers, the Reifels kept a dizzying schedule that took them to every county and most of the towns in the district. It appeared, wrote a reporter, that Reifel enjoyed campaigning. On a typical day, he would arrive at 8:00 a.m. on the main street of a First District town where the local newspaper and radio station had announced his coming. If a Republican volunteer was there to escort him, the two would walk the streets and enter businesses and restaurants where Reifel would introduce himself. If no volunteer was available, Reifel worked alone. He walked briskly, introduced himself to an individual or small group, engaged in brief but warm conversations, extended his card, and moved along to the next voters. On occasion, Reifel would come across a voter as talkative as himself and those conversations might prove harder to break off.[43] It was textbook retail campaigning, and by all accounts, Reifel excelled at it. Staffer Rolly Samp, recalling a reelection campaign in the 1960s, described his former boss as "very outgoing. We would be driving down a highway, and if there was a group of people working on the road, he'd tell me to stop the car. He'd hop out and not just shake hands but have a conversation and ask questions. He wanted to get feedback." Former field representative David Volk remembered Reifel's gentle and personable nature. Reifel was "probably the most unassuming, nicest guy you would ever want to meet. I never saw him lose his temper. I never saw him say an unkind word."[44]

One should consult campaign literature with a degree of skepticism for clues to a politician's character. Nevertheless, a description of Reifel's personality found in a banquet program may not be far from the mark: "He sincerely likes people and enjoys meeting them, and that particular quality is the real secret of his campaign success." He did not behave like a politician, the program continued, and because of that "people seem to like him in return."[45] The *Aberdeen American-News* found that Reifel's supporters in church and civic circles took pains to inform others of his "exemplary character."[46]

As an office seeker of American Indian descent, Reifel did not fit neatly into the white, middle-class mold that characterized congressional candidates of the 1950s and 1960s. Yet there was no denying that he embodied what veteran journalist Theodore White referred to as the "two moods" of the Republican Party: "the old Protestant-Puritan ethic of the small towns of America, of the decent, sober, God-fearing, law-abiding men," and the GOP adherence to "the philosophy of private enterprise, the sense that the individual . . . can build swifter and better for common good than big government."[47] Analysts and Democrats might have retorted that a twenty-two-year veteran of big government makes an unconvincing spokesman for private enterprise. But such an assessment would have mischaracterized Reifel's career at the Bureau of Indian Affairs, where, from the moment he joined the bureau until his retirement, he strived to reduce American Indians' dependency on Washington. Though uncomfortable with the pace and scope of termination programs, he supported the gradual loosening of federal-tribal ties, a process that would restore Indians' dignity and unleash their talents for the common good. Reifel regarded the Republicans as the party most committed to the goal of Indian self-reliance, and he ran under the GOP banner without hesitation.

Supporters saw in Reifel an articulate and politically astute professional who could attract white voters. They assumed his candidacy would energize American Indian voters in East River who, if they turned out on election day, might prove to be a deciding factor in a close race. And yet despite his "fresh face and fresh approach" and a well-earned reputation as a problem-solver, Reifel had his share of doubters. Could a Lakota Sioux with West River roots get elected in a predominantly white congressional district where only forty-five hundred of the state's thirty-three thousand Indians resided? "When Ben Reifel announced," confessed a Republican attorney, "I said to myself 'you poor misguided soul, they'll never vote for an Indian.'"[48]

Reifel was busy testing the attorney's assumption on the main streets and back roads of eastern South Dakota. Though he hoped to secure the Indian vote, he knew that his political future would be decided by whites who had never been asked to vote for an Indian. The small number of registered Indian voters would probably have little effect on the outcome of the 1960 election. Few Indians in the First District (or elsewhere) had gone to the polls in the 1950s, and those who did resided in Democratic-leaning counties—Buffalo, Charles Mix, and Roberts, for instance—that were carried by the 1956 Democratic presidential ticket of Stevenson-Kefauver and by George McGovern in his House race in 1958. Granted, Indian voter registration was on the rise in the late 1950s, but Democrats were the beneficiaries of that trend. In 1957, Helen L. Peterson, an Oglala Sioux and the executive director of the National Congress of American Indians, took notice of the increase in Indian voter registration and concluded that on once Republican-friendly reservations in Arizona and South Dakota,

Indians were expressing their disappointment with Eisenhower's termination policy by voting for Democratic candidates.[49] Three years later, Rosebud Sioux tribal president Robert Burnette, referencing his fellow tribal member's United States House bid, claimed that "Indians were going Democrat two years before Mr. Ben Reifel decided to run for Congress."[50] Results from the elections of 1952 and 1956 bolstered Peterson's and Burnette's observations. In 1952, presidential candidate Eisenhower and Second District Republican congressman E.Y. Berry, himself a proponent of the termination policy, carried Shannon (Oglala Sioux Tribe) and Todd (Rosebud Sioux Tribe) counties in Republican-heavy West River South Dakota. In 1956, both men lost in both counties.[51]

Reifel was aware that Indians were transferring their loyalties to the Democratic Party. In South Dakota's First Congressional District, many Indians lived in Democrat-heavy Buffalo, Charles Mix, and Roberts counties, where Reifel was convinced that "the influence of their [white] neighbors had a lot of bearing on [Indians'] political leanings." Furthermore, Indians had come to identify social welfare programs with the Democrats, a perception that explained their recent voting behavior, which Reifel attributed to the influence of "candidates who promise more and more benefits from the Federal government and protection of the present tribal rights against State and National encroachment."[52]

And yet, despite the decline in American Indian support for Republicans, Reifel was endorsed by some South Dakota Indian leaders. Though members of the Oglala Sioux Tribe could not cast votes in a First District election, their vice president, Sam Stands, ensured Reifel that "the Sioux people are wholeheartedly proud of your qualifications, achievements and leadership." Referring to the pressing civil rights issues facing the nation, Stands thanked Reifel for running for office at a time when Congress was confronted "with the supreme question of how to work out a philosophy of decency and fair play with its minority groups more especially the American Indian."[53] J. W. Thompson, chairman of the Lower Brule Sioux Tribe, lamented Reifel's resignation from the Bureau of Indian Affairs and shared his regret that members of the tribal council were ineligible to vote in First District elections. In language that expressed Reifel's own attitude toward American Indians and public service, Thompson wrote that the Lower Brule council felt "very strongly that more Indians should enter politics as much can be gained for the Indian people if they participate in our government." As a show of their support, the tribal council contributed $150 to Reifel's campaign.[54]

Indians living off the reservation, including the critically acclaimed artist Oscar Howe and the ethnographer and linguist Ella Deloria, applauded Reifel's bid for office. After crediting Reifel with arranging his recent appearance on the television program "This Is Your Life," Howe congratulated Reifel on his decision to run for Congress and informed him that he and his wife Heidi had signed his petition.[55] Deloria expressed her family's pride in Reifel and offered him their "very staunch and complete moral support." Reifel also received the endorsement of Jim Blue Bird, the organizer and overseer of the Native American Church of South Dakota, who promised to campaign on Reifel's behalf.[56]

Though humbled by the support of his fellow American Indians, Reifel resisted being packaged as "the Indian Candidate." Nor did he wish to be the recipient of a sympathy vote. According to Rolly Samp, a central message of the Reifel stump speech was the candidate's desire to be judged on his qualifications and his qualifications alone. "He'd say in speeches 'I'm asking for your vote as Ben Reifel, not as a Native American, not by any other labels.' He didn't back away from being a Native American, but he didn't want that to be what he was known for."[57] The *Aberdeen American-News* drew similar conclusions about Reifel's campaigning. "He did not campaign as an Indian candidate," the paper observed.[58]

Nor did Reifel limit his campaigning to traditional means. In addition to spreading his message on the campaign trail on foot, Reifel took to the airwaves. He embraced the medium of television at a moment when TV and politics were converging to create a new force in electioneering. The number of households with televisions had increased tenfold between 1950 and 1960, the latter year witnessing the advent of the first televised presidential debates between Senator John F. Kennedy and Vice President Richard M. Nixon. On 17 May, Reifel made his television debut, a ten-minute spot on KELO-TV in Sioux Falls, followed by eight five-minute and eighteen twenty-second appearances before the primary election was held on 7 June. His print ads in East River newspapers were reinforced by radio ads.[59] In the radio spots (sometimes narrated by a voice other than Reifel's), the candidate's government service, qualifications, leadership skills, energy, humble background, and compelling personal story were emphasized. When speaking for himself on television or radio, Reifel pointed out that he had "traveled over 15,000 miles in an attempt to see you and to have you see me because I realize the great value in exchanging ideas."[60]

Ultimately it was Reifel's grassroots campaigning that determined the outcome of the primary race and likely the November general election as well. "The campaign was almost entirely on a 'meet the people' plane," wrote the *Aberdeen American-News*. In the primary campaign, issues were less important to Reifel than introducing himself to the voters of the district. "His campaign was face-to-face, personal and seldom involving issues. He said any problem that could be discussed intelligently in a few minutes couldn't be much of a problem."[61] Robert J. Artz, cochair of the Reifel for Congress Club, characterized Reifel's campaign strategy as "primarily that of personal contact with the people of the First Congressional District." Reifel maximized his TV, newspaper, and radio ads and sent campaign literature to every mailbox in the district, and yet according to Artz, it was his travel schedule that defined his campaign. "He is often traveling from 500 to 1000 miles a week and has intensive speaking engagements," Artz told a United Press International reporter.[62] Reifel's disciplined travel schedule was disrupted only once, when he learned in April that his sister-in-law had been killed and his brother John injured in a tragic automobile accident.[63]

Reifel's boundless energy, his appealing personality, and his racially neutral message resonated with the Republican voters of East River South Dakota who, on 7 June 1960, selected him as their party's candidate for the United States House of Representatives. He received 56 percent of the vote in a three-way race and helped turn out over 53,000 Republican voters in the First District, a number far above the 28,000 Democrats who went to the polls. Within days of Reifel's victory, political observers were predicting a Republican win in November in the same district that George McGovern had carried by 14,000 votes in 1958.[64]

Reifel's primary victory brought him national exposure, with wire service stories on "the first Sioux Indian ever nominated for Congress in South Dakota" appearing in urban newspapers from coast to coast. The Salt Lake City *Deseret News*, predicting that "the Reifel story may well be indicative of things to come for the Indian," cited one of Reifel's more popular lines from the campaign trail: "My state, our country and her people have given me the opportunity to receive a meaningful education. I have tried to use that education to help others."[65] Some of the joy of winning the election was dampened when, three weeks after the primary, Reifel learned that a cousin missing for over a year had been murdered in Nebraska, the second family tragedy to strike the Reifels within three months.[66]

After a brief respite following the primary, Reifel prepared for the general election. Having spent most of his money and appreciating his need for better organization, Reifel asked Vernon C. Loen, press secretary for Senator Case, to serve as his campaign manager. Loen agreed and in August arrived at Reifel's headquarters in Aberdeen where he found things, in his words, "in total disarray—utter disarray. He didn't . . . have any money, didn't have any bumper stickers, any buttons, any organization, any fund-raising." Loen immediately began arranging Reifel's schedule and designing TV, radio, and newspaper ads. He joined Ben and Alice on their barnstorming tours, with Alice driving the car, Ben walking main streets and going door to door, and Loen hanging signs and distributing campaign literature. Twenty years after that historic campaign, Loen remembered Reifel's effectiveness at stumping through rural South Dakota. "In Sioux Falls, they don't go for putting posters up in the light poles or telephone poles; it's a lot tougher. You have to go out and work shopping centers for example, and stand by the door and intrude on peoples privacy and Ben didn't like to do that." Reifel was far more comfortable campaigning in small towns. "He was a tremendous walker. Those little towns was where he [was] really at his best. Nobody out walked him that year."[67]

Standing between Reifel and Congress was the Democratic nominee, Ray Fitzgerald, an Aurora County farmer and businessman and former South Dakota secretary of agriculture under Governor Ralph Herseth. A staunch McGovern supporter, an affiliate of the

Farmers Union, and, in Loen's view, a "forceful" candidate who "could really take on the agricultural issues and make points with the voters," Fitzgerald was determined to keep the First District seat in Democratic hands.[68] But he faced an uphill battle from the start, evidenced by the primary vote gap that separated him from his Republican opponent. Furthermore, polling showed Reifel with a sizable lead that he would retain throughout the campaign. Reifel led Fitzgerald by nearly fourteen points in early July, and despite campaigning little in August or the first half of September—Reifel, observed the *Aberdeen American-News* on 13 October 1960, "appeared satisfied to let his opponent carry the campaign" during the late summer—he held a similar advantage over Fitzgerald on election day.[69]

That being said, First District voters were treated to a colorful campaign. The race was between two former public servants with no legislative experience but with legitimate ties to the state's farm economy. South Dakota farmers still exercised considerable political clout in 1960, with nearly 360,000 of South Dakota's 680,514 persons living on farms or in farming communities. But the number of farms was decreasing—from 83,157 in 1935 to 55,729 in 1959—as the average size of farms was increasing—from 672 acres in 1950 to 804 acres in 1960.[70] Both candidates understood that party affiliation was an unreliable predictor of farmers' voting behavior, for, though there were slightly more Democrats than Republicans among them in 1960, South Dakota farmers were, as a group, not strongly identified with either party. The farmers courted by Fitzgerald and Reifel were, in the words of political scientist Alan Clem, "'weak' Democrats or Republicans, independents, or apoliticals" who classified themselves as ideologically moderate to conservative.[71] This political reality forced the two candidates to occasionally distance themselves from national party platforms and to compete for the trust of moderate-to-conservative voters who wanted to know which of the two candidates better represented the rural culture of South Dakota.

In his public remarks, candidate Reifel divulged the political philosophy and issue stances that would guide him through five terms in Congress. In his espousal of Midwestern values, his fiscal conservatism, his sensitivity to minority rights, and his acceptance of some features of the welfare state, Reifel embodied the moderate Robert Taft and Nelson Rockefeller wings of the Republican Party. On the subject of national security, Reifel was a defense hawk in the Rockefeller mold. Reifel championed free enterprise and self-reliance, voiced concerns about the growth of the welfare state, and heralded the dangers of international communism, positions associated with the emerging Barry Goldwater faction of the Republican Party.[72] Taken as a whole, Reifel's philosophy was strikingly consistent with Vice President Nixon's and reflective of what Herbert S. Parmet has classified as "the Age of Nixon," the period from 1946 to 1980 when the former congressman, vice president, gubernatorial candidate, president, and statesman sought "to rationalize two ongoing developments, the progressivism of the New Deal welfare state and the continuing cold war."[73] Nixon's anti-communist credentials, his high-profile performances in the Hiss case and Checkers speech, his exhaustive stumping for Republican candidates, his bridging of the Midwestern old guard and Eastern establishment wings of the GOP, and his substantive responsibilities as vice president had endeared him to the Republican rank-and-file.[74] Despite being cast as an orthodox Republican, Nixon was not interested in dismantling the welfare state. Instead he focused his criticisms on government waste and bureaucratic irresponsibility.[75] He held together the moderate and conservative wings of the Republican Party at a moment when the middle class was recovering from the hangover of the Great Depression and World War II and renewing its faith in American capitalism. The "great silent majority" of middle-class Americans was comprised of acculturated immigrants who had "achieved their security, had faith in the American dream, and contributed a conservative, stabilizing force in the context of American traditionalism." Nixon personified the traditionalists and articulated their priorities.[76]

So did Ben Reifel personify the traditional, middle-class sensibilities of South Dakotans. Reifel enjoyed the support of the vice president, and, in turn, he campaigned hard for Nixon. The two men met at the South Dakota American Legion Convention in Sioux Falls on 19 June and then made a joint appearance in Sioux Falls on 23 September.[77] For Richard and Pat Nixon, Reifel felt "the highest admiration and deepest respect," and he praised the "gracious and undaunted manner" by which the Nixons led the Republican effort in South Dakota and beyond.[78]

Reifel aligned himself with Republican principles that he believed would advantage the nation and the state. On topics of foreign policy and national defense, Reifel emphasized that the preservation of American security depended on the nation's "containment of the communist philosophy." South Dakota producers could contribute to the containment policy by sharing farm surpluses with undeveloped nations, a time-tested deterrent to Soviet and Chinese "aggressive actions to expand their spheres of influence."[79] In contrast to his opponent, who called for a reappraisal of weapons systems and defense contracts so as to eliminate duplication and waste, Reifel underscored the need for a "margin of military superiority" and recommended a congressional review to determine whether current military spending levels were "adequate to insure our safety in the future."[80] Reifel's comments on defense were part of a larger effort by Republican candidates to mollify the Rockefellerites—who asserted that the nation was not doing enough to meet the Soviet threat—but to do so without embarrassing President Eisenhower, who was sensitive to any criticism of his defense budget.[81]

Reifel stood for balanced budgets. Described by a staffer as a fiscal conservative and opponent of Keynesianism who insisted that there was "no way we can spend our way to prosperity," Reifel went to great lengths to position himself as a debt hawk.[82] Congress needed to "hold the line on tempting new programs" typically approved during election years. He favored tax reductions for farmers, wage earners, and small businessmen but cautioned voters not to pin their hopes on a return to small government. "With the people demanding more and more government services and a strong national defense," remarked Reifel, "the outlook for a tax cut is dim indeed."[83]

One of the government services that Reifel was referencing was federal aid to education, which turned out to be a hotly contested issue in the Fitzgerald-Reifel race. The dispute unfolded against the backdrop of a congressional debate over whether an education bill should provide grant money for both school construction and teacher salaries.[84] In the words of a respected national journalist, "there were not enough schools, nor the right kind of schools, nor was there any clear, agreed-on answer on how to build more."[85] Characterizing South Dakota school taxes as "among the highest in the nation," Fitzgerald argued that federal aid was necessary to maintain school facilities at "adequate educational levels." He proposed an education block grant program that would retain local control of Washington dollars but went on to qualify education as a shared responsibility of federal, state, and local governments.[86]

There was nothing controversial about Fitzgerald's call to increase appropriations for school buildings—Reifel shared that position—but Reifel pounced on Fitzgerald's recommendation to supplement teacher salaries with federal dollars, a proposal that placed the Democrat on the wrong side of public opinion. Federal aid for teacher salaries, Reifel warned, would result in "federal domination and control of our schools."[87] Strings attached to federal dollars gave Washington the leverage to "dictate the courses to be taught in our schools or the manner in which they shall be taught."[88] Reminding voters of his years of supervising federally funded schools and his witnessing of the "inevitable controls that accompany" education dollars, Reifel limited his recommendations to federal aid for school construction, building expansions, and maintenance upgrades.[89]

The education issue added color to the campaign and served Reifel's strategy of depicting Fitzgerald as a "let government do it for us" candidate who was out of touch with voters.[90] But the race would not be decided by an education debate. South Dakotans were most interested in the candidates' proposals for fixing the state's sluggish farm economy which in 1959 experienced a staggering 35 percent drop in average net income per farm.[91] Fitzgerald could tout his farming experience and his well-publicized attacks on Eisenhower's secretary of agriculture, Ezra Taft Benson, an unpopular figure among South Dakotan producers. Faced with price-depressing surpluses, shrinking storage capacity, and declining farm income, Eisenhower and Benson had sought to reduce New Deal price support programs that encouraged farmers to produce more but that lacked adequate provisions for marketing farm products. Great Plains farmers interpreted the Eisenhower administration's effort to reduce price supports as a betrayal of the president's 1952 campaign pledge to retain crop prices at 90 percent parity.

When the administration introduced a "soil bank" program that encouraged farmers to reduce crop acreages in return for government certificates redeemable in cash or kind, the response was immediate, intense, and bipartisan. The fiercest opposition came from Farm Belt Republican congressmen running for reelection in 1956. Two years later, their backs pressed against the wall by angry voters, GOP lawmakers banded together to pass a bill to temporarily increase price supports. Though Republicans pleaded with Eisenhower to sign the bill, their appeals fell on deaf ears; the president vetoed it, contributing in no small way to the Republican disaster of 1958.[92]

Fitzgerald tried to link Reifel to Eisenhower farm policies. Secretary Benson's recent endorsement of Nixon was, in Fitzgerald's judgment, a forecast of what South Dakota farmers could expect under Republican leadership in Washington. Campaigning in Redfield, the Democrat characterized Nixon's agriculture agenda as "just a bold extension of the shop worn Benson plan" that Ben Reifel had embraced "in a Johnny-come-lately statement on the question." Citing an Iowa State University study on the projected impact of a Nixon farm program, Fitzgerald told his audience at the Redfield Congregational Church that if GOP free market ideas were ever legislated by Congress, "farmers would take whopping cuts in prices in the next four years," a scenario that "would spell ruin not only for this nation's farmers but for the businessmen on the Main Streets who depend upon farm prosperity for their own success."[93]

In the words of a reporter, "Reifel stood apart from the bipartisan anti-Benson chorus" that accompanied the agriculture debate.[94] He took pains to avoid personal attacks on Benson, who was in Reifel's opinion a good economist, "a fine Christian gentleman," and a dedicated official committed to a long-term goal that he shared: "getting the federal government out of the farm business." But as things stood, Reifel noted, the government was in the farm business and would remain so as long as surpluses undercut prices. Farming was a basic industry and essential to American prosperity and security. Pointing out that the federal government had "subsidized other industries on the basis of far weaker arguments," Reifel called for a farm program that combined a voluntary land retirement and price support plan with payment-in-kind features to encourage producers to retire surplus-producing acreages.[95] He embraced Nixon's farm plan, presented by the vice president to a large audience at the South Dakota Soil Conservation Days in Sioux Falls on 23 September. Nixon focused on the $9 billion crop surplus that was dampening farm income. His solution, recited almost verbatim by Reifel in stump speeches, radio addresses, and television appearances, consisted of two parts. Operation Consume called for an expanded Food for Peace program to reduce surpluses; the creation of a strategic food reserve; payments in kind to farmers who retired lands into conservation; and a program for producing meat, powdered milk, butter, cheese, and eggs for sale overseas or for distribution to the poor. Operation Safeguard involved voluntary expansion of conservation reserves with fair rentals over a three-to-ten-year period, price supports through payments in kind in exchange for acreage reductions, and the substitution of long-term price supports as grain surpluses were reduced.[96]

Nixon distanced himself from the soil bank scheme that Reifel blamed, in part, for declining business conditions in rural towns and the nationwide trend toward fewer farms. Nixon's proposal, Reifel concluded, "recognizes the errors of the past programs and moves to correct them." In the battle for the hearts and minds of small town businessmen, Reifel worked to counter Fitzgerald's claim that Republican policies hurt the farm economy. On the contrary, he said, Nixon's plan realistically addressed surpluses while putting government payments "in the farmer's pocket. And money in the farmer's pocket means money in the tills of our business places."[97] Reifel reminded voters that the Democrats had their shot at making farm policy. "The Democrats have had two to one control of Congress for the last six years and what have they done?" he asked.[98]

At a Farmers Union convention in Huron, at an appearance in Stickney, and in back-to-back debates with Fitzgerald in Aberdeen and Mitchell on 18 and 19 October (two of the five organized debates the candidates engaged in), Reifel defended his farm policies. Conceding that crop reduction and land retirement programs would not bring immediate relief to farmers, Reifel insisted they were necessary if surpluses were to be reduced and demand increased. He also asked producers to consider new endeavors. In what would become a four-year personal crusade, Reifel urged East River farmers to invest in the sugar beet industry, already in its infant stage of development in the James River Valley near Huron. He noted the spin-off effects of beet farming, which included the prospect of an East River sugar refinery and the larger economic benefits that could be derived from the refinery.[99]

While Reifel stuck to the themes of surplus, demand, and diversification, Fitzgerald, in what may have been a Hail Mary pass to energize rural voters, presented a far-reaching plan for farmers to gain control of the production process. The Democrat proposed federal legislation allowing farmers themselves to determine when and how to set crop capacities, a reform that would, in Fitzgerald's view, provide balance to an agriculture sector dominated by industry and labor. During the Mitchell debate, Reifel, who was generally supportive of greater advisory roles for farmers, nevertheless rejected the Fitzgerald plan. Despite its populist appeal, a federal law along those lines, he argued, would prove unworkable. It would be much more difficult for 4 million independent farmers to establish production quotas, he quipped, than for United States manufacturers to establish production controls in their respective industries.[100] Statements like these and others were efforts by Reifel to highlight what he saw as the conflicting means by which he and Fitzgerald would problem solve. Government, agreed Reifel, had a place in the lives of Americans. But it was important to resist the trend toward government solutions to problems that were best resolved by the free market. "Reliance upon free individual enterprise is the principle which has made South Dakota a great state and our country a great country," Reifel proclaimed.[101]

Despite their differences, Fitzgerald and Reifel remained cordial with one another. Though sprinkled with animated exchanges, their joint appearances were, according to a reporter, "marked by lack of public acrimony."[102] On the campaign trail, Reifel exhibited a sharp wit and a disarming sense of humor, best captured in an oft-quoted one-liner meant to deflect suspicions about his Ivy League credentials: "I'm probably the only person to graduate from Harvard and on the way out the door turn to the Right."[103] Reifel's bumper stickers and newspaper ads, typically embellished with an illustration of a rifle or a musket, bore the campaign's central slogan: "Ben Reifel for Congress: A Straight Shooter."

Humor helped Reifel tolerate the distraction of being the state's first American Indian candidate for Congress, a milestone that intrigued political observers. His historic primary win had created a media buzz and earned Reifel a degree of national distinction. As South Dakota voters stood poised to elect an Indian to Congress, journalists pressed the candidate for his thoughts on the gravity of the moment. Reifel's polite response proved disappointing: Race, he said, was not an issue. Instead, his campaign stressed the similarities he shared with non-Indian South Dakotans. A self-described "Indian American," he took pride in his Lakota Sioux heritage but in a way that a Norwegian, Irish, or Swedish American might express pride in his or her ethnicity. Reifel reminded voters that he was a half-German American who had lived in the white man's world and worked for the white man's government for most of his adult life. He classified himself "first and last" as an "American and I would consider it the highest possible honor to serve both the whites and the Indians of this district in the Congress of the United States."[104]

In a post–primary election interview with the *Minneapolis Star Tribune*, Reifel indicated that he had never been "snubbed" because of his race. "When an Indian is dressed and acts presentably, I don't know where he might go that he would be discriminated against." The radicalization of Indian politics was a decade off, so Reifel had yet to encounter "the animosity reservation Indians sometimes show toward the 'white Indian' who has made good." Reifel moved comfortably between two cultures, and his Indian heritage, he confessed, probably enhanced his electability. "When it might have been an element, I think it helped. Club women would say they were voting for me because they felt I could help the Indian problem."[105]

Vernon Loen saw Reifel's racial heritage as an asset. "Everybody was going to know he was an Indian—you took one look at Ben Reifel and you knew he was an Indian," Loen told an interviewer in 1980. An important story line in Reifel's biography was his overcoming of racial adversity by pursuing opportunities that promised success in the white man's world. In the age of television it made no sense to "downplay" Reifel's American Indian heritage, Loen concluded, "so why not seize upon it and show how he had risen above [adversity] in good Republican tradition [by] doing for himself."[106]

First District voters were impressed with Reifel's résumé, his appreciation for rural values, and his commitment to free enterprise. It appeared that he would defend agricultural interests and promote small business while channeling his professional expertise to confront the poverty, unemployment, and crime plaguing the state's Indian reservations. Furthermore, he possessed what the editors of the *Aberdeen American-News* described as a "magic" or "charm" that appealed to voters.[107] He was smart yet sensible, inspirational yet grounded. And he obviously shared a respect for the conservative values that South Dakota voters were determined to preserve. Maybe it was time, voters reasoned, to elect a politician who embodied—literally—the state's bicultural heritage.

In the end, Reifel's experience, personable nature, and exhausting travel schedule won over the citizens of the First District, who defied history and voted for an Indian on 8 November 1960. Reifel defeated Fitzgerald by over 22,000 votes (126,033 to 103,755) while carrying over two-thirds of the district's counties (28 to 13). He won Democrat-friendly Brown County and finished just 81 votes behind Fitzgerald in the Democrat's home county (Aurora). Reifel posted big numbers in Minnehaha (including Sioux Falls) and Brookings counties and won by large margins in several rural counties in the northern and southeastern ends of the district. Though counties with concentrations of Indian populations—Buffalo, Charles Mix, and Roberts—went to Fitzgerald, the American Indian candidate polled well among American Indian voters. In Roberts County, home to Sisseton-Wahpeton Sioux tribal members, Reifel carried three of the five townships that had large numbers of Indian voters, evidence, perhaps, that his Bureau of Indian Affairs and GOP affiliations did not offend them. During the next eight years, Reifel would win the Indian vote in Roberts County in all but the Democratic landslide year of 1964, the same year, ironically, in which he won the larger vote in Buffalo, Charles Mix, and Roberts counties. These results suggest, possibly, that Indians and non-Indians in the three counties were satisfied that their congressman showed no favoritism toward members of either race.[108]

Ben Reifel, a Lakota Sioux Indian born in a log cabin on the Rosebud Sioux Indian Reservation in desolate southwestern South Dakota, was going to Washington. Reifel promised the voters of his district that he would represent the needs of all South Dakotans while upholding the conservative values that defined the state's political culture. His constituents waited to see if his legislative actions would fulfill those promises.

6 CONGRESSMAN REIFEL

On 3 January 1961, Ben and Alice Reifel arrived in Washington, D.C. After moving their belongings into an apartment near the Capitol, Ben moved into his new office, number 348 in the Old (now Cannon) House Office Building, where he was joined by Vernon Loen, who opted to become Reifel's administrative assistant rather than return to Senator Case's office. "Well, I decided to go with Ben," said Loen, who admitted to having "so much admiration for him as a person."[1] As had been the case with every South Dakota legislator before him, Reifel considered it his priority to promote the state's foremost industry. Accordingly, he wasted no time lobbying House Minority Leader Charles A. Halleck of Indiana and House Republican Conference chair Charles B. Hoeven of Iowa for a seat on the House Agriculture Committee. His request was granted, Hoeven informing Reifel that "from the start" the South Dakotan had been on his list of candidates.[2] Subcommittee assignments placed Reifel at the center of deliberations over, among other things, family farms, research and extension services, and wheat, oilseed, and rice programs.[3]

Reifel moved quickly to establish his voice on agricultural matters. Arguing that producers needed to make well-informed decisions on the future of retired farmlands, he pressed President Kennedy's secretary of agriculture, former Minnesota governor Orville Freeman, to clarify the administration's position on conservation programs. South Dakota farmers, Reifel insisted, needed to decide whether they should lease, sell, or resume farming on large tracts of retired acreages. They had "a right to know where the administration stands on this question, so vital to their personal planning and livelihoods in the years ahead."[4] It would be the first of many exchanges between Reifel and the secretary, whose proposals for feed, grain, wheat, and dairy farmers would, in Reifel's estimation, spell ruin for small producers and rural industries such as cheese factories. In his first year in office, Reifel sought to reduce Freeman's authority to shape legislation while he worked with farm groups on designing new commodity programs.[5]

Reifel's maiden speech in the House occurred on 26 July 1961, when he spoke in favor of the Agriculture Act of 1961. Acknowledging the "surplus problem" associated with wheat and feed grains and the need for some level of reserve lands to address the problem, Reifel nonetheless warned against excessive acreage reductions: "our South Dakota wheatgrowers have taken serious acreage cuts in the past in order to comply with the wheat program and they cannot, without running into uneconomic units, now take more than a 10-percent cut in many situations." Reifel was hopeful that the bill would be a step in the development of a long-range program for wheat and feed grains, "the major difficulties faced in our supply-demand balance."[6] To keep constituents abreast of his floor remarks, as well as his bills, committee assignments, and case work, Reifel began mail delivery of a single-page update, *Reifel Shots*, which also included criticisms of Kennedy (and later Johnson) administration programs, as well as his thoughts on issues such as the Kennedy tax cut, civil rights, Vietnam, and United States–Soviet relations.

Highlights of Reifel's first term included his well-publicized opposition to livestock price controls and the passage of his first bill, HR 11413, permitting farmers to grow nonsurplus crops such as flax on diverted wheat and feed grain acreages. Reifel's measure, which passed the House and Senate in a week's time, allowed South Dakota farmers to increase their production of safflower, an oil-producing plant used in margarine, mayonnaise, and other food products, while permitting them to retain up to 50 percent of the diversion payments they would have received had their lands remained idle. The legislation, Reifel reasoned, would reduce grain production yet bolster farm incomes while sensibly utilizing Great Plains farmlands.[7]

Though he was a valuable asset to the Agriculture Committee, Reifel had, within a year of arriving in Washington, set his sights on a more influential committee seat, one that could provide enormous benefits to both non-Indian and Indian South Dakotans. "It has come to my attention," he wrote to colleagues in January 1962, "that several vacancies have developed on the House Committee on Appropriations."[8] It was nothing short of audacious for a first-term representative to seek a seat on the powerful Appropriations Committee. "They said that there was no way a sophomore congressman is ever going to get put on the Appropriations Committee," recalled Vernon Loen.[9] Under the seniority system, the coveted seats on Appropriations typically went to veteran congressmen with noteworthy legislative records. House tradition, however, did not deter Reifel from pursuing a post that would allow him to address problems in Indian country while continuing to exert leverage on agricultural matters. Reifel alluded to his "Indian ancestry and many years of work with the Indian people" as rationales for filling an Appropriations seat, from which he could draw on his past experiences to serve the goal of "accelerating the adjustment process of the Indian American while also remaining in a position to be of service to agriculture."[10] Giving up his Agriculture seat would not be detrimental to South Dakota farmers, he emphasized, especially since he would be reassigned to an "important committee holding jurisdiction over all Federal spending."[11]

In the summer of 1962, Reifel's campaign for an Appropriations seat, not to mention his campaign for reelection, was temporarily interrupted. On 22 June, South Dakotans learned of the sudden death of Senator Francis Case, the victim of a heart attack. More than six months remained on Case's term of office, obliging Governor Archie Gubbrud to choose a successor to serve out the unexpired period. Expressing no personal interest in the position, yet hesitant to act before the Republican State Central Committee met to select their United States Senate candidate for the November election, Gubbrud shifted the responsibility of selecting Case's replacement to the Central Committee. By the time its 126 members gathered in Pierre on 9 July, six candidates—United States Representative Ben Reifel among them—had been nominated to fill Case's seat. The other candidates were former governors Sigurd Anderson and Joe Foss; the current lieutenant governor, Joseph

Bottum; former State House speaker Nils Boe; and attorney general and former United States Senate candidate A. C. Miller.[12]

In choosing Case's replacement, the committee applied a balloting procedure that empowered a county party representative to cast one-half of the vote the county cast for the Republican gubernatorial candidate in 1960. To win the nomination, a candidate needed to capture a majority of all votes cast. Brown County delegates judged Reifel to be the most qualified candidate and were confident that, should the committee become deadlocked, he would prevail. But the selection process favored Bottum, who, like Case, was a popular West River conservative, a tireless campaigner for Republican candidates, and a favorite of key members of the state's party machinery. Reifel, meanwhile, faced serious disadvantages. Though well-educated, a respected civil servant, and an energetic campaigner, he had faced only one electoral test. He possessed fewer party ties than the other candidates and was one of three East River nominees who were destined to divide votes between themselves. Significantly, of the six men vying for Case's seat, only Reifel was absent from the 9 July meeting in Pierre.[13]

The Central Committee required twenty ballots to choose Case's replacement—Joe Bottum—but by the end of the second round of balloting, Reifel had been eliminated as a serious contender. Brown County delegates stood by Reifel until the twentieth ballot, at which time his 6,617 votes passed to Bottum, leaving Reifel and Nils Boe as the only two candidates with no twentieth round votes. It was evident during most of the proceedings that only Brown County and Todd County backed Reifel, who, along with the other East River candidates, was unable to consolidate a large voting bloc.[14]

His pursuit of the Senate vacancy did not interfere with Reifel's reelection campaign—he defeated Democratic challenger Ralph A. Nauman by a 59.2 percent to 40.8 percent margin—nor with his goal of securing an Appropriations seat. On 24 January 1963, a "somewhat flabbergasted" Reifel learned of his appointment to the House Appropriations Committee's Subcommittee on Interior Affairs, a victory aided by the support of Ben F. Jensen of Iowa, the ranking Republican on Appropriations, who was moved by Reifel's assertion that he "could serve effectively for both situations, that is, agriculture in the State and the Indians in South Dakota and the nation generally, by being on this Committee."[15] Congressman Jensen, recalled Reifel's administrative assistant, "was delighted to find somebody that wanted to work with Indian programs, because nobody else did."[16] Reifel's appointment was somewhat historic in that he and Francis Case were the only South Dakotans to have served on the House Appropriations Committee. Furthermore, since Karl Mundt was a member of the Senate Appropriations Committee, Reifel's new seat, Mundt proclaimed cheerfully, gave the state a "'one-two punch' on appropriations committees" that it had not enjoyed for thirteen years.[17]

Though he had vacated his seat on Agriculture, Reifel retained associations with its subcommittees and participated in their affairs. In the spring of 1963, he cosponsored a bill to increase aid to agricultural experiment stations that were exploring new industrial uses for farm products. The legislation specifically benefited South Dakota facilities devoted to dairy research, poultry science, and animal health.[18] In 1968, Reifel testified before the House Appropriations Subcommittee on Agriculture in support of the Soil Conservation Service budget. He praised the service for its contributions to conservation districts and declared it time to reverse budget restrictions on the Soil Conservation Service; not doing so "would be inconsistent with the preserving of the nation's natural resources and development of America's farmland."[19]

In the mid-1960s, Reifel became a leading critic of Democratic farm policies. He brought to light Undersecretary of Agriculture John A. Schnittker's regrettable comment that his department aimed at achieving parity income for "adequate sized commercial farms, but not necessarily for small farms." By Schnittker's definition, adequate farms were those grossing over ten thousand dollars annually, whereas farms with smaller earnings would need to seek assistance from departments other than agriculture. Citing statistics that showed 58 percent of South Dakota farms grossing less than ten thousand dollars, Reifel quipped that under Schnittker's plan, "the Agriculture Department would turn over two-thirds of American agriculture to welfare and poverty agencies for assistance." Reifel accused the Johnson administration of having "failed to strengthen the family farm as it pledged."[20]

Despite his criticisms of the Johnson White House, Reifel showed a willingness to support some Democratic measures, most notably the controversial and closely contested cotton-wheat bill of 1964. The act, shepherded through Congress by Democratic representative of Texas Graham Purcell, a close colleague of Reifel's, rewarded farmers for voluntary acreage reductions. Estimates projected that the bill would generate $18 million in income for South Dakota wheat growers.[21] Reifel sat in when the Agriculture Committee debated the bill and then deviated from the party line to vote for it. He won praise from a constituent who admired Reifel's "strength and good common sense in crossing the political concrete-barbed wire line. He did his share for the farmer, the state and the nation."[22]

Reifel felt the government was not doing enough to curb the flow of foreign commodities. As early as 1963, he was working to reduce the amount of red meat shipped to the United States, beef imports being, in Reifel's words, "a price-depressing factor about which something must be done."[23] In 1967, citing the "irreparable damage" caused by an upward spike in livestock imports, Reifel sponsored legislation to place import quotas on processed beef and veal, approximately 1.2 billion pounds of which had reached American soil in 1966. Federal restrictions on meat imports, Reifel noted, would protect the 70 percent of South Dakota farm income derived from livestock and livestock products, an income threatened by beef importations that climbed over 50 percent from 1966 to 1967.[24] To Reifel's frustration the bill stalled in the Ways and Means Committee, held prisoner, in Reifel's words, by "Social Security bills and the President's proposed tax increase."[25]

Though sometimes stymied in the pursuit of his legislative agenda, Reifel could use his seat on the Appropriations Committee to produce tangible benefits for South Dakota. The most dramatic example of the Mundt-Reifel appropriations "punch" came in 1969, when the two bid to locate the United States Geological Survey's EROS (Earth Resources Observation Systems) Data Center in South Dakota. Reifel and Mundt exercised their influence as ranking Republicans on their respective appropriations committees and as conferees on conference committees to gather support for a Sioux Falls site for EROS, a facility for receiving, processing, archiving, distributing, and researching remote sensory data gathered from earth-orbiting satellites. The Mundt-Reifel staffs were joined by professional lobbyists, the city of Sioux Falls, members of the Sioux Falls business community, and Governor Frank Farrar in pitching the Sioux Falls site as the ideal, middle-of-the-continent location for the new data center. The South Dakota team suffered several setbacks during their two-year fight, none more demoralizing than Senator Mundt's debilitating stroke in November 1969. But on 30 March 1970, the Nixon White House, following a direct appeal from Mundt's staff, broke a funding deadlock and announced Sioux Falls as the location of the EROS Data Center, a political victory that generated hundreds of jobs and established South Dakota as a contributor to the United States space program.[26] The victory was, from the point of view of Vernon Loen, a revealing example of the political clout exercised by the South Dakota delegation in the 1960s. Sioux Falls became the home of EROS through "sheer political muscle when Ben Reifel and Karl Mundt teamed up to put that thing in South Dakota, and it's still there today."[27]

Much of Reifel's effectiveness as a politician could be attributed to his personality. Loen described his boss as a "very personable, down-to-earth" man with a good sense of humor and a love of storytelling. "Well, there's no question that his real strength was his personality—his ability to develop friendships and relationships with his colleagues in either party." Reifel prided himself on cultivating first-name-basis relationships with all of his congressional colleagues. He formed particularly close friendships with, among others, Senator Case and with representatives Hjalmar C. Nygaard, Republican representative of North Dakota; Joe McDade, Republican of Pennsylvania; and Mike Kirwan, Democrat of Ohio. Though he was universally respected for his knowledge of Indian country, he was also "well-liked," and Loen could recall no instance when a legislator said "an ill word about Ben Reifel." He was not driven by ambition and his colleagues viewed him as "a rather quiet legislator with his own district's interests foremost in his mind," qualities that earned Reifel a reputation as a sympathetic and dedicated servant of South Dakota.[28]

One of Reifel's more gratifying services occurred in early 1969, when he teamed with Karl Mundt to win a tax-filing extension for South Dakota producers affected by the paralyzing blizzards of

1968–69. In mid-January East River attorneys notified the two congressmen that severe weather and impassable roads were preventing farmers from reaching their tax preparers' offices by 15 January, the date by which farmers were required to file income tax estimates. Weather conditions created a tax-filing logjam, and, according to one of the attorneys, made it "physically impossible" for tax preparers to meet the 15 February deadline for farmers to file their final tax reports. The attorneys' appeal to the district director of the Internal Revenue Service for a filing extension was followed up by letters to Washington. With the threat of delinquency penalties facing thousands of farmers, Mundt and Reifel were urged to take action, if not through legislation, then through seeking an executive order from the Nixon White House. Describing in dramatic language the (allegedly) surly attitude of dairy farmers who were forced "to dump their milk because they can't get the milk trucks in," an attorney called on the two officials to "proceed to seek administrative relief so that our people will not have the feeling that our Republican legislators and new Republican administration have no interest in this problem which is very real to our people."[29]

It is doubtful that veiled threats dictated the actions taken by Mundt and Reifel, which included Reifel's letter to the Treasury Department and Mundt's letter to John Ehrlichman, special counsel to the president, in which the two men argued that the winter weather more than justified a delay in farmers' tax filings.[30] Farmers affected by the blizzards cheered the outcome of the letters, Mundt's office announcing on 20 February that the White House had ordered the IRS to waive delinquency penalties on South Dakota producers whose tax filings were delayed by adverse weather.[31]

The blizzards were a vivid reminder of the environment's formative impact on South Dakota agriculture. Writing in 1961, the same year Ben Reifel joined the United States House of Representatives, historian Herbert S. Schell concluded that "by virtue of the environmental influences, the history of South Dakota agriculture has been essentially a story of adjustments and modifications in farming methods and land use."[32] Over the next decade it appeared that modern science, civil engineering, and new technologies would enhance those adjustments and modifications, and, in the case of the development of the Missouri River, further irrigation, water supply, and flood control projects to boost the economy of eastern South Dakota.

Following the death of Francis Case, a leading figure in national water development, Reifel labored to, in his words, "master the complicated and tedious steps to develop South Dakota's immense water resources."[33] Over the next eight years, Reifel worked diligently on water development. In his public remarks he often discussed what he saw as the still-unrealized benefits that South Dakota had been promised in the Pick-Sloan Plan. Speaking to the House chamber in 1966 in support of his cosponsored bill to authorize an Oahe diversion project to irrigate 190,000 acres of South Dakota lands, Reifel stated that "the overall impact of the Missouri River Basin project on South Dakota has been negative," with the greatest beneficiaries being out-of-state users of hydroelectricity and "downstream interests" who had gained "at the expense of upstream States." South Dakotans endured many sacrifices to make possible the building of dams within their state. Several hundred thousand acres of land had been inundated. Reductions in property taxes affected schools and local government. Towns, farms, and ranches had disappeared. Thousands of Indians had been forcibly relocated. Because of these and other sacrifices, South Dakota, Reifel declared, was deserving of a water diversion project. Agricultural irrigation, municipal and industrial water access, and provisions for wildlife and recreation development—all recommended in the first phase of the Oahe project—would extend to his constituents the benefits of the Pick-Sloan Plan. In short, a diversion project would "make possible smaller farms, population growth, industrial development, crop diversification—all the things that are needed to help our rural State share more equally in the national prosperity."[34]

Reifel proposed a variety of water plans. He secured appropriations for dam feasibility and construction projects, water storage projects, flood control and bank stabilization studies, irrigation studies, and silt deposit studies. He encouraged James River valley residents to form conservancy subdistricts to investigate flood control plans and identify their irrigation, municipal water, wildlife conservancy, and recreational needs. He threw his support behind the Garrison Diversion Unit which, as originally planned, would have transferred water to Brown and Marshall counties in South Dakota. And Reifel continued his fight for the Oahe irrigation project.[35] In testimony before an appropriations subcommittee in 1969, he reminded his House colleagues of the 34 million acre-feet of water stored behind Missouri River dams. While his state "was proud to assist" in protecting downstream citizens and their properties, it was time for South Dakota to reap the benefits of water development. Speaking on behalf of the people of North Dakota and South Dakota, Reifel urged congressional approval of Garrison and Oahe diversion projects that "may play a significant role in re-establishing the much-needed rural-urban balance."[36]

Congress did not authorize funds for the first phase of the Oahe irrigation project until 1968, and Reifel was still battling for additional funding during his final term in office (1969–71).[37] But his efforts came to naught. According to Michael L. Lawson, "irrigation has become the abandoned orphan of the Pick-Sloan Missouri River Program." Though planners envisioned 5.3 million acres of Missouri River basin lands under irrigation, the Bureau of Reclamation had developed only 465,000 acres by the late 1980s. "The large main-stem projects proposed for the Dakotas never materialized," Lawson writes, the cost of irrigating just the 190,000 acres called for in the first phase having exceeded $1 billion by 1982. "In light of the unit's steadily decreasing benefit-cost ratio, public support for the Oahe project," Lawson concludes, "gradually shifted to alternative water programs, and Congress de-authorized the unit in 1982."[38]

Reifel's attempts to develop the Missouri River were closely linked to another legislative crusade that ended in his greatest political disappointment. During his first year in office, Reifel had grown frustrated with the Democrats for repeatedly blocking legislation that would have expanded the domestic sugar industry. In retaliation, the freshman Republican, determined to create a new source of farm income for his district, began a hard-fought yet futile three-year battle to expand the sugar beet industry in South Dakota.

Sugar legislation was followed intently by a small group of South Dakota farmers who saw in sugar beets, produced commercially in Minnesota, Montana, Nebraska, and North Dakota, an opportunity to capitalize on the shortage stemming from the United States embargo on Cuban sugar that followed Fidel Castro's seizure of American oil refineries in 1960. The ability of Belle Fourche Valley farmers in western South Dakota to harvest enough beets to sustain a sugar plant in the town of Belle Fourche had inspired East River farmers to experiment with a crop less susceptible to the surpluses plaguing the cash grain and feed grain industries.[39] Reifel emphasized the stability that sugar beets might bring to the state's economy at a moment when rural South Dakotans were trying to revive agriculture markets.[40] "Sugar beet cultivation offers our farmers a chance to produce a crop not in surplus and vital to the nation in time of emergency," Reifel said in a press release. He linked beet production to water legislation and predicted that the crop would "slow the trend toward fewer and larger farms, revitalize the small town, bring new industry and assist in irrigation development. This crop could be a significant factor in Missouri River development as well."[41]

From the House floor on 31 August 1961, Reifel remarked that in failing to pass long-term sugar legislation, Congress "has been put in the unfortunate position of failing to keep faith with the farmer" at a moment when 45 percent of the sugar consumed by Americans was imported from foreign markets. In biting language, Reifel railed against acreage limits on beet production, a step that would be interpreted as "discriminatory against the domestic producer" and evidence that the Agriculture and State Departments "think more of the foreign sugar producer than of the American farmer."[42] Reifel cited what he saw as the "huge potential" for sugar beet farming in eastern South Dakota, where the crop would create spin-off industries. "The opportunity to expand production of sugar beets would have a highly favorable impact in stabilizing our up-and-down agricultural economy, preserving the small town, attracting new agricultural-type industries, providing employment, and reversing the trend toward larger and fewer farms," he commented. Sugar beets would be a centerpiece cash crop of the Oahe project but would also possess an added value as a byproduct for livestock feeding, an industry that accounted for 80 percent of South Dakota farm income.[43]

Reifel ended his appeal for increased sugar production by reminding his House colleagues of the consequences of their inactivity. Eastern South Dakota was a promising region for beet farming, an industry that could, in time, create demand for a sugar processing plant. Since economic diversification was essential to the survival of rural America, federal restrictions on United States sugar production "would be a crushing blow to agricultural development in South Dakota as well as other areas of the Nation."[44]

Hopeful about their prospects, farmers in southeastern South Dakota increased their beet acreages in the spring of 1962. That same year a lobbying effort by Reifel and beet producers proved critical in the passing of legislation requiring the Agriculture Department to increase South Dakota's beet allotment to the nineteen-thousand-acre level deemed sufficient for supporting a second processing plant in the state. By early 1963, due to the high cost of freight hauls from East River beet farms to the Utah-Idaho Sugar Company (U&I) Plant in Belle Fourche, sugar processing had become a paramount issue. At the time, U&I was showing interest in building a multi-million dollar plant in southeastern South Dakota.[45] Entering the spring of 1963, Reifel was guardedly optimistic that continued growth in the East River beet industry would justify a new sugar factory to serve southeastern South Dakota as well as northwestern Iowa and northeastern Nebraska.

Reifel's optimism proved to be premature, for his crusade to establish an eastern South Dakota sugar beet industry began to lose momentum. In his enthusiasm to expand beet production in his district, Reifel may not have fully appreciated the demands imposed by the crop, which requires extensive watering to prevent wilting. U&I, citing among other reasons the slow pace of Missouri River irrigation development, announced suddenly in October 1963 that they were no longer proceeding with plans for a factory in eastern South Dakota. An even stronger influence on the U&I decision was the weed problem facing East River beet farmers, a challenge that highlighted the labor intensive nature of sugar beet farming and the manual labor force, comprised of Mexican American or Mexican migrant labor, needed to thin, weed, and hoe the crop.[46] A sector of the South Dakota farm economy had become dependent on migratory labor, but it had become so at the very moment that Mexican migration was under scrutiny by Washington lawmakers.

Consequently, in the fall of 1963, Reifel, determined to salvage his sugar beet project, placed himself at the center of a national debate over the extension of the Mexican Farm Labor Program, popularly referred to as the bracero program.

Based on a 1942 bilateral agreement between the United States and Mexican governments, the bracero program began as a wartime emergency measure to address the labor shortage impacting American agriculture during World War II. The agreement was repeatedly extended and in the process it brought millions of contracted, documented Mexican workers to the United States to perform non-mechanized farm labor. By the early 1960s, however, the bracero program had come under assault. A sharp increase in the machine-harvesting of cotton, growing opposition to the program from labor and social welfare groups, and evidence that the domestic Mexican American workforce was sufficient to meet the needs of California and Southwest producers reduced demand for bracero farmworkers. By 1963, documented Mexican laborers constituted only 0.7 percent of the nation's agricultural workforce. Operators who continued to hire braceros were accused of receiving unfair, federally subsidized advantages. Sensing the shift in political winds, the Kennedy administration began imposing strict standards on import labor to strengthen protections for domestic farmworkers.[47]

In one of the more thoughtful, wide-ranging arguments for bracero labor presented to the House of Representatives, Reifel, during an 31 October 1963 debate on the extension of the Mexican Farm Labor Program, described the importance of temporary work permits for ensuring a stoop labor force for American farms. His was not a congressional district, he admitted, that relied upon Mexican labor. On the contrary, it was the influx of contracted Mexican labor into California and the Southwest that "enables the domestic migratory workers from that area to come up to our part of the country to work on the sugar beet crop." As things stood, political opposition to the farm labor program was scaring away sugar beet investors. A sugar processing company had abandoned its plans to build a factory in South Dakota, a decision based largely on the absence of a bracero policy that would have furthered the expansion of the region's beet industry. South Dakota operators now faced a labor shortage that affected their ability to care for the crop. The absence of migratory farm labor was depriving farmers in the United States heartland of a lucrative alternative to the traditional price-depressed commodities associated with South Dakota and other plains states.[48]

Reifel declared that a vote for the extension of the Mexican Farm Labor Program was "a vote for the small farmer who is seeking to meet his economic problems by shifting from historic cropping patterns which produce surpluses into new specialty crops such as vegetables and sugar beets." To make the transition they "must be assured of an adequate and stable labor force to do the arduous stoop labor that too few domestic workers are willing to do." For those congressmen representing manufacturing districts, Reifel framed the labor program in terms of its impact on factory workers and consumers. Growth of the domestic sugar industry meant lower sugar prices for United States households, reduced dependency on foreign suppliers, and immunity from the uncertainties of international crop conditions. New sugar factories guaranteed new jobs and increased employment opportunities in related industries. Furthermore, employment opportunities for domestic farm laborers would continue to grow, a development that promised to ameliorate the problem of illegal immigration and enhance domestic workers' chances of joining the agricultural job market.[49]

In his closing remarks, Reifel reiterated his cardinal theme: sugar beet farming would reinvigorate South Dakota's stagnant agricultural economy. In his mind, nothing took precedence over that goal. Arguments for improving domestic laborers' wages and living standards were worthy of consideration and should remain features of the national debate. But such arguments must be tempered by the economic realities of rural America. Imposing a minimum wage on farm labor would pinch "the struggling small farmer who already is beset by numerous imponderable, seasonal and economic factors which make such a proposition totally impractical." In recent years, Reifel argued, Congress "dwelt too much upon the needs of the domestic farm laborer and too little upon the needs of the American farmer. For without the farmer, particularly the small farmer, there would be no work at all for the migratory laborer, foreign or domestic."[50]

Though he made a forceful case for expanding sugar beet farming, Reifel's efforts were in vain. It became evident in 1964 that South Dakota would not join her neighboring states as a producer of domestic sugar. The Mexican Farm Labor Program had run its course and expired on 31 December 1964.[51] Plans for an East River sugar factory were scuttled. The Belle Fourche U&I sugar plant closed its doors. Senator Mundt and South Dakota governor Nils Boe briefly entertained the possibility of the state leasing or purchasing the U&I plant and operating it like the South Dakota Cement Plant, but the plan never materialized.[52] South Dakota sugar beet farming died quietly, Reifel's crusade to establish the industry proving no match for the political obstacles that stood in the way of small farmers who experimented with agricultural diversification.

His time-consuming dedication to agricultural issues did not deter Reifel from weighing in on other matters important to his state and party. Ideologically, Reifel could be characterized as a fiscally conservative, taxpayer-conscious, small government Republican who resisted excessive spending and the expansion of the welfare state. "He said no way we can spend our way to prosperity," recalled congressional aide Rolly Samp.[53] Speaking to the South Dakota Young Republicans in Brookings in August 1961, Reifel turned President Kennedy's "Ask not what your country can do for you" inaugural line on its head and suggested that the most likely thing young Americans would do for their country would be to pay "higher taxes . . . in the future in order to finance foreign and domestic giveaway programs today." Democrat-sponsored welfare programs were ushering-in a cradle-to-grave "creeping socialism" that fostered a "morally soft" citizenry who "have forgotten what it is to do for ourselves those things that we can best do for ourselves." In defining "What It Means To Be a Republican," Reifel contrasted the Democrats' approach to government spending with that of South Dakota's, where a Republican governor and legislature practiced a "taxpayer-first, down-to-earth, fiscally responsible government" that Reifel asked the young Republicans to maintain.[54]

Generally speaking, Reifel's actions matched his rhetoric. In 1964, he disclosed to a feature writer that because he had witnessed their failure to impact American Indians, he had little faith in welfare programs and government "handouts."[55] Reifel joined with

E.Y. Berry to vote against a food stamp bill.[56] He voted against a $2.8 billion foreign aid appropriations bill.[57] He opposed the founding of the Peace Corps, which he characterized as "a good program for those who want to see the world, and I doubt that it has much value otherwise."[58] Reifel described Kennedy's "domestic Peace Corps," which under the name of Volunteers in Service to America, or VISTA, was approved as part of the Economic Opportunity Act of 1964, as "an exercise in futility and a complete waste of the taxpayer's money." He likewise took "a dim view" of a Youth Opportunities bill (cosponsored by George McGovern) that would employ unskilled young people at national parks, on Indian reservations, and in urban slums.[59] Reifel proposed the creation of a congressional watchdog committee to investigate the budgets of federal agencies and he voted to sustain President Nixon's veto of a Health, Education and Welfare–Office of Economic Opportunity appropriations bill that the president described as "excessive."[60]

As a budget cutter, Reifel even displayed a willingness to curtail agriculture programs, despite the potential unpopularity of such cuts in South Dakota. At the height of the Vietnam War, Reifel supported cuts to the agriculture budget, impelled, he said, by the worst financial crisis since 1931. Since federal spending reductions would affect basic services such as rural electricity, soil and water conservation, and farm loans, "then every other agency of the government should [also] be required to take equally significant cuts." Reifel warned his constituents that, budget reductions or no budget reductions, "a tax increase will be inevitable due to the proliferate spending policies of the both gun-and-butter era."[61]

Reifel's budget-mindedness explains his resistance to the Kennedy administration's high-profile $11 billion tax cut plan, passed by the House on 25 September 1963. In voting against the bill, Reifel aligned himself with conservative colleagues who were apprehensive about deficit spending. Republican economists argued that tax cuts must be paired with spending cuts, a position taken by House Republicans, who classified the Kennedy tax reductions as reckless.[62] "A tax cut," Reifel reasoned, "is something that we as a nation ought to earn. To do so, we should set priorities, deny ourselves things that are desirable but not absolutely essential—just as you are forced to do in handling your family or business budget."[63] Reifel's opposition to a tax cut mirrored the attitude of the general public, who, in the words of Allen J. Matusow, "found it offensive both to common sense and morals that the president wished to increase spending by $4 billion while cutting taxes a net $11.4 billion." Voters expressed a reluctance to lower taxes if it meant a larger deficit, a mood manifested in a *New York Times* poll that revealed "a deep worry about the size of the national debt." An effort by Republicans to tie tax cuts to spending limits failed, though it showcased the GOP's desire to restrain government growth.[64] Later, Reifel voted for the continuation of a Johnson-era surtax of 10 percent on personal and corporate income taxes to finance the Vietnam War, another example of his balanced budget priorities.[65]

Reifel rarely commented on Vietnam, though when he did, he defended Johnson's and Nixon's war strategies. "Ben was a hawk on the war," noted Vernon Loen, "but he didn't . . . make a repetition defending it."[66] In the midst of the Tet Offensive of 1968, he urged South Dakotans to support Johnson during a critical moment of the war.[67] He helped introduce a House resolution commending Nixon's "Great Silent Majority" speech of 3 November 1969, in which the president asked the nation to support his strategy for ending the war.[68] On the question of American POWs, Reifel called on Hanoi to release the names of prisoners and allow for inspections of POW compounds.[69] In the larger arena of international affairs, he took a special interest in United States–Mexico relations, on four occasions serving as a representative on the United States delegation of the Mexico–United States Inter-Parliamentary Group.[70] As a member of his United States Army Reserve unit, Lieutenant Colonel Reifel toured military installations in Europe and Africa, deployments that gave him the opportunity to monitor security conditions on two continents.[71] Reifel also traveled to Alaska and to Guantanamo Bay, Cuba, in early 1963, several months after the Cuban Missile Crisis. In classic Cold War language he reminded voters that Castro had created "a closed, totalitarian society" and that Cuba "function[ed] as a base from which communism can be exported to other nations of the hemisphere."[72] Later, in marking the one-year anniversary of the missile crisis, he asked his constituents to treat with skepticism the Kennedy administration's "oft-repeated belief that the Soviet

Union is mellowing and that it is seeking peace and understanding with the West."[73]

Reifel found a few elements in President Johnson's sweeping domestic agenda to his liking, most notably the National Endowments for the Arts and Humanities. Vernon Loen remembered Reifel feeling "very deeply about" the arts and humanities and using his position on appropriations to secure funding for the National Endowments for the Arts and Humanities.[74] Reifel went to great lengths to promote American Indian artists, who he hoped would be some of the chief beneficiaries of NEA resources. He had befriended Oscar Howe, one of South Dakota's greatest artists, in the early 1940s and had done much to advance Howe's career, including purchasing his paintings for display in the Aberdeen Bureau of Indian Affairs Office and arranging Howe's appearance on the television show "This Is Your Life."[75] On one occasion, Reifel stood on the House floor to discuss a particular book, "Noble Living and Grand Achievement: Giants of the Republic," that had "inspired" him because it showed "how people could succeed if they would go out and work for it and persevere." Loen described Reifel's floor remarks, made during a debate over federal funding for the humanities, "as a very moving little speech which helped secure the first appropriations for the humanities."[76] In 1968, Reifel joined with three other representatives to send a letter to House members calling on their support for HR 11308, a bill that included amendments to the Arts and Humanities Act of 1965.[77]

Despite his championing of federal assistance for the arts and humanities, Reifel fretted over what he considered to be the burdensome costs and unrealistic expectations created by the Great Society and War on Poverty. "He voted against practically all the Great Society programs," Loen told an interviewer.[78] But there was little that Republicans could do to halt Johnson's legislative steamroller. For Democrats 1964 had been a landslide year, one in which they won their largest congressional majority since 1936. Republicans were left in the unenviable position of being able to critique, but not obstruct, the Democrats' agenda. Nevertheless, GOP legislators assailed the costs of LBJ's social programs. Reifel told South Dakotans that Johnson could not wage war on poverty and build a great society within the budgetary limits he had established. Costly new programs "seemed to be out of tune" with the president's "economizing" rhetoric. "The President would be something of a magician if he could persuade Congress to pass all those welfare programs . . . and yet cut federal spending." Nor was Reifel, who was the consummate farmer's advocate, happy with what he believed to be Johnson's ignoring of American producers in his quest to uplift "other groups" through his social programs.[79]

Reifel remained sensitive to the needs and wishes of his older constituents and thus, while harboring reservations about the cost of the Medicare program, he accepted the inevitability of its passage. He worked closely with Wilbur Mills, an Arkansas Democrat and the chairman of the House Ways and Means Committee, and others to help shepherd a Medicare bill through the House. He contributed to the Medicare debate by cosponsoring a bill to provide for a voluntary health insurance plan to pay medical costs and doctors' bills for those sixty-five and older. He also proposed amending the Social Security Act to provide increases in cash benefits to cover expenses for health insurance and expand coverage for dependents and widows.[80]

But when it came to social welfare issues, Reifel's first priority was American Indians. Though he worked tirelessly for all South Dakotans, Reifel's heart lay in Indian country. Indian education and health care depended on federal appropriations, and Reifel was in a position to secure those dollars. Yet he was also determined to use his national platform to advance the integration of American Indians. He would do so at a moment when Indian activists were repudiating integration, placing Reifel in the difficult position of asking Congress to be patient with Indian country while he appealed to Indians to accept change and let go of those cultural practices that prolonged their plight.

William ("Shorty") Reifel, Rosebud, S.Dak. *South Dakota State University Archives*

Benjamin Reifel, age two, c. 1908.
South Dakota State University Archives

Reifel as a freshman at South Dakota State College, 1928. *South Dakota State University Archives*

Reifel and Alice Johnson, c. 1931. *South Dakota State University Archives*

John Collier, 1933. *Library of Congress*

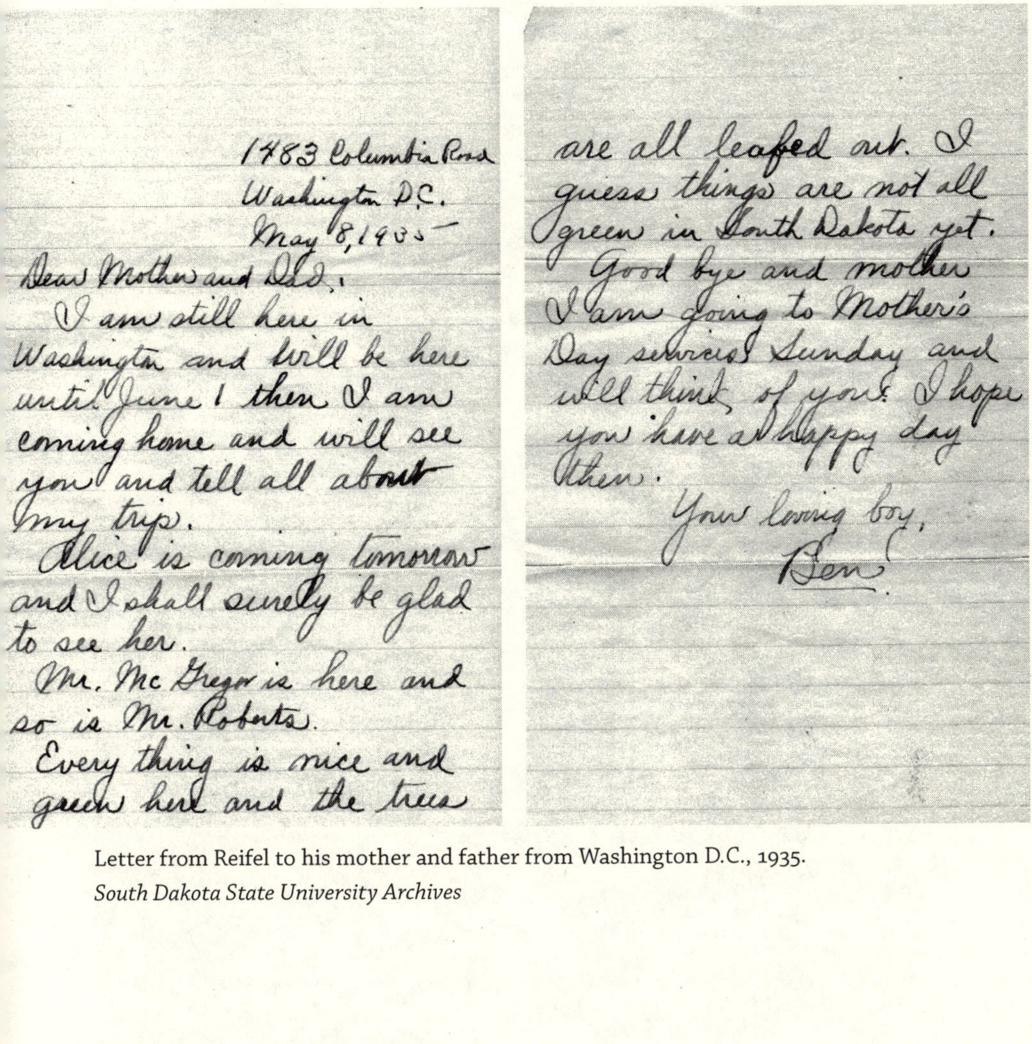

1483 Columbia Road
Washington D.C.
May 8, 1935

Dear Mother and Dad:

I am still here in Washington and will be here until June 1 then I am coming home and will see you and tell all about my trip.

Alice is coming tomorrow and I shall surely be glad to see her.

Mr. McGregor is here and so is Mr. Roberts.

Every thing is nice and green here and the trees are all leafed out. I guess things are not all green in South Dakota yet.

Good bye and mother I am going to Mother's Day services Sunday and will think of you. I hope you have a happy day then.

Your loving boy,
Ben

Letter from Reifel to his mother and father from Washington D.C., 1935.
South Dakota State University Archives

Lucy Burning Breast, Reifel's mother, holding Loyce Reifel, Rosebud, S.Dak., 1936. *South Dakota State University Archives*

Army training, c. 1942. *South Dakota State University Archives*

Reifel and military police jeep, c. 1942. *South Dakota State University Archives*

Reifel while superintendent of Fort Berthold, N.Dak., c. 1946.
South Dakota State University Archives

The Reifel family at Thanksgiving, 1946. *South Dakota State University Archives*

Reifel campaigning in Aberdeen, S.Dak., for the First House District, 1960.
South Dakota State University Archives

Reifel speaks with a store owner and employee during campaign, 1960. *South Dakota State University Archives*

Reifel in Washington, D.C., affixes a Hobo Day bumper sticker to his car, 1961. *South Dakota State University Archives*

Reifel visits with Richard Nixon, 1964. *South Dakota State University Archives*

Karl Mundt and Reifel, c. 1969. *South Dakota State University Archives*

From left, A. E. Crook, Spink County GOP chairman, Reifel, and William E. Bergeson, Utah-Idaho Sugar Company in Belle Fourche, S.Dak., holding sugar beets, c. 1963. *South Dakota State University Archives*

Reifel visiting an Oscar Howe exhibit in the South Dakota Art Museum, Brookings, c. 1965. *South Dakota State University Archives*

Reifel and other members of the House Committee on Appropriations, 1966; from left: George Evans, Joe McDade, Reifel, Winfield Denton, Mike Kirwan, Julia Hansen.
South Dakota State University Archives

Reifel, second from left, and others at the Sisseton High School groundbreaking, 1968.
South Dakota State University Archives

Reifel, with second wife, Frances (Colby) Reifel, is sworn in as commissioner of Indian affairs by Tom Kleppe, 1976. *South Dakota State University Archives*

7 NO MAN MORE FAMILIAR WITH INDIAN PROBLEMS

Indian affairs was a focus of Ben Reifel's political career and a policy arena in which he exercised considerable influence. Reifel won his House seat by earning the trust of white voters who encouraged him to address the problems plaguing Indian country. He did not disappoint them or the American Indian beneficiaries of his efforts. "By far his leading interest was to do something to better the lives of Indian people," observed one of his aides. "That was his foremost concern."[1] Congressman Reifel was a respected authority on Indian affairs, his record reflecting a conviction that American Indians, though in possession of some extraordinary legal rights, must immerse themselves into white society if they hoped to escape the poverty and social distress that defined their condition. Though his signature accomplishments came in the areas of Indian education and tribal justice, his seat on the Appropriations Committee positioned Reifel to address a broad range of issues affecting Indian country. Described as a provincial legislator narrowly dedicated to his district's needs, Reifel was, when it came to the subject of Indian affairs, national in his outlook. Here was a congressman, said a staffer, who "would go to bat for Indians wherever they lived."[2] Reifel's colleagues in Congress valued his expertise and looked to him for advice on strategies to alleviate reservation poverty. By the time he retired from Congress in 1971, Ben Reifel was, arguably, the nation's most influential American Indian.

Just weeks after arriving in Washington in January 1961, Reifel began working to fulfill a government pledge to compensate the Crow Creek Sioux Tribe for lands inundated by reservoir waters from the Big Bend Dam. In the 1950s, the Crow Creek and Lower Brule Sioux had negotiated with Congress, the Corps of Engineers, and the Bureau of Indian Affairs to reach a settlement for lands condemned by the building of the Fort Randall Dam. The two tribes endured a second round of negotiations and land losses, this time as a result of the Big Bend Dam, designed to eliminate surges when the Oahe Dam released large amounts of water. Having originally planned to locate the dam thirty-five miles northwest of the town of Fort Thompson, the corps changed its mind and selected a site adjacent to Fort Thompson, an adjustment that would flood the town of Lower Brule, inundate Crow Creek and Lower Brule bottomlands, and displace hundreds of reservation residents. Dam construction began in September 1960. Two compensation bills had been introduced the previous spring, at which time the Crow Creek and Lower Brule Sioux had requested settlements of approximately $4.9 million per tribe.[3]

Reifel inherited the Crow Creek settlement question and on 2 March 1961 introduced HR 5165 to compensate the tribe. It was a propitious time to author the bill since legislators, writes Michael L. Lawson, "appeared to feel some guilt for the treatment of the Lower Brule and Crow Creek tribes in regard to the Fort Randall settlement," as well as for their losses from the Big Bend Dam.[4] Some of the guilt could be attributed to Reifel. Characterizing his bill as "eminently fair and humanely considerate," he prevailed upon Congress to approve a settlement that would provide just compensation for some of "the most needy and impoverished of our citizens" whose annual per-capita income, Reifel disclosed, was only $260. If enacted into law, HR 5165 would ensure that "once again justice to the Indian American in this situation has been exhausted in full measure," affording the Crow Creek people "a great opportunity which will help this needy group to find a new day in their own land."[5]

As the bill wended its way through Congress, committees in both chambers chipped away at the compensation figure. Alarmed at additional Senate cuts to the already lower than expected $4.64 million settlement approved by the House, a concerned Crow Creek citizen traveled to Washington to press Reifel to increase the compensation level above the approximately $4.3 million figure fixed by the Senate. Moved by the personal appeal, Reifel helped arrange for a meeting between himself, Karl Mundt, E.Y. Berry, and Democratic senator Clinton Anderson of New Mexico, the powerful chairman of the Senate Interior Committee. The three South Dakotans lobbied emphatically for the restoration of the settlement money removed by the Interior Committee but Anderson rejected their plea. Reifel informed the Crow Creek representative that Mundt "really talked hard for getting more money for the Crow Creek people," only to be warned by Anderson that sending the bill back to the Interior Committee for reconsideration would result in their "try[ing] to cut us back even more."[6]

With negotiations closed, HR 5165 and HR 5144, the Berry-introduced bill to compensate the Lower Brule Sioux, became law on 3 October 1962. The two settlements brought an end to Pick-Sloan land condemnations. Despite the lower than requested sums received by the Crow Creek and Lower Brule Sioux, the two tribes were, relative to the other tribes impacted by Pick-Sloan, the most generously compensated by the federal government, a testament to the legislative efforts of Reifel and the rest of the South Dakota delegation.[7]

Reifel's long career in Indian country had helped him win a seat on the House Appropriations Committee's Subcommittee on Interior Affairs in January 1963. Interior Secretary Stewart L. Udall sang Reifel's praises to the subcommittee's members. "Ben Reifel, a longtime employee of our Department, is one of the best area directors we had in the entire Bureau of Indian Affairs," Udall remarked. "I think you are going to find that you can saddle him with a lot of responsibility in this field. He will know a lot . . . without even having to ask a question."[8] In offering Reifel his congratulations following the congressman's reelection in 1964, Indian Commissioner Philleo Nash echoed Udall's sentiment that the Bureau of Indian Affairs was well served by Reifel's presence in Congress. "I have long appreciated your understanding of Indian affairs and your support of programs realistically related to the work that needs to be done," Nash wrote. "The prospect of continuing to work together with you pleases all of us at the Bureau of Indian Affairs."[9]

Reifel's membership on the House Appropriations Committee—"one of the great satisfactions that comes to me as a member of Congress," he proclaimed—was advantageous for South Dakota Indians. Between 1963 and 1970, he was able to secure millions of dollars for reservation and off-reservation projects "to help the Indian people on the road to a better way of life."[10] In March 1964, for instance, he secured funds to build a community center on the Lake Traverse Indian Reservation, the construction of which provided twenty-four months of employment for certain Sisseton-Wahpeton Sioux residents.[11] Later that year he procured a $285,000 appropriation for alterations and renovations to the Public Health Service Indian Hospital in Wagner, a feat that impressed the state's senior senator. "The Reifel action resulted in a *speed-up by four years* of beginning the necessary improvements," Senator Mundt wrote.[12]

Reifel took a special interest in Indian education, though he qualified his support by reiterating that American Indian equality hinged on the enrollment of American Indian students in integrated schools. According to Vernon Loen, his boss "felt that the only way that Indians could compete on a par with non-Indian Americans was for them . . . to sit along side their non-Indian colleagues in school, and to learn to compete on the same basis that non-Indians do."[13] To underscore his position, Reifel demanded that monies appropriated for Indian education go toward schools that brought together Indian and non-Indian students under one roof. He was willing to defend his ground against critics such as the influential Wayne Morse, Democrat from Oregon and one of the more acerbic members of the United States Senate. After reviewing a proposal by Morse to convert an abandoned naval base in Astoria, Oregon, into an all-Indian school for a thousand students from the American Southwest, Reifel, joined by Democratic representative Julia Butler Hansen of Washington, called on the House to reject the plan. Reifel and Hansen argued that Indian students, if they were to adjust to white institutions, must not be segregated from white students. If monies were to be spent on Indian education, they said, let it go toward the construction of dormitories to house Indian students enrolled in integrated public schools.[14]

During hearings on the Morse proposal, Reifel charged that Indian youth were being "sacrificed" to create an alternative use for an abandoned government facility. "Do with it whatever seems appropriate," he told Indian Commissioner Nash, "but don't use the Indian kids as a reason for this sort of thing." Reifel's argument carried the day in the House, as it did in the Senate, where Morse, despite a two-hour harangue against the appropriations committees of both chambers, saw his Indian school project go down to defeat.[15]

Reifel's advocacy for integrated public schools was well-received in his home state, which benefited immensely from his seat on the Appropriations Committee. "If it was a matter of constructing a school, and they had ten Indian schools on the priority list all over the country," recalled a Reifel aide, "you can bet that [the] South Dakota school got to the top of the priority list."[16] Reifel obtained millions of dollars for school construction projects on the Lake Traverse Reservation in Roberts County and the Rosebud Sioux Reservation in Todd County. As early as 1965, Reifel had informed Commissioner Nash of the need for upgrading educational facilities in the Sisseton area of Roberts County, where some American Indian students were opting to attend schools in North Dakota or transferring to the Indian boarding school in Flandreau, South Dakota. Reifel's goal was to apply Bureau of Indian Affairs money toward the building of an integrated school, and the following year, due largely to Reifel's lobbying efforts, the Bureau of Indian Affairs made a Roberts County school complex a priority project.[17] The procurement for the new Sisseton High School and Peever Elementary School totaled over $4.5 million, making it the largest single South Dakota project in the Interior Department's budget for the 1968 fiscal year.[18] The Roberts County schools were built to serve both Indian and non-Indian students, an arrangement that, in Reifel's estimation, proved of greatest benefit to Indian students. In the over three decades since he had graduated from a white college, Reifel had witnessed others like him "shake off the bonds of reservation life. It has convinced me more than ever that education in integrated surroundings—not in remote reservation schools—is essential to successful adjustment." Now that a seat on the Appropriations Committee gave him the opportunity to put his "philosophy into practice," Reifel was determined to bring together Indians and non-Indians to "compete together—as equals—on the playground, in the classroom, on the football turf and in the gymnasium."[19]

Even before the federal dollars for the Sisseton schools were secured, Sisseton's residents were thanking Reifel for his unparalleled support of their community. "Should this become a reality," a school board member said of the proposed facilities, "it will be the greatest thing that has ever happened in this area."[20] In 2018, the Ben Reifel Gymnasium at Sisseton High School continues to honor the memory of the man whose efforts made the building possible.

Reifel was especially proud of the $4.9 million expenditure that made possible the Todd County school complex, a modern facility that included boys and girls dormitories, teacher housing, classrooms to serve at least six hundred junior and senior high students, and the spacious two-thousand-seat Ben Reifel Auditorium. During the April 1963 hearings that reviewed the school proposal, Reifel, who first conceived of a Todd County school while serving as the Aberdeen Area Bureau of Indian Affairs director, confessed his personal interest in the approval of a federally funded project outside his House district. "Mr. Chairman, the Rosebud Tribe is my tribe and this is my childhood school." It was Reifel's firsthand knowledge of the tribe's poor educational facilities, limited to the boarding school that he had attended in his elementary years, that made his testimony compelling. He explained how schools for the Cheyenne River, Pine Ridge, and Standing Rock reservations had been constructed in the 1930s before World War II suspended building projects. Now the Rosebud Sioux Tribe deserved its turn. Centrally located in the town of Mission, the new school would serve the whole of Todd County, which, in Reifel's words, was "one of the few counties in the United States that has an over-all, one-county school system which enables it to coordinate the whole business, cut out little school districts and therefore provide a more efficient educational system."[21] Moreover, a Todd County school would satisfy Reifel's integrationist purpose. "I wanted a central system where you'd have all the kids in Todd County come, Indians and whites," he told an interviewer in 1988.[22]

At first, Indian Commissioner Nash showed only a token interest in a Todd County school. The Bureau of Indian Affairs had not budgeted for a school to serve the Rosebud Sioux Tribe, and when pressed by Reifel to explain the prospects for such a school, Nash could only respond that it was on a priority list. Reifel continued: "I said, 'How high on the priority list?' He mumbled around, well fairly high." At that point Representative Winfield K. Denton, an

Indiana Democrat who Reifel described as "a great friend," admonished Nash for failing to provide "a very good response to . . . an active member of this Committee when he was asking about his alma mater." Denton's remarks stunned Nash—and Denton's colleagues. "We fell out of our chairs," Reifel recalled. Minutes later, Reifel came across Nash in a House hallway. "'Well Mr. Commissioner what do you think about [the Todd County school]?' He said, 'I got the message.' We got a $5 million school at Mission, with the dormitories and beautiful building."[23]

In remarks at the dedication of the Todd County school complex, held in the Ben Reifel Auditorium on 7 May 1966, Reifel apprised the assembled students of the opportunity provided them by generous American taxpayers. He then challenged them to live up to the financial sacrifices made by millions of ordinary citizens. While it was fitting that their generation had better school facilities than his, it would still "be up to every young man and woman to prove to the American people that their investment was a good one—that they will get more back than they have spent in this institution by educating young men and women to find their place in society."[24]

After securing funding for the Sisseton and Todd County school complexes, Reifel asked the Bureau of Indian Affairs to investigate the feasibility of a school to serve the students of the Crow Creek and Lower Brule reservations as well as the non-Indian students residing in that area of central South Dakota. Reifel envisioned a new school located west of the Missouri River in Lyman County that would bus-in students from the two reservations and from the white communities and ranches of the area.[25] The plan did not come to fruition, but it further illustrated Reifel's resolve to establish integrated public schools in rural South Dakota.

Despite his earnestness to improve the lives of young American Indians, Reifel's fiscal conservatism, reflected in his remarks at the Todd County School dedication, conditioned his approach to Indian affairs. Reifel never hesitated to acquaint politicians with the low graduation rates and high unemployment rates suffered by American Indians. But neither did he lose faith in the full integration of American Indians into mainstream life. Hilton M. Briggs, a former South Dakota State University president and a friend of Reifel's, recalled the congressman's belief that more attention to formal education would change American Indians' lives. During a visit to Reifel's office in Washington, Briggs witnessed his friend interacting with an Indian delegation. "Ben sat down and talked to those people like no white man could ever talk to them. I thought, 'What a man.'"[26]

Reifel rejected dismal assessments that, by their nature, American Indians were doomed to lives of poverty, alcoholism, and social dysfunction. "Practically my entire adult life has been spent in trying to help these underprivileged Americans break through this endless circle and take their place as responsible, taxpaying citizens," he wrote. "I know it can be done because it happened to me."[27]

Nowhere was Reifel's optimism more thoughtfully expressed than during the 30 March 1965 House debate on the Interior Department budget for 1966. Reifel began one of his longest congressional speeches by calling attention to the budget cuts made by his appropriations subcommittee, the body responsible for the Interior Department and its most heavily funded agency, the Bureau of Indian Affairs. The 6 percent reduction worked out by the subcommittee had, in Reifel's opinion, created "a budget free of frills and unnecessary expenditures. The American taxpayer will receive a dollar's worth of service for every dollar spent under this budget."[28]

His cost-cutting credentials established, Reifel felt it necessary to justify the largest spending line in the budget, the $203 million allocated to the Bureau of Indian Affairs. The public, many of whom "still think that every Indian receives some kind of a welfare check from Uncle Sam," deserved to know if their tax dollars were improving conditions to the point where reservation residents were becoming more self-reliant. "What advances," Reifel asked rhetorically, "are the Indian people themselves making as a result of these appropriations?" There was no denying that the government's goal of transitioning Indians to "the ways of our society" had been impeded by the "unique problems" faced by reservation residents. "Progress is undeniably slow," he admitted. But Reifel reminded his congressional colleagues that he had once been a reservation Indian with an eighth-grade education and might have remained so had it not been for a federal loan that allowed him and a few other Indians to attend college. Now, thirty-six years later, 5,900

American Indians were enrolled in college, and, due largely to government assistance, American Indian students in elementary and secondary schools matriculated in grade levels compatible with their ages.[29]

Education, Reifel continued, was but one of the government services that addressed the "social and economic standards of the Indian American." Counseling and guidance services, child welfare services, mental health services, and other types of assistance equipped Indians "to cope with the serious problems facing them." No taxpayer could question the positive impact made by annual appropriations to the Indian Health Service, which, through its recent efforts, had raised the average life expectancy for American Indians from forty-two years in 1955 to sixty-three years in 1965. On the other hand, little impact had been made in the field of public housing, "one of the great unsolved problems on today's reservations," Reifel emphasized. After informing House members that nearly 90 percent of Indian housing was "far below any standard of decency," he read a letter from a Catholic priest on the Rosebud Reservation. The priest, who had been taking communion to shut-ins in the middle of the winter, described four homes that "were like iceboxes" and yet inhabited by elders and school-age children who could not catch their buses because their homes were "too cold for human functions." While there were similar circumstances on other reservations, the one bright spot in the Indian housing crisis, Reifel noted, was the participation of more tribes in government housing programs.[30]

Reifel asked taxpayers—and their representatives in Congress—to remain patient. "The record is clear that our public investments in these Indian programs are paying bigger dividends every year," he asserted. The road to American Indian equality was "a long one and we cannot expect to reach our destination overnight. The distance between the world of the Indian past to that of the Indian American today requires a long bridge of understanding and patience."[31]

Reifel's eloquent speech on the condition of American Indians was well-received, with Republican Frank T. Bow of Ohio commenting that, in reference to his colleague from South Dakota, "there is probably no man in this House more familiar with the Indian problems in the United States than the gentleman now in the well." In response to Bow's kind remarks, Reifel conceded that he and other middle-class Indians were in a far different situation than the 450,000 enrolled tribal members who remained on reservations. Reifel had left the reservation with the help of the government, which, after having provided him with a start in life, "assumes no further responsibility." His success story aside, Washington's responsibility to American Indians would continue. "We are trying to merge them into present-day society. This is not easy even for fairly well-adjusted American citizens in our time." In Reifel's mind, Indians' adjustment was contingent upon integrated education. "Indians will adjust if we provide the educational opportunities," Reifel concluded, "and . . . once they raise themselves up to the level of living commensurate with the world about them . . . there will be no economic and social problem which can be described as a peculiarly Indian problem."[32]

Reifel's use of the appropriations process to highlight American Indian acculturation supplemented the efforts of Secretary of the Interior Stewart L. Udall, a former Arizona congressman and Kennedy appointee with a genuine interest in Indian affairs. "Never before has such dedicated concern [for the Bureau of Indian Affairs] been shown by a Secretary of the Interior," Reifel said of Udall.[33] Shortly after his appointment, Udall formed a task force to study Indian affairs and offer recommendations for improving the bureau's effectiveness. The final report of the task force (which included in its membership the next Indian commissioner, Philleo Nash) recommended the cancellation of the termination policy and a continued federal presence to help Indians achieve "equal citizenship, maximum self-sufficiency, and full participation in American life." Task force members were convinced that Indians could "retain their tribal identities and much of their culture" while adjusting to mainstream society, which itself would be enriched by Indian talents and contributions. Hence, concluded the task force, it would be "in our best interests" if Indians were working to adapt to modern living.[34]

Reifel could not have better articulated his own philosophy of Indian affairs. From his seat on the Appropriations Committee, he supported any program to facilitate Indian participation in American life. This meant occasionally tolerating Democratic initiatives that he might otherwise have opposed. Though the proliferation of War on Poverty programs caused great confusion on Indian reservations, the programs sometimes augmented Bureau of Indian Affairs objectives. The Office of Economic Opportunity, for instance, provided resources for Operation Head Start, the best-funded of the Office of Economic Opportunity programs.[35] Unfortunately, despite the presence of programs funded by Office of Economic Opportunity aid, the office made little impact on reservation life. Identifying qualified persons to serve as Head Start, day care, and remedial education workers proved difficult. Reservation residents were soon complaining that the Office of Economic Opportunity created too few jobs and benefited too few people. If the goal of Office of Economic Opportunity programs was to lift Indians out of poverty, the programs were clearly a failure and did little to convince American Indians of the immediate benefits of federal spending.[36]

While at the Bureau of Indian Affairs, Reifel was on occasion the target of anger directed at bureau officials by reservation residents who were frustrated with stagnant economic conditions. In some ways, the stagnation validated Reifel's thesis that until more educated residents moved away from overpopulated reservations the general condition of Indians would not improve. But until that day arrived, public dollars and public services would act as stopgaps to prevent a further decline in the Indian standard of living. Conditions in Indian country were bad, though without the Bureau of Indian Affairs—an agency, Reifel remarked, that "many across the country and . . . a few in Congress . . . would like to see . . . done away with"—they would be much worse. Reifel noted that "frontal attacks" by Bureau of Indian Affairs critics typically overlooked the bureau's primary objective, which was not fighting poverty but adjusting American Indians to the dominant society, an outcome that would ultimately eliminate the so-called Indian problem.[37]

Reifel's faith in the Bureau of Indian Affairs mission was evident during April 1966 hearings before the Senate Interior and Insular Affairs Committee on the nomination of Robert L. Bennett as commissioner of Indian Affairs. Reifel's longtime friend and his former colleague at the Aberdeen Area Office, Bennett became the first person of American Indian descent to fill the position since 1871. The two men shared much in common. Both were raised on Indian reservations and both received encouragement from white neighbors and Bureau of Indian Affairs employees to continue their schooling. "Independent of each other," Reifel testified before the committee, "we decided over 30 years ago to repay some of our debt to our country and the Indian people by helping the BIA to aid others as we have been assisted to find a meaningful place in our dominant society."[38] Reifel and Bennett were unwavering in their belief that the bureau, while deserving of some criticism, remained essential to the modernization of Indian tribes. The Bureau of Indian Affairs represented the best of the federal government in its desire to "meet the peculiar needs of the Indians to enable them to find hope, not despair; opportunity, not discouragement, sharpened aspirations, not continued frustration. Put simply, just to have a chance and an effective chance."[39]

Aside from his official responsibilities, Congressman Reifel used his national platform to profess his belief that American Indians were independent economic actors, not slaves of reservation circumstances. But by urging educated Indians to join the American mainstream, he roiled a younger generation of Indian activists who were denouncing middle-class values, resurrecting tribal traditions, and demanding the return of former tribal lands. Red Power radicals of the 1960s and 1970s were anti-assimilationist and, due to the urban roots of many of their leaders, more militant than the previous generation of American Indian activists. Their cultural-nationalist and separatist ideology contrasted sharply with Reifel's integrationist message. The radicals proposed a withdrawal of Indians from American life, whereas Reifel was encouraging Indians to experience American institutions, embrace the concept of private initiative, and contribute to the larger society through hard work and the fulfillment of their civic duties.

In defending integration, Reifel was also expressing a desire for national unity. One of the more telling examples of Reifel's patriotic loyalty was his opposition to a congressional resolution to establish American Indian Day. To know Reifel was to know of his love for Lakota culture. "When he was in Congress, he used to call me after 5 o'clock, every day, so he could speak Lakota with me and keep his Indian language going," recalled Nellie Menard, a Reifel cousin from Mission, South Dakota. "Out in Washington, of course, he had no one he could talk Indian to. He said he didn't want to forget it."[40] And yet in 1964, despite his undisguised respect for his Indian heritage, Reifel declined to join Republican senator Jacob K. Javits of New York in introducing a joint resolution to create an American Indian holiday to be observed on the fourth Friday of September. Reifel did, however, surprise observers by declaring his support for a "Leif Erickson Day" to recognize the Viking's "courageous explorations . . . [which] could be compared with our space explorations of today." A tribute to Erickson, he added, would highlight Scandinavian-Americans' record of "populating and developing South Dakota and other plains states."[41]

In explaining his opinion about an American Indian holiday, Reifel stated that he was not opposed to Congress recognizing an individual American Indian for notable contributions to American history. But he reiterated his belief that "Indian Americans" were, first and foremost, Americans. "I dislike the tendency to emphasize racial and ethnic differences among the American people," he told reporters. "After all, we all are Americans whether we have Jewish or Negro or Indian ancestry."[42] In 1965, Reifel objected to another American Indian Day bill introduced by Representative John Tunney, Democrat of California. For his stance, Reifel came under attack from American Indian supporters of the bill. Rupert Costo, a Cahuilla Indian and president of the American Indian Historical Society, described Reifel as "one of the fractionated Indians who have lost track of their own beginnings—nothing could be further from the truth than the way he thinks." Reifel held his ground and reasserted his melting pot interpretation of American history. "I feel we have matured as a country, where we are all—Indian, Norwegian, Italian, Irish—Americans."[43]

Nor had Reifel silenced the "time, work, save" message he honed while superintendent of the Pine Ridge Indian Reservation in the mid-1950s. To an audience at the National Seminar of American Indian Women, held in Fort Collins, Colorado, in August 1970, Reifel proposed that Indian mothers bore the chief responsibility of training children to survive in the modern world. Indian women, he said, must inculcate their children to the white man's conceptualizations of time and property. "If we want to hold jobs, have nice homes, and educate our children, we have to have a sense of time. We have to get to jobs on time and be concerned with time. We must learn to save and manage our incomes for the future."[44] There was no reason why "economically and socially adjusted" American Indians could not participate fully in American society.[45] Conversely, "lack of planning for the future, sharing all one has, lack of concern for time, savings, and work—all operating together, make it extremely difficult for the Indian, who is plagued by any one of them, to make a satisfactory adjustment in our competitive society."[46]

Reifel's reference to "competitive society" revealed his undiminished commitment to Indian relocation. Though American Indians were, like many other rural Americans, reluctant to leave their childhood homes, they could adjust to urban life if they were adequately educated and assisted. Agricultural mechanization and rising Indian populations were shrinking the reservation property base and making schools to prepare students to "go anyplace else and survive" the fundamental institutions in Indian country. "And this is my interest," Reifel told an interviewer: "I keep telling the young people that [education is] the great opportunity in America for all of us. The only thing we have to do, primarily, is to fit into our system." Schools, Reifel emphasized, groomed American Indian youth to fit into the American system.[47]

Among other things, fitting into the system meant submitting to American legal practices and Western notions of individual rights and liberties. A longtime observer of the tribal justice system, Reifel had become critical of tribal courts that were not, in his opinion, adequately protecting the rights of individual Indians. His confidence in the American justice system shaped Reifel's attitude toward tribal courts, which he maintained were crucial to the development of competent, forward-thinking tribal councils. Owing to his two decades of work with Indian tribes, coupled with an ambition to improve their courts, the former Bureau of Indian Affairs officer turned congressman was asked to testify during hearings on the groundbreaking Indian Civil Rights Act, submitted as Title II of the Civil Rights Act of 1968.

Reifel's advocacy of civil rights was well-known to South Dakota voters. During his tenure as Aberdeen area director, he had served as a member of the South Dakota Advisory Committee of the United States Commission on Civil Rights. The committee's report for 1959 bore Reifel's imprint, especially in its conclusion that, despite the poor condition of Indian housing in South Dakota, Indians seeking off-reservation housing were not being discriminated against by white property owners. The housing problem, the report stressed, was "based on the economic condition of our Indian people," and where there was a "reluctance on the part of landlords to rent quarters to them," the evidence suggested that those same landlords had opposed renting to anyone—non-Indian or Indian—"who are known to be generally careless, destructive, untidy, or unclean." The committee noted that there was "no discrimination in education in South Dakota" and that the low scholastic performance of Indian students "was attributable to their parents' failure to give them encouragement, and to insist on desirable study habits and regular attendance."[48]

At the national level, Reifel supported, as did most Republicans, the civil rights initiatives of the Kennedy and Johnson administrations. During his 1960 campaign, Reifel proclaimed the GOP as the civil rights party. "Our party cares fundamentally about people," he insisted. "It was born of leaders that snapped the chains of slavery," and it was the Republican Party that extended "universal voting rights for the Indian American."[49] During the fall of 1963, when President Kennedy was pressing Congress to pass legislation that would, among its other provisions, require hotels, motels, and restaurants to desegregate their premises, Reifel announced that he would "vote for the strongest civil rights bill that is brought to the floor of the House."[50] A year later he did just that, joining with 137 other House Republicans in voting for the sweeping Civil Rights Act of 1964.

His vote exposed Reifel to some political backlash. A Sioux Falls insurance salesman, for instance, was "convinced that if a strong candidate were to use Reifel's vote on this particular bill as the basis for his campaign to beat Mr. Reifel in his bid for re-election that he would have an excellent chance to do so."[51] Reifel's support for civil rights may have shaped his attitude toward the candidacy of Barry Goldwater, the Republican nominee for president in 1964 and an opponent, on constitutional grounds, of the Civil Rights

Act. Though a loyal Republican, Reifel was probably lukewarm in his support for Goldwater. South Dakota Republican leaders were clearly divided over sending a Goldwater-pledged delegation to the Republican National Convention in San Francisco. In an internal debate that a South Dakota newspaper referred to as "a threat . . . to party solidarity," Reifel sided with the unpledged faction, whose chief spokesman was Governor Archie Gubbrud. As the convention drew near, Gubbrud questioned whether state party leaders could "sell Goldwater to South Dakota Republicans." If the leadership sent a Goldwater-pledged delegation to California, Gubbrud reasoned, they "would be indicating that Goldwater already has been sold to our people." Yet polls indicated that among rank-and-file Republicans, Richard Nixon and Henry Cabot Lodge Jr., the United States ambassador to South Vietnam, were more popular than Goldwater.[52] As late as July, a nationwide poll showed Republican voters favoring Pennsylvania governor William W. Scranton over Goldwater by a 60 percent to 34 percent margin.[53]

Reifel asked not to be considered as a delegate to the convention, citing his wish that the delegation, which arrived in San Francisco uncommitted to any candidate, reflect the geographical makeup of party volunteers. He remained confident that South Dakota's delegation would "make decisions reflecting state-wide Republican sentiment back home."[54] Reifel's support for civil rights influenced the thinking of delegates like Karl Mundt, who grew concerned that differences of opinion over the party platform might affect the relationship between Reifel and E.Y. Berry, who had split their votes on the Civil Rights Act.[55] And while there is no evidence that Reifel actively opposed the nomination of Goldwater, the record suggests that he was conflicted during the primary season and might have welcomed another Republican candidate for the presidency.

The Goldwater issue had no impact on Ben Reifel's 1964 reelection bid; he defeated Democratic challenger George May by over thirty-two thousand votes. Lyndon Johnson, on the other hand, defeated Goldwater in South Dakota by almost thirty-three thousand votes, evidence, possibly, that the voters' views on civil rights aligned with those of their First District representative.[56]

Reifel cast a vote for the Civil Rights Act of 1964. He would play a much larger role in the passage of the Civil Rights Act of 1968, also known as the Fair Housing Act, to which the Indian Civil Rights Act (ICRA) was attached as a rider. Before 1968, constitutional protections did not always apply to tribal members. Simply put, there existed no constitutional or legislative provisions to prevent incompetent or culturally conservative tribal judges from denying individual Indians their basic rights. Puzzled as to how an individual's rights could be denied on account of tribal customs, Senator Samuel J. Ervin, the Democratic chair of the Judiciary Committee's Subcommittee on Constitutional Rights, moved for the adoption of an Indian Civil Rights Act, attaching his legislation to the high-profile Fair Housing Bill being debated in the late winter and early spring of 1968. Ervin's objective was to secure clauses for freedom of expression, free exercise of religion, defendant's rights, and Fourteenth Amendment protections, thus assuring that constitutional law applied to all tribal courts.[57]

The Fair Housing Bill, President Johnson's endeavor to prohibit discriminatory practices in the sale and leasing of houses, passed the Senate but stalled in the House Rules Committee where it was seen as an election year liability by Democrats trying to distance themselves from "LBJ's bureaucrats."[58] Reifel, who viewed the ICRA section of the bill as "very important legislation [that would] grant to the American Indians many of the rights presently denied them," testified before the House Rules Committee on behalf of the legislation, and in the process, provided valuable support for Johnson's civil rights agenda.[59]

Reifel believed that the ICRA would create an "Indian bill of rights" to protect individuals tried in tribal courts, address shortcomings in the quality of justice administered by those courts, and empower tribes to resist state efforts to assume jurisdiction on their lands without their consent. Taking up the third purpose first, Reifel reminded the committee that PL 280, the Eisenhower-era statute designed to extend the jurisdictional reach of states into Indian County, had already granted jurisdiction over civil and criminal matters on Indian reservations to six states. He recalled the "major battle" that occurred in his home state after Governor Archie Gubbrud signed HB 791 into law in 1963, empowering South Dakota, pursuant to PL 280, to assume jurisdiction of criminal and civil cases on the state's Indian reservations.[60] In a repeat of the events of 1957, when the State House passed HB 892 in an attempt to extend jurisdiction to reservations without the tribes' consent, South Dakota once again sought to force PL 280 upon the state's Indian citizens.

This time the tribes resisted. In March 1963 tribal leaders organized the United Sioux Tribes of South Dakota and chose the state's referendum instrument to block the implementation of HB 791.[61] Their mobilization drive to collect the fourteen thousand signatures to place the referendum on the ballot was aided by the Maurice Paulsen Advertising firm of Sioux Falls, cash-strapped county officials who opposed the assumption of criminal jurisdiction, and the considerable political influence of Congressman Ben Reifel. Together, their efforts proved successful. Attorneys for the United Sioux Tribes filed a petition with twenty thousand signatures to assure that the referendum would appear on the ballot for the 3 November 1964 election. The voters, troubled by the fact that the Sioux had not consented to state jurisdiction, roundly rejected HB 791, with 79 percent of South Dakotans casting "no" votes against the termination bill.[62] "I am proud I have played a substantial role in that effort," Reifel told the House Rules Committee, adding that over the years there had occurred too many instances where states had "failed to give adequate protection to members of the tribes because the States are unwilling to commit the necessary resources to properly enforce their laws."[63]

Reifel assumed that even the proponents of state jurisdiction would approve the ICRA goal of gradually incorporating reservation citizens into the legal mainstream, albeit without "unnecessarily disrupting the values, traditions and customs of these people." He agreed that some tribes were well suited for state jurisdiction and regulation. "If a state is particularly well equipped in a particular field, such as mental health or facilities for juvenile delinquency, the State would assume jurisdiction in these areas without having to assume jurisdiction in all fields." Still, despite his approval of some PL 280 applications, Reifel upheld the independence of tribal governments because he believed that, as sovereign entities, they were free to exercise jurisdiction in most matters without interference from state governments.[64]

Conversely, though he was sympathetic to tribes' judicial independence, Reifel pointed to the weaknesses inherent to tribal systems of law and order. He had witnessed firsthand how tribal judges ignored individual rights.[65] To demonstrate how an individual's rights could be violated on a reservation, Reifel recalled the time when his younger brother was arrested by tribal police for his alleged involvement in a fight. His brother was arrested the day after the fight in question, "but there was no warrant issued, no written charge was given to my brother; he was held in jail for several days without a hearing and without being advised by counsel or family." Seeing that no tribal official was prepared to release his brother, Reifel intervened on his behalf, organizing a meeting with "a Federal official, not a tribal official," who convinced the tribal jailers to release the prisoner.[66]

Reifel could not accept the existence of tribal courts as courts of last resort, which they too often were, in many cases denying defendants the right of appeal or review. He explained that "although an Indian who appears before the state court or a Federal court is given full rights of the Constitution, when that same Indian appears before the Indian tribunals, he has no assurance of receiving such protections." When an Indian is denied his or her constitutional rights in tribal court, Reifel continued, "there is no power in any Federal court to review the matter and set things straight." The ICRA corrected these shortcomings, extending to American Indians freedom of expression, freedom from unreasonable search and seizure, and all other freedoms "essential to the maintenance of a free and democratic society. It is difficult to see how such a provision would interfere with legitimate tribal interests."[67]

Committee members from both parties, impressed with Reifel's grasp on tribal justice systems, praised his testimony. Del Latta, Republican of Ohio, called Reifel's testimony "one of the finest statements we have heard made to the committee." Ray J. Madden, a Democrat from Indiana, remarked that Reifel had offered "the most illuminating statement as far as so-called civil rights justice is concerned . . . that I have heard in all the testimony . . . on this bill." John B. Anderson, Republican from Illinois, noted that Reifel's testimony "perhaps more than any other today has served to underscore the fact that these hearings . . . are serving to illuminate the bill and to educate the members of this committee and I think

Members of the House on how important and how fundamental some of these provisions of the bill are."[68]

Reifel's convincing testimony helped win passage of the Indian Civil Rights Act, which, with some exceptions and accommodations, replicated the guarantees and protections of the Bill of Rights.[69] American Indian reaction to the ICRA, however, was mixed. Though there was widespread support for repeal of PL 280, some tribal leaders insisted that the other features of the act undermined tribal sovereignty by interposing federal judges between tribal courts and individual Indian citizens. If Indian tribes were to retain the authority to designate and interpret the rights of their members, then what, they asked, would the extension of constitutional guarantees to those members do to the sovereign standing of tribal governments?[70] These fears were not shared by Reifel, who detected "nothing bad in this legislation. It is good legislation. It does protect the individual and his civil rights." The ICRA, he declared, was an important vehicle for adjusting Indians to American institutions. It respected tribal sovereignty, but not, argued Reifel, at the expense of individual liberty, nor, in a larger sense, the individual Indian's "gradual movement into the general stream of legislative machinery that we all recognize the need for."[71]

Years later, proponents of the ICRA were stunned by the Supreme Court's decision in *Santa Clara Pueblo v. Martinez* (1978), which barred most ICRA suits against tribes and tribal officials in federal courts. "The Court's holding," writes Dennis R. Holmes, "was based on the principle that tribes retain the internal government powers of a sovereign" and that Congress's objective in protecting American Indians' rights, as outlined in the ICRA, "could be achieved in tribal courts without federal interference." Holmes concludes that the "*Santa Clara* decision has all but destroyed any possible federal court protection of Indian political rights," though he adds that "ongoing upgrading" of tribal courts may create a "better" legal environment than that which existed before the passage of the ICRA.[72]

The reservation legal climate did not necessarily improve, and in retirement, Reifel would continue to share his ideas for improving tribal justice and law enforcement. But in 1968 he had a campaign to run. Reifel's testimony on behalf of the ICRA occurred as he was running for what would be, he had decided, his fifth and final House race. Staff member Rolly Samp recalled that Reifel had taken a pledge in 1960 to serve only five terms in the House of Representatives. "He came from the philosophy that those serving in the House should serve the people and then just leave."[73] Still popular with East River voters but unwilling to break his promise, Reifel entered the 1968 campaign with a desire to win the election, serve out his term, and walk away from the House of Representatives.

The campaign ended in Reifel's victory over Democratic challenger Frank E. Denholm, though the political events of that year nearly turned out differently. Having been encouraged by friends and supporters to challenge George McGovern, Reifel considered running for the United States Senate in 1968. He had, after all, been critical of McGovern's liberal voting record and begun to question whether the senator was representative of the state's political culture. "It is not enough that the incumbent be a 'nice guy' and have an attractive family," Reifel said of McGovern. "He should vote in a manner reflective of South Dakota thinking. As things now stand, Senator Mundt's vote is being cancelled out on every major issue."[74] But after months of "prayerful consideration"—and after reviewing poll numbers that showed him trailing McGovern —Reifel informed the Republican State Central Committee on 6 September 1967 that he would "not be a candidate for the United States Senate next year. That decision is final." His senior standing on the Appropriations Committee had put him in line for the chairmanship of the Interior Affairs subcommittee, should the Republicans have won control of the House in 1968. "Such a position is far more meaningful than that of a junior senator," he told state party leaders.[75]

Privately, Reifel listed his age—he turned 61 in 1967—as an important factor in his decision not to run for the United States Senate.[76] But there were also nonpolitical opportunities that would allow him to shape Indian affairs and advance his cause of integrating American Indians. As he prepared to retire from politics and pursue those opportunities, Reifel could take pride in what he referred to as "his most important work" as a United States representative: his efforts to improve the living standards of American Indians. Reflecting on his political career a few years after retiring from Congress, Reifel recalled that he had "tried to make members of Congress become more aware of the needs of the Indians." While educating his House colleagues about the "two life styles of the Indians and the whites," he also "tried to make Indians themselves aware that this is the problem," that the Indian lifestyle was not suited for the white man's world. Reifel's philosophy remained unchanged. "Indians must move forward," he maintained.[77]

In 1971, Ben Reifel prepared to move forward. He was beginning the final phase of his life, a period of active retirement during which he heralded his vision of Indian country while strengthening bridges of understanding between the two cultures he embodied.

8 THE BEST OF BOTH CULTURES

During his final years in Congress, Ben Reifel formed a working relationship with George B. Hartzog Jr., the head of the National Park Service and, according to former National Park Service chief historian Robert M. Utley, one of its greatest directors. Having already undertaken an unprecedented expansion of the nation's parks, wildlife refuges, and historic sites, Hartzog had begun to explore how the National Park Service might assist Indian tribes in developing tourism opportunities on reservations adjacent to national parks and monuments. An "empire builder" with a personal vision that "fit right into Lyndon Johnson's Great Society ideas," Hartzog hoped that tribal economies could reap benefits from their proximity to National Park Service sites.[1]

Sometime in 1970, Hartzog, intent on placing more minorities in National Park Service leadership roles, asked Reifel, one of the park service's staunchest defenders on the House Appropriations Committee, to join his staff. Reifel "possessed a wealth of experience and knowledge," said Hartzog, who saw in the soon-to-be-retired congressman a person who would "materially enhance [National Park Service] efforts to support and assist the Indian Tribes, many of whom are close neighbors of the national parks."[2] Reifel did not accept a full-time position—he told Hartzog that he was "not interested in . . . [g]oing to work at eight o'clock every morning"[3]—but he agreed to become the "Assistant Director for Indian Affairs" on a part-time and voluntary basis. In exchange for reimbursements of their fuel expenses, Ben and Alice Reifel, towing an Airstream trailer behind their 1969 Lincoln Continental, began traveling to Indian reservations, where Ben met with tribal representatives to explore ways to develop campgrounds, parks, and recreational programs on Indian lands. The Reifels spent time in Alaska, Arizona, California, Colorado, North Carolina, and Utah and consulted with Oglala Sioux representatives on the prospects of building a motel near the Badlands National Park in South Dakota.[4]

Reifel served the National Park Service in an advisory role until 1974, at which time he concluded that, unfortunately, the reservation tourism program was not working. In an interview, Reifel described National Park Service–sponsored tribal development as "very limited" and almost exclusively dependent upon location. Whereas the Eastern Band of Cherokees and some Southwestern tribes were perfectly placed to benefit from park traffic, many reservations were too far removed from National Park Service sites to gain any economic advantage.[5] Despite his inability to make the impact he desired, Reifel's efforts did not go unnoticed or unappreciated. In recognition of his legislative support for the National Park Service and his more recent attempts to develop tourism on Indian reservations, the Cedar Pass Visitor Center at the Badlands National Park was renamed the Ben Reifel Visitor Center in October 1990, nine months after Reifel's death. In a letter to former Reifel aide Rolly Samp, United States Senator Larry Pressler of South Dakota, sponsor of the amendment to rename the visitor center, wrote that honoring Reifel's memory in such a fashion was "the least we can do to show our appreciation for his lifetime of service."[6]

At about the same time that he began working for the National Park Service, Reifel received news that President Nixon had appointed him to a two-year term as chairman of the National Capital Planning Commission, a twelve member body that meets on a monthly basis "to adopt, approve, or provide advice on plans and projects that impact the nation's capital and surrounding areas." Comprised of planners, architects, urban designers, and other professionals, the National Capital Planning Commission mission is in some respects similar to that of the Park Service in that it is charged with preserving and enhancing the cultural, historic, and natural resources and assets of the capital region.[7] The National Capital Planning Commission chairmanship was a good fit for Reifel. He and Alice had grown fond of Washington—the capital remained their home of residence—and Ben, whose wonderment at being part of the American government had never flagged, welcomed the opportunity to help preserve the nation's capital for future generations.

While in the capital in February 1972, Ben suffered a devastating personal loss. On 4 February, Alice complained of a sore throat and exhibited some symptoms of influenza. Two days later, she was admitted to Walter Reed Hospital where she was diagnosed with pneumonia. Her condition deteriorated rapidly over the next forty-eight hours, and on 8 February, at the age of sixty-two, Alice died, leaving behind her husband, her daughter Loyce and son-in-law Emery Anderson, and three granddaughters. A grieving Ben, who had rarely been separated from Alice during their year of travel with the National Park Service, flew her body back to South Dakota. Following a funeral at Saint Mark's Episcopal Church in Aberdeen, she was buried near her parents in her hometown of Erwin.[8]

Just two and a half weeks after Alice's death, Reifel shocked South Dakota voters by announcing his desire to return to politics. His wife's recent death had altered his retirement plans, he said. "The reason I stepped aside [in 1971] was our desire to spend more time together. Now that reason no longer exists."[9] GOP leaders and rank-and-file Republicans who thought they had seen the last of candidate Reifel began offering their advice. Some urged Reifel to run for governor. Others recommended that he win back his House seat or throw his hat into the 1972 Senate race that was wide open due to Karl Mundt's stroke in November 1969.[10] After weighing his options, Reifel announced on 15 March his intention to seek the United States Senate seat. Though sixty-six years old, he insisted that he still had "years of productive service to offer the people of my native state."[11]

And then suddenly, after what can only be described as one of the shortest—and most unusual—campaigns in South Dakota history, Reifel withdrew from the race. On the morning of 22 March, just one week after confidently declaring his candidacy, Reifel told a gathering in Huron that they must raise $50,000 by 5 p.m. that day or he would drop out of the Republican primary. Supporters dug into their pockets and worked the phones and raised $35,000 before the deadline, at which time Reifel abruptly announced that he was quitting the race. Contributions, however, continued to roll in and later that evening reached Reifel's $50,000 mark. But despite having amassed a not inconsiderable amount of cash in a short period of time, Reifel refused to reconsider his decision, stating that since he could not get firm commitments of support to mount a campaign, he would not run for office. "This has been a traumatic experience for me," he commented, "and I don't want to go through it again."[12]

Reifel's behavior must have left supporters wondering what "traumatic experience" he was referring to. Had it been the ordeal of raising campaign cash, or was he expressing his emotions over the sudden loss of Alice? Five times in the 1960s Reifel had run a congressional campaign, with each race requiring the raising of money and the personal solicitations and fundraising events that attended that process. Since his Huron followers had just collected tens of thousands of dollars in fewer than twelve hours, one must assume that Reifel's talent for generating campaign contributions remained intact. This is not to say that the process of filling a campaign coffer is not accompanied by its share of doubt and anxiety. But be that as it may, it is difficult to escape the conclusion that Ben's reason for dropping out of the Senate race was attributable to his state of mind in the wake of Alice's untimely death. His wife had been by his side in five previous campaigns, an indispensable partner and constant supporter whose face and voice were recognized by voters on both sides of the Missouri River. Now Ben was on the verge of another tough race, this one a statewide contest against the likely Democratic nominee, James Abourezk, who was polling well ahead of his primary opponent. It is possible that the thought of running a pressure-packed campaign without his beloved Alice caught up with Ben in Huron on 22 March. Despite his well-earned reputation for prudence and composure, Ben Reifel was human, after all, and jumping into a high-profile race so soon after Alice's death might have proved too much for him to bear.

Now that he had decided against running for office, Reifel, when not absorbed by his volunteer activities or board assignments, sought out the company of old friends, one of whom was a college classmate, Frances Ryland Colby. Ben had known Frances since the late 1920s, when she and her former husband, Irving Colby, began palling around with Ben and Alice at SDSC. On 14 August 1972, Ben and Frances were wed in Durango, Colorado. They lived in Washington, D.C., until 1973, when they returned to South Dakota to make their home in Aberdeen. "I've enjoyed a happy relationship with South Dakota," Reifel told a reporter. "That's why I stay here."[13] The couple relocated to Sioux Falls in 1976 and then moved again three years later to a cabin on the north shore of Lake Poinsett near Estelline, South Dakota. From there they wintered for several years in Largo, Florida, in the Tampa–Saint Petersburg area.[14]

Frances found herself wedded to a man who was involved in many causes and who appeared to be just as busy in retirement as he had been during his professional days. In addition to retaining his connections at the National Park Service and National Capital Planning Commission, Reifel accepted the chairman's post for the South Dakota Easter Seal Society and threw himself into raising money for community and county programs that served handicapped children and adults in need of financial assistance.[15] Reifel remained in high demand as a public speaker, appearing, for instance, in Lawrence, Kansas, as the master of ceremonies at the American Indian Hall of Fame induction of their inaugural class of American Indian athletes, a group that included Jim Thorpe and baseball legend Chief Bender.[16]

In 1973, Reifel became a founding member of the American Indian National Bank of Washington, an institution dedicated to serving Indian communities and which dealt with such specific matters as assisting credit unions in Indian country. Other prominent members of the bank's board, of which Reifel served as chairman from 1974 to 1976, included William W. Keeler (Cherokee), the CEO of Phillips Petroleum Company; Peter McDonald, chairman of the Navajo Tribe; and Barney Old Coyote (Crow), director of the American Indian Studies program at Montana State University.[17] Reifel also served as president of Arrow, Inc., an Indian service organization, and he was a member of the National Advisory Council of the Boy Scouts of America. He was appointed to the Council of Trustees of the Freedom Foundation at Valley Forge, and President Gerald Ford, a close Reifel friend from their days together in the United States House of Representatives, made him a member of the National Advisory Council for the Education of Disadvantaged Children.[18]

A more prestigious appointment awaited Reifel; on 7 December 1976, President Ford named him the nation's forty-eighth commissioner of Indian Affairs. Reifel had been considered as a candidate to succeed Commissioner Louis R. Bruce in 1972, but, at age sixty-six, was probably seen by the Nixon White House as too old to perform the duties of office. The Ford administration saw otherwise, though Reifel's appointment was, unfortunately, only a recess appointment, made necessary by Ford's defeat by Jimmy Carter and Morris Thompson's resignation as Indian commissioner on 3 November 1976, the day after the election. Recognizing that it was unlikely that Carter, a Democrat, would retain him as commissioner, Reifel nevertheless prepared himself for what he believed would be several months as head of the Bureau of Indian Affairs. On 7 December, he was sworn in by Interior Secretary Thomas S. Kleppe, the man who recommended him for the commissionership. "I feel like I'm going home," Reifel said of his return to the Bureau of Indian Affairs.[19]

He would inherit a bureau that was still recovering from a decade of American Indian dissent that shook the confidence of bureau employees. American Indian radicals, most notably the members of the militant American Indian Movement (AIM), depicted the Bureau of Indian Affairs as the source of many of the "evils" endured by Indian people over the decades. Among other events, AIM's takeover and ransacking of the Bureau of Indian Affairs headquarters in Washington in November 1972 and AIM's armed occupation of the symbolic hamlet of Wounded Knee, South Dakota, in February 1973 had exposed philosophical divisions within the bureau itself. To make matters worse, nonactivist, law-abiding tribal leaders were concerned about their future with the Bureau of Indian Affairs. Commissioner Thompson, an Athabascan Indian from Alaska, had shown himself to be a stalwart defender of the Nixon administration's "Indian self-determination without termination" policy, for which the Indian Self-Determination and Education Assistance Act of 1975 provided a legal basis. And yet the act's intent—to transfer more control over federal programs and services to Indians themselves—received a tepid response from tribal leaders who, because of their concern that they might fail to uphold new contractual obligations, demonstrated a "reluctance . . .

to embrace the opportunities provided by the Self-Determination Act."[20]

Commissioner Reifel met these and other challenges head-on. In the course of his administration—the shortest in the history of the Bureau of Indian Affairs—Reifel dazzled those around him by demonstrating a grasp on the workings of both the bureaucracy and Congress. A contemporary within the Bureau of Indian Affairs described him as "probably . . . the best-qualified person ever appointed to head the Bureau of Indian Affairs." Unlike other short-term political appointees who had no time to acquaint themselves with the key personalities upon whom their agencies depended, Reifel had worked with many of the current area directors, tribal chairs, and congressmen who shaped the administration of Indian affairs. "He was not awed by personalities or titles" and his "no-nonsense manner" won over legislators, Bureau of Indian Affairs staff, and tribal representatives who witnessed how a person of Reifel's experience and professional caliber "could revitalize the bureau and imbue its personnel with a new sense of purpose."[21]

Above all else, Commissioner Reifel was decisive. Reflecting on his short stint as commissioner, Reifel gave himself high marks for avoiding bureaucratic snarls and red tape. "I think most of the time an administrator who has authority delegated to him to exercise, if he goes ahead and exercises, he and everybody else are better off if he does it," he said in an interview in 1979. "He may make a mistake, but if he doesn't do anything it's a worse mistake than doing something about it."[22] Michael T. Smith writes that Commissioner Reifel's decisiveness was refreshing. "This in itself was a change," especially since Reifel was "able to put the concerns of the Indian people first and deal with other interested parties later. Given the opportunity, his administration could have demonstrated that people come before politics."[23]

Unfortunately, Reifel was not given the opportunity. On 28 January 1977, a bureaucrat sent on behalf of the Carter White House asked Reifel for his resignation. Reifel immediately complied. "He didn't deserve to be fired like that," noted Mark Trahant, an *Arizona Republic* reporter who knew Reifel and had followed his career. Though a Republican by preference, Reifel's first loyalty was to American Indians, and for that reason he would have been loyal,

Trahant argued, "to any president. Yet under orders he left office quietly and entered . . . retirement quietly." As was his nature, Trahant added, "he never complained either. Reifel had just been serving his country again."[24]

It may have been Reifel's good fortune to be replaced as commissioner, for, as previously alluded to, the dynamics of American Indian politics had changed dramatically, and in some ways permanently, in the 1960s and 1970s. As was the case in many quarters of American government in those turbulent decades, Indian affairs transpired in a tense, emotionally charged political environment marked by rising minority consciousness, a growing acceptance of cultural pluralism, and increased grassroots activism, which was, in the case of American Indian activism, nourished by what one historian has referred to as "a pervasive public guilt for crimes committed against indigenous peoples."[25] Indians became politically emboldened during Reifel's decade in Congress. The American Indian Chicago Conference of 1961 and the formation of "New Indian" groups like the National Indian Youth Council planted the seeds of a Red Power movement that demanded action on such issues as tribal sovereignty, religious freedom, and fishing, hunting, mineral, and water rights. But it took the Indian occupation of a former federal prison, Alcatraz Island, in November 1969 to bring national exposure to Indian causes. The occupiers, whose sardonic Alcatraz Proclamation declared the island suitable for a reservation since it was now inhabited by a people that "has always been held as prisoners," attracted media attention and received visits from Jane Fonda, Anthony Quinn, and Buffy Sainte-Marie. Safety concerns and troubles resulting from drug and alcohol use, vandalism, and fights brought the occupation to an end in June 1971, at which time the symbolism of the Alcatraz Island takeover was still lingering in the minds of both red and white Americans.[26]

It was the American Indian Movement that most affected South Dakota reservations and, not surprisingly, young Lakotas' attitudes toward Ben Reifel. Founded in the Twin Cities in 1968 as a watchdog organization to monitor interactions between local police and American Indians, AIM received a boost in 1970 when Russell Means, an Oglala Sioux who had lived in the Bay Area and Cleveland, joined their ranks. Together, Means, Dennis Banks

(Chippewa), Clyde Bellecourt (Chippewa), and John Trudell (Santee Sioux) organized demonstrations like the 4 July 1971 "counter-celebration" at Mount Rushmore and the painting (with red paint) of Plymouth Rock on Thanksgiving 1971. AIM activities took a decidedly militant turn in the fall of 1972. Determined to draw attention to their grievances by staging a high-profile demonstration in the nation's capital, American Indian activists, in a manner intended to be reminiscent of Martin Luther King Jr.'s March on Washington, organized the Trail of Broken Treaties. Caravans from around the country concentrated in Minneapolis where Hank Adams produced a document, "The Twenty Points," that called for a return to bilateral treaty arrangements, the restoration of traditional lands, the abolition of the Bureau of Indian Affairs, tribal control of reservation affairs, and religious freedom.[27]

When the protestors reached Washington, D.C., on 3 November, they suffered from the poor advance work of their organizers. Marchers descended on the Bureau of Indian Affairs headquarters building, where at 5 p.m. they were told to disperse. They resisted. Within minutes, some four hundred demonstrators occupied the building and began raising barricades to block the entrances. As police surrounded the building, the occupants attacked its interior, breaking furniture, knocking out windows, defacing walls, and, in a testament to the senselessness of their action, slashing and smashing pieces of Indian art. Bureau files that were not destroyed—and many were—were smuggled out and with them went property records, trust accounts, probates of estates, and water documents that were of immeasurable value to individual Indians. If the rioters were looking for a confrontation with police, they were disappointed, for law enforcement officers were determined to avoid violence. Conceived by its organizers as a peaceful demonstration with spiritual overtones, the Trail of Broken Treaties had descended into a destructive melee that bore no resemblance to the March on Washington.[28] Leonard Garment, a member of President Nixon's White House staff, writes that AIM "left behind not only a devastated building but a very bad taste in the mouths of many Americans, including a good number of previously sympathetic editorial writers and federal political figures."[29]

And AIM leaders were not finished. Two months after the Washington riot, they gathered in Custer, South Dakota, to protest the events surrounding the death of Wesley Bad Heart Bull. AIM members clashed with police, and the offices of the Custer Chamber of Commerce were set on fire. In February AIM shifted its focus to the nearby Pine Ridge Indian Reservation, where the Oglala Sioux Tribe found itself divided between supporters and opponents of tribal chairman Dick Wilson. AIM swung its muscle behind the opponents of Wilson, who was himself well protected by an armed security force known as goons. As scores of federal officers and state police rushed to the reservation to preserve order, Russell Means and Dennis Banks, inspired by an Oglala elder who encouraged AIM to "make [a] stand," led a caravan to the village of Wounded Knee, where the militants occupied Sacred Heart Catholic Church, a few houses, and the local trading post, which was raided for rifles, shotguns, and ammunition.[30]

Federal officials sealed off Wounded Knee, and for the next seventy-one days a national television audience followed the standoff, which has been described by one author as "the apex moment of Indian militant activism."[31] The historian Francis Paul Prucha characterized AIM leaders as "astute propagandists who fed the media their views and staged events that the television cameramen eagerly reported."[32] Though the two sides traded gunfire and two Indians died during the confrontation, law officers chose not to assault the militants, who on 8 May withdrew from Wounded Knee. In the legal proceedings that followed, only 10 percent of the Indians involved in the events at Pine Ridge were convicted of crimes. Nevertheless, the halcyon days of Indian activism were nearing an end. Most AIM members had come to accept the futility of violent protest, and the organization itself was wracked by factionalism and a host of internal problems. Moreover, by the mid-1970s the leaders of AIM had lost their audience, the American public having grown weary of their militant theatrics.[33]

Ben Reifel counted himself among the AIM-weary. He worried that his vision of American Indian progress would henceforth be dismissed by young Lakotas who were taken-in by the spectacle of AIM radicalism. Despite his traditional upbringing with a Lakota mother and his command of the Lakota language, he knew that some Lakotas "resented" him. "Full-bloods" labeled him "an outsider," a "mixed-blood apple Indian" whose red skin covered a white identity. "Most of us who are mixed-blood, I think we're regarded as being white," he admitted.[34]

Yet Reifel understood that it was more than his blood quantum that drew the skepticism if not the outright ire of the "New Indians." His call for Indians to "meet the behavior expectations of society" by adopting the "time-work-savings syndrome and future orientation" clashed with the activists' devotion to traditional customs and beliefs. The activists' literary voice and a hero of many young Lakotas was Vine Deloria Jr., author of the popular *Custer Died for Your Sins: An Indian Manifesto* (1969), in which Deloria celebrated Indian people's resiliency, resourcefulness, and resolve to preserve their cultural heritage. Sounding a note of optimism, Deloria predicted a future in which the "greater strength" of American Indians "shall wear down the white man and finally outlast him."[35] He credited American Indian revolutionaries with reviving tribal languages and rituals and inspiring Indians to resurrect old customs to replace modern legal institutions. Deloria pressed Indian communities to reconsider the definition of *tribe*. Was a tribe a traditional organization bound by custom and under the political leadership of chiefs and medicine men, he asked, or was it "a modern corporate structure attempting to compromise with modern white culture?"[36]

The back-to-the-past theme promulgated by Deloria and others concerned Reifel, who feared that such thinking would frustrate the adjustment of American Indians to modern life. He acknowledged that the political landscape of Indian country had changed and confessed that because of his adherence to integration he "couldn't be a superintendent or area director today under the circumstances."[37] And yet despite the activists' contempt for his integrationist philosophy, Reifel refused to surrender the argument to them. In the 1970s and 1980s he took advantage of newspaper and magazine interviews to refute their claim that Indians should retreat from American life. There would be no outlasting of Euro-American culture, he warned. "The Indian cannot go back to the buffalo economy, and they know it. Romanticists want to keep them the same as they were, but Indians have to accommodate to today."[38]

Reifel challenged American Indian radicals to pay closer attention to American Indian history, which was replete with stories of cultural adaptation and evolution. "Take the Sioux Indians," he said. Once woodsmen armed with bows and arrows in the Great Lakes region, they had been driven from their homelands by Chippewa Indians armed with guns and powder. They relocated to the northern plains, where they were transformed. They "conquered the horse, then the buffalo. They transferred their religion to the sun." The Sioux culture, once shaped by forests and lakes, was reconstituted by a semiarid grasslands into "an entirely different cultural system, an entirely different set of religious symbols." Imagine, Reifel asked readers, what would have become of the Sioux Indians had they not relocated from the woods to the prairie. In 1800, a Sioux traditionalist might have argued that his people "should have kept what they had in the woodlands." But had the Sioux not moved, had they not adapted to a new place and a new material order, "they would have perished."[39]

And therein lies the lesson for contemporary American Indians, whose fate would be determined by the acceptance or rejection of the modern economic order. Indians who adopted the white man's time-work-savings complex, Reifel argued, gained their independence, whereas those who did not resigned themselves to a life of dependency and destitution. While Vine Deloria Jr. was demanding from the establishment "a cultural leave-us-alone agreement in spirit and fact," Reifel was calling on Indian students to take advantage of educational opportunities "available to them under the Establishment." The socioeconomic problems plaguing reservation Indians would not be alleviated by turning back the clock. It was time, Reifel argued, that American Indians embarked upon a new migration, a migration of the mind in which they adjusted to the values of the dominant society so that they could begin reaping the benefits of that society.[40]

Though the American Indian Movement's symbolic occupation of Wounded Knee had placed South Dakota at the center of a national debate about Indian-white relations, Reifel could find nothing constructive that resulted from AIM's actions. "I don't think it's done any good," he said of AIM during an interview in

1980. "I don't think it's changed anything. My inclination is that it may have done more harm than good, because it may have caused some turmoil on the reservations."[41] Most of the militants' goals had focused on the attainment of tribal sovereignty, a term which, when uttered by radical separatists, was vague and in some cases altogether extraneous. A people's self-rule derived from their economic independence. But that condition did not exist among the northern plains tribes. By seeking to "build up their own system in isolation from the majority system," activists defeated any hope of reservation economic development, and yet without that development, Reifel stressed, there would be no forces to "break the circle" of social problems that were the byproduct of widespread reservation unemployment. Maybe it was time, Reifel submitted, that Indian leaders "come to the realization that we can sacrifice some sovereignty for the development of our people. Sovereignty may be an empty concern if it doesn't provide security."[42]

It came as no surprise to Reifel's critics that he pinned his hopes for economic security on Indian people's conforming to the American education system. To an even greater degree than they had been in the 1950s and 1960s, Reifel's remarks on Indian education could be jarring, for at the heart of his message lie the question of cultural values. Though he retained "a deep-seated respect" for his mother's ancestors, their traditional culture had vanished. Keeping alive traditional customs, such as the practice of sharing one's material possessions with extended family or friends, "militates against the current system of saving for tomorrow."[43] Repeating the message he shared with Oglala parents in the 1950s, Reifel asked a new generation of Indian parents, many politicized by the events of the 1960s and 1970s, to allow schools to "inculcate" their children to the value of saving money. "By saving, I mean investing in the future," he explained. Drawing a loose comparison to traditional Lakota beliefs about sharing, Reifel noted that by saving money now and thus stabilizing his or her financial situation, an individual Indian could "give away and share" in the future.[44]

Particularly controversial were Reifel's comments on the value of the Lakota language, the survival of which was a basic objective of Lakota activists. His bilingual skills aside, Reifel did not wish to see poverty-affected Indian children spending a portion of their school day learning the rudiments of an inessential language. "I can't see any supporting cultural value in speaking the Lakota language," he said, noting that it was "a dying language." Reifel fielded criticism for promoting ad nauseam his "time, work, saving, sharing within reason" philosophy, but that philosophy reinforced goals like "learning the English language and picking up [those] ways of the dominant society" that were necessary for the advancement of the Indian race. American Indians had once consulted medicine men for their ailments, but today "when we become sick and want to get well, we have to go to a doctor." In the same way, Indian youth desiring a better life must entrust themselves to the mores of the Western education system. "We have to live in the present," Reifel implored.[45]

Despite his willingness to engage activists in debates about modern reservation life, Reifel did not let those debates define his work with American Indians. In the summer of 1979, for instance, he traveled to North Carolina to chair several sessions that culminated in a new constitution for the Eastern Band of Cherokee Indians. Several hundred tribal members gathered at the opening session, held in the Cherokee High School auditorium, to approve the constitution's preamble, adopted with only one dissenting vote. Honored to have been chosen to draft "a constitution that will go before the tribal members in secret vote," Reifel took special pride in the establishment of a judicial system that would, in his words, "be independent of both the executive and legislative branches of tribal government. So many [tribal] courts have been creatures of council to where the judges lack freedom."[46]

As an authority on Indian affairs, Reifel was asked his opinion on how the Sioux tribes should respond to a United States Court of Claims settlement, affirmed by a 1980 Supreme Court ruling, which awarded $106 million to the Sioux for the government's taking of the Black Hills in 1877. The tribes refused the award—they asked for the land instead—but Reifel told a gathering in Brookings that he did not think the Sioux "will get anywhere in trying to get the Black Hills back." Nevertheless, he was pleased with the court's decision and suggested that a portion of the settlement monies go toward a scholarship fund. The Sioux tribes could purchase land in the Black Hills with their money, but many of the poorer tribal members, Reifel pointed out, were in need of immediate relief, so pooling the settlement money to buy land might prove unpopular.[47]

The 1980s witnessed Reifel's involvement in a range of organizations and causes. He continued to serve on the Boy Scouts' national and regional boards. When they formed a Blue Ribbon Task Force on Indian Affairs, the National Committee on Indian Work of the Episcopal Church selected Reifel, a longtime lay leader in the church, as one of its first appointees.[48] Late in life, Reifel noted with pride that he had served as chairman of the Lower Brule Sioux Tribe Farm Corporation, an organization dedicated to irrigation development and farm management improvements on the Lower Brule Reservation.[49]

Of special importance for future generations of South Dakotans were Reifel's contributions to the South Dakota Art Museum in Brookings. He was named a museum trustee in 1977 and served as museum board president in 1982 and 1983. Before the museum had acquired any American Indian art work, Reifel donated his entire American Indian collection. He then secured several Oscar Howe paintings. His prediction that his gifts would encourage other donations of American Indian art proved accurate, for at the time of his death in 1990, nine collections totaling 680 objects had been cataloged by the museum. One of the rarest pieces in the South Dakota Art Museum is a turn-of-the-century Crow Tribe eagle feather headdress presented to Reifel by Henry Kills Warrior of Oglala, South Dakota, in 1935.[50]

Joe Stuart, a former director of the museum, remembered Reifel as an avid supporter of the arts. He found Reifel's generosity and his attitude toward material objects especially remarkable. Stuart recalled how one day Reifel arrived at the museum, asked for a knife, and then proceeded to remove a feather from an Arikara headdress that he had donated with his private collection. The feather was to go to a nephew participating in a special ceremony. "He was not so much interested in material things as in what they meant," Stuart said of Reifel, who, in his approach to politics, was also atypical. Though "a good politician," his outlook was that of a bygone era. "He was a politician sort of in the old Sioux spirit of a leader who was concerned about everybody," Stuart mused.[51] "He feels that all people are equal in the eyes of God."[52]

Many awards befell Reifel in retirement. He received honorary doctorates from Northern State College, South Dakota State University, and the University of South Dakota. In 1984, Reifel, along with baseball icon Henry "Hank" Aaron and ten others, was the recipient of the prestigious Boy Scouts Silver Buffalo Award for distinguished service to youth.[53] In recognition of his many years of lay work, the Episcopal Diocese of South Dakota presented Reifel with their Saint George Award, while the South Dakota Board of Regents paid tribute to him by naming him a South Dakota Centennial Alumnus.[54] Reifel was in the first class inducted into the South Dakota Western Heritage Hall of Fame, and in 1976 the South Dakota Committee on the Humanities made him the first recipient of its Distinguished Award in the Humanities.[55] During the awards ceremony, John Barcroft, a representative from the National Endowment for the Humanities, identified Congressman Reifel as "one of a handful of men who helped support and foster the [NEH] program. This led the way to the broad bipartisan support the program now has." Reifel's political career, Barcroft concluded, was illustrative of "the optimism and promise of South Dakota."[56]

Though out of politics for good, Reifel occasionally lent his support to candidates, including one controversial candidate for president. State GOP leaders must have been surprised and not a little frustrated by Reifel's announcement in July 1980 that he would be endorsing Independent candidate John Anderson, rather than Republican candidate Ronald Reagan, for the presidency. After indicating that George Bush had been his first choice for the Republican nomination, Reifel explained his support for Anderson, a liberal Republican congressman from Illinois and a former House colleague to both Reifel and Bush. Reifel had hoped "to stay with the party," but he and Anderson "went to Congress together and we worked well together. When he put his name in the pot, I said I would support him and contributed money to his efforts."[57] Reifel's endorsement had no impact on the race—South Dakota's four electoral votes went to Reagan—but the episode speaks volumes about the enduring relationships that Reifel forged with members of the United States House of Representatives.

Unfortunately, Reifel's career in Congress created a bitter moment for him when in September 1988, the editors of the *Sioux Falls Argus Leader*, in a column critical of wasteful government spending, reported that he was one of three retired congresspersons to earn more than $1 million in federal retirement benefits. The editors, who seem to have erroneously concluded that all of Reifel's retirement pay stemmed from his salary as a congressman from 1961 to 1971, deplored the benefits as "indicative of the nation's serious financial woes" and suggested that federal legislators "suffer and enjoy the same economic realities as other Americans." Better homework and some deliberation on the part of the *Argus Leader* staff would have revealed that, in addition to his years in Congress, Reifel's well-earned federal pension was derived from his two decades with the Bureau of Indian Affairs and his career as a United States Army officer on active duty and reserve rosters. And yet, despite the implication that he was one of the "members of Congress . . . [who] are capable of devising ingenious perks for themselves to assure that they retire in luxury," there appears to be no evidence that Reifel responded to the opinion piece.[58]

Reifel's decision not to rise to his defense was probably a reflection of his age. Once a tireless dynamo whose schedule and pace during early retirement were that of a man twenty years younger, Reifel had slowed down considerably in the late 1980s. He rarely appeared or spoke at public events, and aside from the occasional interview, he spent his days fishing or playing cards with family and friends on Lake Poinsett. Reifel remained intimately connected with his grandchildren and great-grandchildren as well as his nieces and nephews. A great-niece recalled that his "home was always open," and a granddaughter remembered him being more like a parent than a grandparent.[59] He remained close with former congressional aides and staffers whom he now counted as friends. Former staffer and South Dakota state treasurer David Volk, who credited Reifel with giving him his start in politics, described his old boss as "one of those guys who stayed loyal to the people who worked with him."[60]

In 1989, Reifel was generally healthy for his age at eighty-two. But that summer he was diagnosed with cancer, and in August, with his health deteriorating, he was admitted to the Good Samaritan Nursing Home in Sioux Falls. There he passed his final days visiting with his wife Frances and with family and friends. In September Reifel mustered his strength to join his former House colleague—and now former president of the United States—George H. W. Bush at a rally to celebrate the South Dakota Centennial. Emotionally moved after being recognized by the president, Reifel reflected on how far he had come since his birth in a log cabin on the Rosebud Sioux Indian Reservation in 1906. "Isn't that something?" he said, his wonderment at achieving the American dream still very much evident. "An Indian who grew up on the reservation getting introduced like that by the President of the United States."[61]

Ben Reifel's extraordinary life journey came to an end in the Sioux Valley Hospital in Sioux Falls on 2 January 1990. He was eighty-three. In attendance at his funeral at the Calvary Episcopal Cathedral in Sioux Falls on 6 January were many Republican politicians and party members, senior citizens who knew Reifel, and, in the words of a newspaper writer, his "countless Sioux friends." Honorary pallbearers included President Gerald Ford, Senator Robert ("Bob") Dole, former congressmen, Bureau of Indian Affairs officials, South Dakota officials, attorneys, and college presidents. Reifel was eulogized as a hero whose generosity, humility, and listening skills endeared him to those who knew him. Several speakers emphasized his lifelong commitment to American Indians and his crusade to enhance race relations. A Reifel relative noted that he "did as much as anyone in South Dakota to bridge the gap between the Lakota and non-Indian cultures." A granddaughter remembered him as a tolerant, color-blind man who "believed it was possible to acknowledge different cultures and seek out the best people from every culture." Following the funeral, Reifel's body was taken to Erwin, South Dakota, and laid to rest next to Alice Reifel. Florentine Blue Thunder sang a Lakota honor song that brought the graveside service to a close.[62]

In the days that followed his death, political commentators, professors, friends, and South Dakota politicians from both parties took the measure of Reifel's legacy. United States Representative Tim Johnson, a Democrat, described Reifel as "a leader for all of

South Dakota" and a public servant who worked for "the betterment of white and Indian relations to the very end."[63] The Democrat who succeeded Reifel in the House in 1971, Frank Denholm, discussed Reifel's sterling reputation in Washington and added that he had "earned his reputation as a man, not because he was a minority."[64] Loren Carlson, a University of South Dakota professor of political science, lauded Reifel for his remarkable ability "to relate, better than anyone I had heard up to that time, the concepts Indians had believed in and interpreted them so non-Indians could understand them."[65] Rolly Samp, in addition to characterizing Reifel as "a very wonderful role model for Native Americans," rated him as one of the few South Dakota politicians who lacked political enemies.[66] Samp also recalled the "diligent," and sometimes humorous, way that Reifel performed constituent services. On one occasion, Reifel sent Samp to a Veterans Administration center to find a man's false teeth. "You either find the man's false teeth or find out what happened to them," Reifel ordered Samp—who eventually found the man's misplaced dentures.[67]

One of Reifel's oldest friends, Harold Shunk, a member of the Yankton Sioux Tribe, called Reifel an historic figure for having broken down racial barriers in South Dakota. He was never discriminated against, Shunk said, and "the fact that he was a Native American and was elected five times proves that people don't look at color line. It depends on who that color is." In reflecting on Reifel's legacy, political observers commented on his quiet influence in Congress. The editors of the *Sioux Fall Argus Leader*, who a year and a half earlier had raised concerns about Reifel's retirement pension, now portrayed him as a popular, well-liked, and effective legislator and Indian advocate who "was not loud or flashy" but who "kept trying to bring Indians and non-Indians closer together." It was the opinion of the *Argus Leader* staff that "as time goes on, Ben Reifel's stature in South Dakota history likely will grow."[68]

Whether Reifel's stature in American Indian history will grow is more difficult to ascertain. Current conditions on the nation's Indian reservations suggest that Reifel's half century of service as a Bureau of Indian Affairs official, politician, and Indian advocate made little impact. Naomi Schaefer Riley points out that "American Indians have the highest rate of poverty, the highest rate of gang involvement and the highest rate of alcohol-use disorders of any ethnic group in the country."[69] Schools on Indian reservations suffer from a myriad of problems, none more paralyzing than their failure to retain qualified teachers who are committed to educating children. Sadly, teacher shortages are sometimes self-imposed by dysfunctional schools and tribal governments that oppose "white" or "Western" thinking in the classroom.[70] In Montana in 2014, teacher shortages were highest on Indian reservations or at schools near reservations. Of the forty Montana school districts in which American Indians made up at least half of the student body, thirty-four did not meet No Child Left Behind standards, a sign of the widening achievement gap separating Indian and non-Indian students.[71] To these discomforting figures one must add the serious problem of suicide in Indian country, where the rate of suicides among American Indians 15 to 34 years in age is 4 times the national average. In one month in 2014, 17 died by suicide on the Pine Ridge Indian Reservation.[72] Between December 2014 and July 2015, 11 people, ranging in age from 12 to 24, killed themselves on the Pine Ridge Reservation. A suicide-prevention outreach worker at Pine Ridge describes the reservation as being in a "state of emergency and it hasn't slowed down."[73]

Viewed within the context of the current state of affairs, one might conclude that Reifel's crusade to steer Indians off the reservation and into the mainstream was not embraced by reservation residents, and that his time, work, save philosophy was ignored by three generations of Indian peoples. But such an assessment would tell only half of the story. For it can be argued that Reifel's exit ramp toward educational success, employment, and economic self-reliance remains intact and is a visible, maybe even a desirable, alternative for many American Indians. As early as the 1970s, as a result of rising numbers of urban Indians earning college degrees, an Indian middle class began to emerge. Exposed to the benefits of the mainstream United States, "these enterprising individuals," writes Donald L. Fixico, "wanted something better for their children." Seeing schooling "as the key to their success," members of the Indian middle class "borrowed many values from the urban mainstream culture." The degree to which individual American Indians assimilate European American values varies, according to

Fixico. Nevertheless, as they pursue better-paying jobs for themselves and their children, "these successful individuals," whether they "choose to retain their Indian identity" or not, "live a lifestyle that combines tribal ways with those of the mainstream culture."[74]

Ben Reifel recounted his personal life story to scores of American Indian audiences because he wanted them to know how poor he had once been, how rurally isolated he had once been, how educationally deprived he had once been, how scared of the outside world he had once been. But in seizing educational opportunities and learning to accept middle-class values, he moved beyond the circumstances of his youth. He remained American Indian, but he was no longer defined by socioeconomic conditions on the Rosebud Sioux Indian Reservation. And now other American Indians follow the path blazed by Ben Reifel, their ambition being to escape the poverty of reservation life without cutting ties to their cultural heritage.

Reifel was not so gullible as to believe that reservations would eventually disappear. Nor did he believe that, even if poverty-ridden reservations did somehow dissolve as features of the American landscape, the gap between Indians and non-Indians would suddenly close.[75] Nevertheless, Reifel did not want American Indians defined by reservations. More than just tracts of land or political units, reservations were cultural confinements that held back their occupants. To break free of their mental confinement, Reifel urged, Indians should imagine their lives without reservations. He had learned to do so, and the consequence was not just his materially improved condition but a fulfilling life wherein he preserved his American Indian identity while enjoying the fruits of American citizenship.

It was in this spirit that at his funeral, Reifel's great-niece, Gayle Teachout Hare, asked American Indians to reflect on the teachings of her great uncle: "I think if Indian people stopped and seriously considered what he said all his life, our lives would be easier by following his suggestions."[76]

Those who knew Reifel observed that the young man who left the Rosebud Sioux Indian Reservation at age nineteen never stopped being an American Indian. At his core, Ben Reifel remained American Indian. But being rooted in one life did not prevent him from branching out into another. Reifel felt it important "to keep the heart of an Indian and be a member of American society," noted one journalist to whom Reifel had made it clear that "it's not a conflict to do both."[77] He was "someone who had kept his values but assimilated very successfully into another culture," recalled Hare.[78] "We can be proud of our heritage," Reifel once told a group of American Indian students, "without preventing us from enjoying the things that are part of America."[79]

After conducting an interview with Reifel ten years before the congressman's death, Chuck Raasch, a reporter for the *Sioux Falls Argus Leader*, described Reifel as having "the best of both cultures."[80] It was an apt analysis because it underscored Reifel's conviction that American Indian and European American cultures were not incompatible. By his example, Reifel showed American Indians that they could be productive members of a modern technological society while remaining authentic to the traditional values that shaped their personalities. A healthy bicultural balance could be struck, one in which the individual did not have to feel that he or she was renouncing his or her cultural core.

Ben Reifel struck the balance. He embraced and flourished in both cultures, and he did so without reservation.

NOTES

CHAPTER 1

1. Paul L. Hedren, *After Custer: Loss and Transformation in Sioux Country* (Norman: University of Oklahoma Press, 2011), pp. 25–26.

2. Francis Paul Prucha, *The Great Father: The United States Government and the American Indian*, vol. 2 (Lincoln: University of Nebraska Press, 1984), pp. 631–33; Rani-Henrik Andersson, *The Lakota Ghost Dance of 1890* (Lincoln: University of Nebraska Press, 2008), pp. 13–16.

3. Robert M. Utley, *The Last Days of the Sioux Nation* (New Haven: Yale University Press, 1963), pp. 22–23; Robert M. Utley, *The Indian Frontier of the American West, 1846–1890* (Albuquerque: University of New Mexico Press, 1984), pp. 236–40; Paul H. Carlson, *The Plains Indians* (College Station: Texas A&M University Press, 1998), pp. 163–64; Luther Standing Bear, *Land of the Spotted Eagle* (Boston: Houghton Mifflin, 1933), pp. 237–38; Frederick E. Hoxie, "From Prison to Homeland: The Cheyenne River Indian Reservation before WWI," *South Dakota History* 10 (Winter 1979): p. 3; John A. Anderson, Henry W. Hamilton, and Jean Tyree Hamilton, *The Sioux of the Rosebud: A History in Pictures* (Norman: University of Oklahoma Press, 1971), pp. 110–11; Herbert S. Schell, *History of South Dakota* (Lincoln: University of Nebraska Press, 1961), p. 316; Hedren, *After Custer*, p. 164.

4. George E. Hyde, *Spotted Tail's Folk: A History of the Brulé Sioux* (Norman: University of Oklahoma Press, 1961), p. 309; George E. Hyde, *A Sioux Chronicle* (Norman: University of Oklahoma Press, 1956), p. 40.

5. Prucha, *The Great Father*, 2:631; Hedren, *After Custer*, pp. 51, 91.

6. Anderson, *The Sioux of the Rosebud*, pp. 16, 83–85; Utley, *The Last Days of the Sioux*, pp. 23–26; Carlson, *The Plains Indians*, p. 170; Schell, *History of South Dakota*, p. 327; Guy Gibbon, *The Sioux: The Dakota and Lakota Nations* (Malden, Mass.: Blackwell, 2003), pp. 119–20; Hedren, *After Custer*, p. 164.

7. Schell, *History of South Dakota*, p. 327; Hyde, *A Sioux Chronicle*, pp. x–xi.

8. Quoted in Utley, *The Last Days of the Sioux*, p. 24.

9. Quoted in Thomas Biolsi, *Organizing the Lakota: The Political Economy of the New Deal on the Pine Ridge and Rosebud Reservations* (Tucson: University of Arizona Press, 1992), p. 3.

10. In 1947, the official name of the organization primarily responsible for managing the federal government's relations with Indian tribes was changed from Office of Indian Affairs to Bureau of Indian Affairs. For the sake of consistency and to avoid

confusion for the reader, the author will use the title Bureau of Indian Affairs to designate the organization that manages the nation's Indian affairs. See Prucha, *The Great Father*, 2:1227–29, for a brief discussion of the "Nomenclature of the Bureau of Indian Affairs."

11. Quoted in Prucha, *The Great Father*, 2:703–4.

12. Utley, *The Last Days of the Sioux Nation*, pp. 36–37; Schell, *History of South Dakota*, pp. 326–27; Anderson, *The Sioux of the Rosebud*, p. 141; Margaret Connell Szasz, *Education and the American Indian: The Road to Self-Determination Since 1928*, 3rd ed. (Albuquerque: University of New Mexico Press, 1999), pp. 8–12; Estelle Fuchs and Robert J. Havighurst, *To Live on This Earth: American Indian Education* (Garden City, N.Y.: Anchor Books, 1973), pp. 225–26; Robert J. Karolevitz, *With Faith, Hope and Tenacity: The First One Hundred Years of the Catholic Diocese of Sioux Falls, 1889–1989* (Mission Hill, S.Dak.: Dakota Homestead Publishers, 1989), pp. 181–85; Hedren, *After Custer*, p. 165.

13. 24 U.S. Statutes at Large, 1887, pp. 388–91; D. S. Otis, *The Dawes Act and the Allotment of Indian Lands*, ed. Francis Paul Prucha (Norman: University of Oklahoma Press, 1973), pp. 19–20, 32; Andersson, *The Lakota Ghost Dance of 1890*, p. 4; Carlson, *The Plains Indians*, pp. 176–77; Prucha, *The Great Father*, 2:667–68.

14. Harry F. Thompson, ed., *A New South Dakota History* (Sioux Falls, S.Dak.: Center for Western Studies, Augustana College, 2005), p. 90; Utley, *The Indian Frontier*, pp. 246–47.

15. Andersson, *The Lakota Ghost Dance of 1890*, pp. 21–29; Utley, *The Last Days of the Sioux Nation*, pp. 69–70; Prucha, *The Great Father*, 2:726–27; Carlson, *The Plains Indians*, pp. 179–80; Schell, *History of South Dakota*, p. 321.

16. Robert M. Utley, *The Lance and the Shield: The Life and Times of Sitting Bull* (New York: Ballantine Books, 1993), p. 285.

17. Utley, *The Last Days of the Sioux Nation*, pp. 3, 69–70, 83, 230; Schell, *History of South Dakota*, pp. 320–23; Carlson, *The Plains Indians*, pp. 179–81; Prucha, *The Great Father*, 2:726–29.

18. Prucha, *The Great Father*, 2:760–61.

19. Carlson, *The Plains Indians*, p. 181.

20. Biolsi, *Organizing the Lakota*, pp. 23–27; Hoxie, "From Prison to Homeland," pp. 59–61; Hyde, *A Sioux Chronicle*, pp. xi.

21. Joseph H. Cash, *The Sioux People* (Phoenix: Indian Tribal Series, 1971), p. 65; Schell, *History of South Dakota*, pp. 330–31; Biolsi, *Organizing the Lakota*, pp. 13–17, 25; Carlson, *The Plains Indians*, pp. 110–11.

22. Graham D. Taylor, *The New Deal and American Indian Tribalism: The Administration of the Indian Reorganization Act, 1934–45* (Lincoln: University of Nebraska Press, 1980), p. 5.

23. Biolsi, *Organizing the Lakota*, pp. 13–14.

24. In *Lone Wolf v. Hitchcock* (1903), a case involving a suit brought on behalf of the Kiowa, Comanche, and Apache Indians of Oklahoma Territory, the Supreme Court asserted that a treaty "cannot be adjudged to materially limit and qualify the controlling authority of Congress . . . and to deprive Congress . . . of all power to act if the assent of three fourths of all the male Indians could not be obtained. Congress has always exercised plenary authority over the tribal relations of the Indians and the power has always been deemed a political one not subject to be controlled by the courts." 187 U.S. Reports, 1903, pp. 553–54.

25. For an account of the opening of the Rosebud Sioux Indian Reservation, see Sean J. Flynn, "Western Assimilationist: Charles H. Burke and the Burke Act" (Master's thesis, Texas Tech University, 1988), pp. 28–47.

26. Prucha, *The Great Father*, 2:875–76. For a thorough analysis of the Burke Act and its implications, see Flynn, "Western Assimilationist," pp. 51–94.

27. Prucha, *The Great Father*, 2:761–62.

28. Ben Reifel, interview by John Painter, 30 May 1979, Folder Reifel Ben AIH 79-50, Box 67, John S. Painter Papers, Richardson Collections, Archives and Special Collections, University of South Dakota, Vermillion; "Ben Reifel," in *Notable Native Americans*, ed. Sharon Malinowski (New York: Gale Research, 1999), p. 357; John S. Painter, "Transitional Sioux Leader: Benjamin Reifel," in *South Dakota Leaders, From Pierre Chouteau, Jr., to Oscar Howe*, ed. Herbert T. Hoover and Larry J. Zimmerman (Vermillion: University of South Dakota Press, 1989), p. 333; Ben Reifel to H. T. Reifel (copy), 3 Apr. 1965, Folder 3, Box 10, MA 9.6; biographical material prepared for Harry Jones by the Congressional Office of Representative Ben Reifel, 1964, Folder 10, Box 9, MA 9.6; Ben Reifel, interview by Barbara Fitzgerald, n.d., Box 30.1, MA 9-0043av (hereafter cited as Fitzgerald interview), Benjamin Reifel Papers, University Archives, South Dakota State University, Brookings.

29. Will Spindler, "New Agent Sees Education as Only Salvation of Sioux," *Rapid City Daily Journal*, 3 Oct. 1954; Ben Reifel, interview by John Painter, 30 May 1979, Painter Papers.

30. The Rosebud Reservation had been the scene of a rivalry between Catholic and Episcopal missionaries since President Grant's decision to allow the Episcopal Church to monopolize religious and educational institutions on the Red Cloud and Spotted Tail agencies. In the 1880s, the Catholic Church, represented by Bishop Martin Marty of Dakota Territory and with the financial support of Katharine Drexel, established its presence on the Spotted Tail Agency. Chief Spotted Tail referred to the Catholic priests as Black Robes and the Episcopalians as White Robes. Though he demonstrated little personal interest in Christianity, Spotted Tail very nearly sent a daughter to a Catholic convent in Kansas City in 1876. Nonetheless, three years

later, after succumbing to pressure from the Indian Office, he recognized the Episcopal Church's privileged status on his agency. Hyde, *Spotted Tail's Folk*, pp. 235–37, 276; Karolevitz, *With Faith, Hope and Tenacity*, pp. 181–85.

31. Painter, "Transitional Sioux Leader," pp. 332–33; marriage license of William M. Reifel and Lucy Burning Breast (copy), Folder 18, Box 11, MA 9.7, Reifel Papers.

32. Mildred Fielder, *Sioux Indian Leaders* (New York: Bonanza Books, 1975), p. 127; Painter, "Transitional Sioux Leader," p. 333; Ben Reifel, interview by John Painter, 30 May 1979, Painter Papers.

33. Bernie Hunhoff, "Ben Reifel's Search," *South Dakota Magazine*, Jan./Feb. 1989: 11–12; Fielder, *Sioux Indian Leaders*, p. 127.

34. Spindler, "New Agent."

35. Chuck Raasch, "Reifel: He Has the Best of Both Cultures," *Sioux Falls Argus Leader*, 21 July 1980; Ben Reifel, interview by John Painter, 8 Oct. 1980, Folder Reifel Ben AIH 80-114, Box 67, Painter Papers; Wesley G. Pippert, "Ex-Congressman Ben Reifel: 'Turn Your Back on the Past; Adapt,'" *Omaha World-Herald*, 10 Feb. 1971.

36. Quoted in Painter, "Transitional Sioux Leader," p. 333.

37. Ben Reifel, speech notes from 1960 congressional campaign, Folder 4, Box 5, MA 9.4, Reifel Papers; Fielder, *Sioux Indian Leaders*, p. 127; Ben Reifel, interview by John Painter, 30 May 1979, Painter Papers.

38. Fitzgerald interview.

39. Loyce (Reifel) Anderson, interview with author, Delta, Colorado, 17 Oct. 2015; Ben Reifel's eighth-grade report card, Folder 17, Box 11, MA 9.7, Reifel Papers; Painter, "Transitional Sioux Leader," p. 334; James Denney, "South Dakota's Ben Reifel: That 'Poor Indian Boy' in Congress," *Sunday Omaha World-Herald Magazine of the Midlands*, 5 Apr. 1970, p. 7; Fitzgerald interview; Ben Reifel, interview by John Painter, 30 May 1979, Painter Papers.

40. Anson Yeager, "Photos Show Sioux Pride," *Sioux Falls Argus Leader*, n.d., clipping in Folder 1, Box 6, MA 9, Reifel Papers; Ben Reifel, interview by John Painter, 30 May 1979, Painter Papers.

41. Fielder, *Sioux Indian Leaders*, p. 128.

42. Ibid.; Hunhoff, "Ben Reifel's Search," p. 12.

43. Ben Reifel, interview by John Painter, 30 May 1979, Painter Papers.

44. Ibid.; Spindler, "New Agent"; *Norfolk* (Neb.) *Daily News*, 5 Jan. 1957, clipping in Box 31, Jennewein Files, Dakota Wesleyan University Archives, Dakota Wesleyan University, Mitchell, S.Dak.; *Phreno Cosmian*, 26 May 1965; Painter, "Transitional Sioux Leader," pp. 333–34; Fielder, *Sioux Indian Leaders*, p. 128.

45. Painter, "Transitional Sioux Leader," p. 334; Hunhoff, "Ben Reifel's Search," 12; Ben Reifel, interview by John Painter, 30 May 1979, Painter Papers.

46. John E. Miller, *South Dakota State University: A Pictorial History, 1881–2006* (Virginia Beach, Va.: Donning, 2005), pp. 31–32.

47. Vernon Loen to George H. Phillips (copy), 23 Apr. 1964, Folder 10, Box 9, MA 9.6, Reifel Papers.

48. "U.S.'s First Indian Congressman Dies," *Sioux Falls Argus Leader*, 3 Jan. 1990.

49. Ibid.; Painter, "Transitional Sioux Leader," pp. 333–34; Fielder, *Sioux Indian Leaders*, p. 129; Ben Reifel, interview by Tom Biolsi, Aug. 1984, Folder Reifel Ben AIH 84-155, Box 67; Ben Reifel, interview by John Painter, 30 May 1979, Painter Papers. Prepared at the request of the Department of the Interior, the Meriam Report, published under the title "The Problem of Indian Administration," recommended increased appropriations for Indian education, Indian health care, and tribal economic development as a means of accelerating Indian self-support and eventually dissolving federal support for Indian tribes.

50. Clipping from an unidentified newspaper, likely the *Brookings Register*, Folder 15, Box 5, MA 9.5, Reifel Papers.

51. Ibid.; James H. McGregor to C. J. Rhoads (copy), 18 Feb. 1932, Folder 007, Box 147, Pine Ridge Agency General Records, Record Group 75, Records of the Bureau of Indian Affairs, National Archives and Records Administration, Kansas City, Mo., hereafter cited as RG 75 NARA; "Ben Reifel, Distinguished Alumnus, South Dakota State University," Ben Reifel Biography File, South Dakota State Historical Society Archives, Pierre; Fielder, *Sioux Indian Leaders*, p. 129; Painter, "Transitional Sioux Leader," p. 335; Spindler, "New Agent"; *Phreno Cosmian*, 26 May 1965; Alpha Zeta induction certificate for Benjamin Reifel, 20 May 1931, Folder 11, Box 3, MA 9; ROTC certificate of appointment for Benjamin Reifel, 30 Jan. 1928, Folder 19, Box 11, MA 9.7, Reifel Papers.

52. McGregor to Rhoads, 18 Feb. 1932, RG 75 NARA.

53. Painter, "Transitional Sioux Leader," p. 335; Fielder, *Sioux Indian Leaders*, p. 129; Loen to Phillips, 23 Apr. 1964; Ben Reifel, interview by John Painter, 29 May 1979, Folder Reifel Ben AIH 79-49; Ben Reifel, interview by John S. Painter, 9 Oct. 1988, Folder Reifel Ben AIH 88-152, Box 67, Painter Papers.

54. Robert P. Frazier, "The Hare Industrial School," Folder 1, Box 1, Object No. 40007.09.01, Bishop Hare Industrial School, Episcopal Diocese of South Dakota Archives, Center for Western Studies, Sioux Falls; Ben Reifel, interview by John S. Painter, 9 Oct. 1988, Painter Papers.

55. Prucha, *The Great Father*, 2:928–30.

56. W. Carson Ryan, Jr., "Federal-State Cooperation in Indian Education," *School and Society* 34 (26 Sep. 1931): 418–23; "Societies and Meetings: Educational Conference of Indian Service Superintendents," *School and Society* 34 (5 Dec. 1931): 764–65.

57. Numerous accounts of South Dakota reservation schools during the 1930s and early 1940s can be found in *Indians at Work*, a newsletter published from 1933–45 by the Office of Indian Affairs in the U.S. Department of the Interior, Washington, D.C. Editions of *Indians at Work* consulted for the aforementioned descriptions of

day schools include vol. 2, no. 23 (15 July 1935): 26–28, and vol. 6, no. 2 (Oct. 1938): 6–25. These and other editions of *Indians at Work* are located in the SDSHS Archives.

58. *Indians at Work* 6, no. 2 (Oct. 1938): 4–6, 9–12, 21–25, 50–51.

59. Lewis Meriam, "Indian Education Moves Ahead," *The Survey* 66 (1 June 1931): 254–55.

60. Daniel Tanner and Laurel N. Tanner, *Curriculum Development: Theory into Practice* (New York: Macmillan, 1975), pp. 525–32.

61. Geoffrey Perrett, *America in the Twenties: A History* (New York: Simon and Schuster, 1982), pp. 436–37.

62. Ben Reifel, interview by Joseph H. Cash, Summer 1967, in *The Plains Indians of the Twentieth Century*, ed. Peter Iverson (Norman: University of Oklahoma Press, 1985), pp. 116–17.

63. Ben Reifel, interview by John Painter, 29 May 1979, Painter Papers; Painter, "Transitional Sioux Leader," p. 335; Fielder, *Sioux Indian Leaders*, p. 129; Loen to Philips, 23 Apr. 1964.

CHAPTER 2

1. Francis Paul Prucha, *The Great Father: The United States Government and the American Indian*, vol. 2 (Lincoln: University of Nebraska Press, 1984), pp. 917–19; Kenneth R. Philp, *John Collier's Crusade for Indian Reform, 1920–1954* (Tucson: University of Arizona Press, 1977), p. 244; Graham D. Taylor, *The New Deal and American Indian Tribalism: The Administration of the Indian Reorganization Act, 1934–45* (Lincoln: University of Nebraska Press, 1980), p. 139; S. Lyman Tyler, *A History of Indian Policy* (Washington, D.C.: U.S. Department of the Interior, Bureau of Indian Affairs, 1973), pp. 146–47; Herbert T. Hoover and Carol Goss Hoover, *Sioux Country: A History of Indian-White Relations* (Sioux Falls, S.Dak.: Center for Western Studies, Augustana College, 2000), p. 203.

2. Taylor, *The New Deal and American Indian Tribalism*, pp. 32, 150.

3. Lawrence C. Kelly, *The Assault on Assimilation: John Collier and the Origins of Indian Policy Reform* (Albuquerque: University of New Mexico Press, 1983), pp. 119–20.

4. Ibid.; Philp, *John Collier's Crusade*, pp. 9–10, 24.

5. Kelly, *The Assault on Assimilation*, pp. 135, 218, 347, 375; Prucha, *The Great Father*, 2:798–805; Philp, *John Collier's Crusade*, pp. 57–58, 67–69.

6. Prucha, *The Great Father*, 2:941–45; Philp, *John Collier's Crusade*, p. 115.

7. Philp, *John Collier's Crusade*, pp. 120–29.

8. Major provisions of the Indian Reorganization Act included the permanent suspension of the allotting of tribal lands to individual Indians, the empowerment of tribes to devise their own constitutions and bylaws for self-government, the extension of charters of incorporation to tribes to grant them the right of control over their properties, the establishment of a revolving credit fund to promote tribal eco-

nomic development, the facilitation of Indian employment in the Indian service, and the annual appropriation of funds for Indian vocational and trade school education. Lawrence C. Kelly, *The Navajo Indians and Federal Indian Policy, 1900–1935* (Tucson: University of Arizona Press, 1968), pp. 163–66.

9. Kenneth R. Philp, "John Collier, 1933–1945," in *The Commissioners of Indian Affairs, 1824–1977*, ed. Robert M. Kvasnicka and Herman J. Viola (Lincoln: University of Nebraska Press, 1979), p. 277.

10. Taylor, *The New Deal and American Indian Tribalism*, p. 39.

11. John Collier, untitled, *Indians at Work* 3 (1 Oct. 1935): 1–4.

12. Ben Reifel, interview by John Painter, 8 Oct. 1980, Folder Reifel Ben AIH 80-114, Box 67, John S. Painter Papers, Richardson Collections, Archives and Special Collections, University of South Dakota, Vermillion.

13. Philp, *John Collier's Crusade*, p. 143.

14. Taylor, *The New Deal and American Indian Tribalism*, pp. 22–23.

15. Prucha, *The Great Father*, 2:960.

16. Taylor, *The New Deal and American Indian Tribalism*, p. 24.

17. John S. Painter, "Transitional Sioux Leader: Benjamin Reifel," in *South Dakota Leaders: From Pierre Chouteau, Jr., to Oscar Howe*, ed. Herbert T. Hoover and Larry J. Zimmerman (Vermillion: University of South Dakota Press, 1989), pp. 335–37.

18. Ben Reifel, interview by Tom Biolsi, Aug. 1984, Folder Reifel Ben AIH 84-155, Box 67, Painter Papers.

19. Painter, "Transitional Sioux Leader," p. 337.

20. Ben Reifel, interview by John Painter, 8 Oct. 1980, Painter Papers.

21. Mildred Fielder, *Sioux Indian Leaders* (New York: Bonanza Books, 1975), pp. 129–30.

22. Thomas Biolsi, *Organizing the Lakota: The Political Economy of the New Deal on the Pine Ridge and Rosebud Reservations* (Tucson: University of Arizona Press, 1992), p. 59.

23. Painter, "Transitional Sioux Leader," p. 338.

24. Tyler, *A History of Indian Policy*, pp. 146–47.

25. James H. McGregor to Robert Bad Wound, 26 Jan. 1934 (copy) and John Collier to James H. McGregor, 30 Jan. 1934 (copy), Folder 7, Box 179, Pine Ridge Agency General Records, Record Group 75, Records of the Bureau of Indian Affairs, National Archives and Records Administration, Kansas City, Mo., hereafter cited as RG 75 NARA.

26. Taylor, *The New Deal and American Indian Tribalism*, p. 25; Philp, *John Collier's Crusade*, pp. 145–46.

27. Biolsi, *Organizing the Lakota*, pp. 65–66.

28. Ben Reifel, interview by Tom Biolsi, Aug. 1984, Painter Papers.

29. Biolsi, *Organizing the Lakota*, p. 66.

30. *Minutes of the Plains Congress* (Lawrence, Kans.: Haskell Institute, 1934), pp. 4–8.

31. Biolsi, *Organizing the Lakota*, pp. 68–70; Philp, *John Collier's Crusade*, pp. 146–47.

32. Prucha, *The Great Father*, 2:958; Philp, *John Collier's Crusade*, pp. 147, 156; Biolsi, *Organizing the Lakota*, p. 70.

33. *Minutes of the Plains Congress*, p. 11.

34. Biolsi, *Organizing the Lakota*, pp. 70–72.

35. Philp, *John Collier's Crusade*, p. 149.

36. Ibid., p. 159.

37. Interview of Ben Reifel in *Indian Self-Rule: First-Hand Accounts of Indian-White Relations from Roosevelt to Reagan*, ed. Kenneth Philp (Logan: Utah State University Press, 1995), p. 76.

38. Ibid., pp. 76–78.

39. Ibid., pp. 77–78.

40. Ibid., pp. 76–77; Biolsi, *Organizing the Lakota*, pp. 73–75.

41. Philp, *John Collier's Crusade*, pp. 157–58; Prucha, *The Great Father*, 2:960–61.

42. Philp, *John Collier's Crusade*, pp. 157–58; Prucha, *The Great Father*, 2:961–62.

43. Philp, *John Collier's Crusade*, pp. 158–59.

44. Taylor, *The New Deal and American Indian Tribalism*, pp. 27–28.

45. Ibid., p. 28.

46. Painter, "Transitional Sioux Leader," p. 339.

47. Quoted in Prucha, *The Great Father*, 2:964.

48. Interview of Ben Reifel in *Indian Self-Rule*, p. 76.

49. Akim D. Reinhardt, *Ruling Pine Ridge: Oglala Lakota Politics from the IRA to Wounded Knee* (Lubbock: Texas Tech University Press, 2007), p. 38; Painter, "Transitional Sioux Leader," p. 339; Ben Reifel, interview by Tom Biolsi, Aug. 1984, Painter Papers.

50. Interview of Ben Reifel in *Indian Self-Rule*, p. 77.

51. Ben Reifel, interview by Joseph H. Cash, Summer 1967, in *The Plains Indians of the Twentieth Century*, ed. Peter Iverson (Norman: University of Oklahoma Press, 1985), pp. 109–10.

52. Ibid., p. 110; Painter, "Transitional Sioux Leader," p. 340.

53. Painter, "Transitional Sioux Leader," p. 340; Ben Reifel, interview by Joseph H. Cash, in Iverson, *The Plains Indians of the Twentieth Century*, p. 111; Biolsi, *Organizing the Lakota*, p. 77.

54. Peter Nabokov, ed., *Native American Testimony: A Chronicle of Indian-White Relations from Prophecy to the Present, 1492–1992* (New York: Viking Press, 1991), pp. 327–28.

55. Interview of Alfred DuBray by Herbert T. Hoover, 28 July 1970, in Iverson, *The Plains Indians of the Twentieth Century*, p. 127.

56. Ibid., p. 126.

57. James H. Hyde to Commissioner of Indian Affairs, 17 Dec. 1935 (copy), Folder 020, Box 150A, Legislation Wheeler-Howard Act, RG 75 NARA.

58. Newspaper clipping from the *Sioux Falls Argus Leader*, n.d., Folder 020, Box 150A, Legislation Wheeler-Howard Act, RG 75 NARA.

59. John Henry Glover, *Tribal Sovereigns of South Dakota: A Description of Contemporary Sioux Governments* (Rapid City: Chiesman Foundation for Democracy, 2005), pp. 22, 31, 48, 80, 92, 103–4.

60. Vote Wheeler-Howard or Indian Reorganization Bill, Pine Ridge Reservation, 27 Oct. 1934, Folder 020, Box 150A, Legislation Wheeler-Howard Act, RG 75 NARA; Biolsi, *Organizing the Lakota*, p. 78.

61. Biolsi, *Organizing the Lakota*, pp. 78–84.

62. Ibid., p. 79.

63. Ben Reifel, interview by Joseph H. Cash, in Iverson, *The Plains Indians of the Twentieth Century*, p. 111.

64. Ben Reifel, interview by Tom Biolsi, Aug. 1984, Painter Papers.

65. Ibid. In 1934, 172 tribes accepted reorganization while 73 rejected it. In a startling decision, the nation's largest Indian tribe, the Navajos, rejected the IRA. See Taylor, *The New Deal and American Indian Tribalism*, p. 32, and Prucha, *The Great Father*, 2:965.

66. John Collier to Members of Tribal Councils, Indians, Reservation Superintendents, Employees, and Others Interested in Indian Reorganization, Folder 2, Box 180, Pine Ridge Agency General Records, RG 75 NARA.

67. Taylor, *The New Deal and American Indian Tribalism*, p. 38.

68. Quoted in Prucha, *The Great Father*, 2:967.

69. Fielder, *Sioux Indian Leaders*, pp. 130–31; Ben Reifel, interview by Joseph H. Cash, in Iverson, *The Plains Indians of the Twentieth Century*, p. 111.

70. Taylor, *The New Deal and American Indian Tribalism*, p. 51.

71. Ben Reifel, interview by John Painter, 8 Oct. 1980, Painter Papers; Taylor, *The New Deal and American Indian Tribalism*, pp. 96–97; Philp, *John Collier's Crusade*, p. 164.

72. Painter, "Transitional Sioux Leader," pp. 340–41.

73. Ibid., p. 341; Biolsi, *Organizing the Lakota*, pp. 86–87.

74. Biolsi, *Organizing the Lakota*, pp. 87–88; Ben Reifel, interview by Tom Biolsi, Aug. 1984, Painter Papers.

75. Taylor, *The New Deal and American Indian Tribalism*, p. 95.

76. Ibid., p. 94.

77. Biolsi, *Organizing the Lakota*, p. 88.

78. Ibid., pp. 88–91; Ben Reifel, interview by Joseph H. Cash, in Iverson, *The Plains Indians of the Twentieth Century*, p. 111.

79. Glover, *Tribal Sovereigns of South Dakota*, pp. 69–73, 209–18.

80. Reinhardt, *Ruling Pine Ridge*, p. 39; Taylor, *The New Deal and American Indian Tribalism*, pp. 96–97.

81. Ben Reifel, interview by Joseph H. Cash, in Iverson, *The Plains Indians of the Twentieth Century*, p. 113.

82. Painter, "Transitional Sioux Leader," p. 341.

83. Ben Reifel, interview by Joseph H. Cash, in Iverson, *The Plains Indians of the Twentieth Century*, pp. 118–19.

84. Ben Reifel, interview by Tom Biolsi, Aug. 1984, Painter Papers.

85. Ben Reifel, interview by Joseph H. Cash, in Iverson, *The Plains Indians of the Twentieth Century*, p. 119.

86. *Moody County Enterprise*, 26 Sep. 1935, clipping in Ben Reifel Biography File, South Dakota State Historical Society Archives, South Dakota Cultural Heritage Center, Pierre.

87. Fielder, *Sioux Indian Leaders*, p. 132.

88. Minutes of the Oglala Sioux Tribal Council meeting of 27 Sep. 1935, Folder 3; Minutes of the Oglala Sioux Tribal Council meeting of 25 June 1935, Folder 2, Box 180, Pine Ridge Agency General Records, RG 75 NARA.

89. Biolsi, *Organizing the Lakota*, p. 95; James H. McGregor to John Collier, 4 June 1935 (copy), Folder 2, Box 180, Pine Ridge Agency General Records; Joe Jennings to John Collier, 2 July 1935 (copy), Folder 020, Box 150A, Legislation Wheeler-Howard Act, RG 75 NARA.

90. Biolsi, *Organizing the Lakota*, p. 95.

91. H. Scudder Mekeel to James H. McGregor, 17 Oct. 1935, Folder 3, Box 180, Pine Ridge Agency General Records, RG 75 NARA.

92. Ben Reifel, interview by Tom Biolsi, Aug. 1984, Painter Papers.

93. Ben Reifel, interview by John Painter, 8 Oct. 1980, Painter Papers.

94. Benjamin Reifel to Commissioner of Indian Affairs, 27 Oct. 1935 (copy), Folder 3, Box 180, Pine Ridge Agency General Records, RG 75 NARA.

95. Ballot for the IRA constitution and bylaws referendum on the Pine Ridge Reservation, Folder 11, Box 181, Pine Ridge Agency General Records; Ben Reifel to "Dear Sir," 4 Dec. 1935 (copy), Folder 020, Box 150A, Legislation Wheeler-Howard Act, RG 75 NARA; Biolsi, *Organizing the Lakota*, pp. 95–98; Taylor, *The New Deal and American Indian Tribalism*, p. 89.

96. Painter, "Transitional Sioux Leader," pp. 341–42; Ernest L. Schusky, *The Forgotten Sioux: An Ethnohistory of the Lower Brule Reservation* (Chicago: Nelson-Hall, 1975), p. 201; Ben Reifel, interview by Tom Biolsi, Aug. 1984, Painter Papers.

97. Quoted in Taylor, *The New Deal and American Indian Tribalism*, p. 116.

98. Ben Reifel, interview by Tom Biolsi, Aug. 1984, Painter Papers.

99. Benjamin Reifel, "Organizing the Sioux," *Indians at Work* 6 (June 1939): 29–30.

100. Ibid., p. 30.

CHAPTER 3

1. Copies of Reifel's semi-monthly Indian Organization Field Reports for 1940 are found in Folder 300:0 Land—Ft. Belknap, 1940–54 Reifel, Box 13, and Folder 160.2 Reifel, Benjamin, Box 44, John S. Painter Papers, Richardson Collections, Archives and Special Collections, University of South Dakota, Vermillion.

2. Correspondence, schedules, minutes, and other materials associated with the Dakotas-Nebraska Superintendents' Council and its conferences for the period 1939–41 are found in the following locations in Record Group 75, Records of the Bureau of Indian Affairs, National Archives and Records Administration, Kansas City, Mo. (hereafter cited as RG 75 NARA): Folder 18, Box 3 and Folders 1, 2, 4, and 5, Box 4, Aberdeen Area Office, Fort Berthold Agency, Subject Correspondence Files, 1864–1962; Folder 6, Box 180, Pine Ridge Agency, General Records.

3. Francis Paul Prucha, *The Great Father: The United States Government and the American Indian*, vol. 2 (Lincoln: University of Nebraska Press, 1984), pp. 994, 1002; Graham D. Taylor, *The New Deal and American Indian Tribalism: The Administration of the Indian Reorganization Act, 1934–45* (Lincoln: University of Nebraska Press, 1980), pp. 141–42.

4. Prucha, *The Great Father*, 2:994, 1002; S. Lyman Tyler, *A History of Indian Policy* (Washington, D.C.: U.S. Department of the Interior, Bureau of Indian Affairs, 1973), p. 136.

5. Benjamin Reifel to Richard Whalen, 6 Mar. 1941, Folder 6, Box 180, Pine Ridge Agency, General Records, RG 75 NARA; Tyler, *A History of Indian Policy*, pp. 136–40; Prucha, *The Great Father*, 2:994–97.

6. Prucha, *The Great Father*, 2:994–1000; Tyler, *A History of Indian Policy*, pp. 136–41; John S. Painter, "Congressional Conservatism and Federal Indian Policy, 1928–1950" (paper presented at the annual meeting of the Organization of American Historians, Detroit, 2 Apr. 1981).

7. Quoted in Prucha, *The Great Father*, 2:1001–2.

8. Ibid., p. 1007; Taylor, *The New Deal and American Indian Tribalism*, pp. 140–41; Tyler, *A History of Indian Policy*, pp. 141–43.

9. Gerald D. Nash, *The American West Transformed: The Impact of the Second World War* (Lincoln: University of Nebraska Press, 1985), pp. 128–35, 139.

10. Ibid., pp. 128–29, 135–36, 141–45.

11. Prucha, *The Great Father*, 2:1009.

12. Nash, *The American West Transformed*, p. 129.

13. "Outstanding Sioux Indian Leaves Indian Service for Active Duty as Army Officer," *Indians at Work* 9 (Apr. 1942): 17.

14. Robert K. Wright Jr., *Military Police* (Washington, D.C.: United States Army Center of Military History, 1992), pp. 8–10.

15. Ibid., pp. 10–11.

16. Ibid., pp. 210, 214; Loyce (Reifel) Anderson, interview with author, Delta, Colorado, 17 Oct. 2015; Mildred Fielder, *Sioux Indian Leaders* (New York: Bonanza Books, 1975), p. 133; 545th Military Police Company Association, "Fort Chaffee," http://www.545thmpassn.com/FtChaffey.htm (accessed 16 July 2014); certificate of Ben Reifel's completion of the advanced military police course at Fort Custer, 8 Jan. 1943, in the possession of Loyce Anderson.

17. John S. Painter, "Transitional Sioux Leader: Benjamin Reifel," in *South Dakota Leaders: From Pierre Chouteau, Jr., to Oscar Howe*, ed. Herbert T. Hoover and Larry J. Zimmerman (Vermillion: University of South Dakota Press, 1989), p. 343.

18. Ibid.; Fielder, *Sioux Indian Leaders*, pp. 133–34.

19. Gordon McGregor, "The Resources, People and Administration of Fort Berthold Reservation North Dakota," Missouri River Basin Investigations (MRBI) Report No. 60, prepared for the Department of the Interior, Bureau of Indian Affairs (24 Aug. 1948), p. 5; Gordon McGregor, "Attitudes of the Fort Berthold Indians Regarding Removal from the Garrison Reservoir Site and Future Administration of Their Reservation," MRBI Report No. 69 (30 Nov. 1948), pp. 18–20; Roy W. Meyer, "Fort Berthold and the Garrison Dam," *North Dakota History* 35 (Summer/Fall 1968): 234–37.

20. McGregor, "Attitudes of the Fort Berthold Indians," pp. 9–13; Meyer, "Fort Berthold and the Garrison Dam," pp. 237–38; George F. Will, "On the Road to Civilization: A Visit to the Fort Berthold Reservation," *North Dakota History* 15 (Jan. 1948): 10–12; Paul VanDevelder, *Coyote Warrior: One Man, Three Tribes, and the Trial That Forged a Nation* (Lincoln: University of Nebraska Press, 2004), pp. 92–93; *Waterbuster*, DVD, film by J. Carlos Peinado (New York: Brave Boat Productions, 2006).

21. McGregor, "Attitudes of the Fort Berthold Indians," pp. 22–23.

22. Meyer, "Fort Berthold and the Garrison Dam," p. 237.

23. For a lively summary of the origins and approval of the Pick-Sloan Plan, see Michael L. Lawson, *Dammed Indians Revisited: The Continuing History of the Pick-Sloan Plan and the Missouri River Sioux* (Pierre: South Dakota State Historical Society Press, 2009), pp. 7–24.

24. Ibid., pp. 52–55; Roy W. Meyer, *The Village Indians of the Upper Missouri: The Mandans, Hidatsas, and Arikaras* (Lincoln: University of Nebraska Press, 1977), pp. 212–13; Meyer, "Fort Berthold and the Garrison Dam," pp. 239–43.

25. Prucha, *The Great Father*, 2:1013–15, 1023.

26. Ibid., pp. 1023–25.

27. Meyer, *The Village Indians of the Upper Missouri*, p. 213; Meyer, "Fort Berthold and the Garrison Dam," pp. 245–47; Lawson, *Dammed Indians Revisited*, pp. 52–53.

28. Lawson, *Dammed Indians Revisited*, p. 54.

29. United States Civil Service Commission Position Description for Benjamin Reifel, 12 Nov. 1946, Folder 1, Box 4, MA 9.3, Benjamin Reifel Papers, South Dakota State University Archives, South Dakota State University, Brookings, hereafter cited as Position Description for Ben Reifel.

30. Meyer, "Fort Berthold and the Garrison Dam," p. 249; Meyer, *The Village Indians of the Upper Missouri*, p. 214.

31. Position Description for Ben Reifel.

32. Ibid.

33. Painter, "Transitional Sioux Leader," pp. 344–45.

34. McGregor, "The Resources, People and Administration of Fort Berthold," pp. 10–12.

35. Ibid., pp. 3, 13–14.

36. Ben Reifel, "Relocation on the Fort Berthold Indian Reservation: Problems and Programs" (Ph.D. dissertation, Harvard University, 1952), pp. 410–12, in Box 1, Series 10608, Ben Reifel Papers, Archives of the State Historical Society of North Dakota, Bismarck, North Dakota.

37. McGregor, "The Resources, People and Administration of Fort Berthold," pp. 8, 15.

38. Reifel, "Relocation on the Fort Berthold Indian Reservation," pp. 113–15.

39. McGregor, "The Resources, People and Administration of Fort Berthold," p. 7.

40. Ibid.

41. Ben Reifel to Commissioner of Indian Affairs, 6 June 1949 (copy), Annual School Report 1947–1948 folder, Box 1, Reports Relating to Indian Schools 1890–1957, Fort Berthold Agency, Aberdeen Area Office, RG 75 NARA, hereafter cited as Indian Schools Reports.

42. Ben Reifel to Willard W. Beatty, 21 July 1947 (copy), Folder 1, Box 1, Correspondence with Educational Administrators, 1916–1953, Fort Berthold Agency, Aberdeen Area Office, RG 75 NARA.

43. Ben Reifel to Willard W. Beatty, 19 Oct. 1948 (copy), Folder 9; "Educational Conference-Fort Berthold Problems," Folder 10, Box 1, Correspondence with Educational Administrators, 1916–1953, Fort Berthold Agency, Aberdeen Area Office, RG 75 NARA.

44. "Come to the Army Recruiting Program," in Indian Schools Reports.

45. McGregor, "The Resources, People and Administration of Fort Berthold Reservation," pp. 7–8.

46. Ibid., pp. 8–9, 15.

47. Ibid., p. 14.

48. Painter, "Transitional Sioux Leader," pp. 343–44.

49. Copies of Reifel's notes from the public meetings on the government's lieu lands proposal to the Three Affiliated Tribes, as well as copies of some official correspondence from the period, are found in the Ben Reifel and Fort Berthold Materials Folder, Box 85, Painter Papers.

50. Copy of "Resolution concerning the Lieu Lands Offer of the Secretary of War," 11 Dec. 1946 Ben Reifel and Fort Berthold Materials Folder, Box 85, Painter Papers; Meyer, *The Village Indians of the Upper Missouri*, pp. 214–16; Meyer, "Fort Berthold and the Garrison Dam," pp. 250–55.

51. Meyer, *The Village Indians of the Upper Missouri*, p. 216.

52. Reifel, "Relocation on the Fort Berthold Indian Reservation," p. 10.

53. Meyer, *The Village Indians of the Upper Missouri*, pp. 216–17; Meyer, "Fort Berthold and the Garrison Dam," pp. 257–59.

54. Ben Reifel, "The Problem of Relocating Families on the Fort Berthold Reservation," *Journal of Farm Economics* 32 (Nov. 1950): 644–46; Reifel, "Relocation on the Fort Berthold Indian Reservation," 3; Meyer, *The Village Indians of the Upper Missouri*, pp. 217–19.

55. Reifel, "Relocation on the Fort Berthold Indian Reservation," p. 12.

56. Meyer, *The Village Indians of the Upper Missouri*, p. 219.

57. Ibid.

58. Painter, "Transitional Sioux Leader," pp. 344–45.

59. Allen Cross and Martin Cross, interview by Mike Schatz, 23 June 1999, Oral Histories, Garrison Dam Relocation, Archives of the State Historical Society of North Dakota, Bismarck, North Dakota, hereafter cited as Garrison Dam Relocation Interviews.

60. Carl Whitman Jr., interview by John S. Painter, 3 June 1982, Folder Whitman, Carl Jr. AIH 82–133, Box 67, Painter Papers.

61. Marilyn Hudson, interview by Larry Volk, 23 June 1999, Garrison Dam Relocation Interviews.

62. Ben Reifel to Allan G. Harper, 24 Mar. 1949 (copy), Folder 3, Box 8, MA 9.6, Reifel Papers.

63. Allan G. Harper to Charles R. Cherington, 6 Apr. 1949 (copy), Folder 3, Box 8, MA 9.6, Reifel Papers.

64. Charles R. Cherington to Ben Reifel, 30 Apr. 1949 and 10 June 1949, Folder 3, Box 8, MA 9.6; John D. Black, "Higher Education for Farm Counselors: Need to 'Keep on Learning' Urged on the People of Today," *Christian Science Monitor*, 15 July 1950, n.p., clipping in Folder 15, Box 5, MA 9.5, Reifel Papers.

65. Milton R. Young to Ben Reifel, 30 Aug. 1949 and 3 Oct. 1949, Folder 3, Box 8, MA 9.6, Reifel Papers.

66. Fielder, *Sioux Indian Leaders*, p. 136; *El Comercio* (Lima, Peru), 22 June 1949,

clipping in Folder 18; Dean Acheson to U.S. Embassy, Lima, n.d., Folder 17, Box 11, MA 9.7, Reifel Papers.

67. Transcript for Benjamin Reifel, Harvard University Graduate School of Public Administration, 27 June 1950, Folder 17, Box 11, MA 9.7, Reifel Papers.

68. Painter, "Transitional Sioux Leader," p. 345.

69. Fielder, *Sioux Indian Leaders*, p. 138.

70. Robert C. Weaver to Benjamin Reifel, 23 Apr. 1951; "Opportunity Fellowships: John Hay Whitney Foundation," Folder 17, Box 11, MA 9.7, Reifel Papers.

71. Reifel, "The Problem of Relocating Families," pp. 644–46.

72. J. M. Cooper to Ben Reifel, 19 July 1951, Folder 4, Box 8, MA 9.6; Ben Reifel, "Plan for Work," Folder 17, Box 11, MA 9.7, Reifel Papers.

73. Louis Holloway to Bruce McKee, 20 July 1951, Folder 4, Box 8, MA 9.6; unknown author from Missouri River Basin Project to Ben Reifel, 17 Aug. 1951; Ben Reifel to John Cooper, 27 July 1951, Reifel Papers.

74. James Denney, "South Dakota's Ben Reifel: That 'Poor Indian Boy' in Congress," *Sunday Omaha World-Herald Magazine of the Midlands*, 5 Apr. 1970, p. 7, clipping in Ben Reifel Biography File, South Dakota State Historical Society Archives, Pierre.

75. Reifel, "Relocation on the Fort Berthold Indian Reservation," pp. 22, 87, 90, 446.

76. Ibid., pp. 6, 26, 34, 100–101.

77. Ibid., pp. 22, 26.

78. Ibid., pp. 17–19, 446.

79. Ibid., pp. 26, 33, 105, 125, 138.

80. "Reveals How Prejudice Is Reduced," *National Fellowship of Indian Workers*, Spring 1953, clipping in Folder 16, Box 3, MA 9.3, Reifel Papers.

81. Reifel, "Relocation on the Fort Berthold Indian Reservation," pp. 29–30, 122–23.

82. Ibid., pp. 20, 279, 341, 447.

83. Ibid., pp. 357–61.

84. Ibid., pp. 363–64, 450.

85. Denney, "South Dakota's Ben Reifel," p. 7.

86. John M. Gaus to Dillon S. Myer, 3 June 1952, Box 1, Series 10608, Ben Reifel Papers, Archives of the State Historical Society of North Dakota, Bismarck, N.Dak.

CHAPTER 4

1. Roy W. Meyer, "Fort Berthold and the Garrison Dam," *North Dakota History* 35 (Summer/Fall 1968): pp. 265–67; Mildred Fielder, *Sioux Indian Leaders* (New York: Bonanza Books, 1975), p. 139; M. F. Peterson to Ben Reifel, 31 Oct. 1952, Folder 5, Box 8, MA 9.6, Benjamin Reifel Papers, South Dakota State University Archives, South Dakota State University, Brookings.

2. Roy W. Meyer, *The Village Indians of the Upper Missouri: The Mandans, Hidatsas, and Arikaras* (Lincoln: University of Nebraska Press, 1977), p. 224.

3. Ibid., p. 223.

4. Ibid., pp. 221, 227; Meyer, "Fort Berthold and the Garrison Dam," pp. 270–71, 275, 281, 290; *Fort Berthold Agency New Bulletin*, 17 Aug. 1953.

5. Kenneth R. Philp, *Termination Revisited: American Indians on the Trail of Self-Determination, 1933–1953* (Lincoln: University of Nebraska Press, 1999), p. 165.

6. *Fort Berthold Agency News Bulletin*, 22 June 1953; Meyer, "Fort Berthold and the Garrison Dam," p. 290.

7. *Bismarck Tribune* and *Fargo Forum*, 6 May 1953; *Minot News*, 12 Jan. 1954; Francis Paul Prucha, *The Great Father: The United States Government and the American Indian*, vol. 2 (Lincoln: University of Nebraska Press, 1984), pp. 1041–42.

8. Prucha, *The Great Father*, 2:1013–15.

9. Philp, *Termination Revisited*, pp. 162–65; Meyer, *The Village Indians of the Upper Missouri*, p. 231.

10. "Address to be Delivered by Commissioner of Indian Affairs Glenn L. Emmons At Meetings with Indian Tribal Groups During Sep. and Oct., 1953," Folder 5, Box 8, MA 9.6, Reifel Papers; *Fort Berthold Agency News Bulletin*, 21 Sep. 1953.

11. Ben Reifel to Simeon Rozonowski, 27 Oct. 1960 (copy), Folder 5, Box 9, MA 9.6, Reifel Papers.

12. Ben Reifel, "Relocation on the Fort Berthold Indian Reservation: Problems and Programs" (Ph.D. dissertation, Harvard University, 1952), pp. 332–34, 338–40, 349–51, in Box 1, Series 10608, Reifel Papers.

13. Ibid., pp. 349–50, 449.

14. Meyer, "Fort Berthold and the Garrison Dam," pp. 271, 282–83; Meyer, *The Village Indians of the Upper Missouri*, pp. 224–25.

15. Ben Reifel to Aberdeen Area Director, 26 Nov. and 22 Dec. 1952, Folder 8, Box 5, Chronological Correspondence Relating to Schools, 1890–1955, Fort Berthold Agency, Aberdeen Area Office, Record Group 75, Records of the Bureau of Indian Affairs, National Archives and Records Administration, Kansas City, Mo., hereafter cited as RG 75 NARA.

16. Ben Reifel to Aberdeen Area Director, 9 Feb. 1953, Folder 9, Box 5, Chronological Correspondence Relating to Schools, 1890–1955, Fort Berthold Agency, Aberdeen Area Office, RG 75 NARA; *Fort Berthold Agency News Bulletin*, 22 June 1953.

17. *Fort Berthold Agency News Bulletin*, 21 Sep. 1953.

18. Rose Ellen Doyle to Benjamin Reifel, 17 Dec. 1952, Folder 4, Box 1, Correspondence with Educational Administrators, 1916–1953, Fort Berthold Agency, Aberdeen Area Office, RG 75 NARA.

19. Ben Reifel, interview by Barbara Fitzgerald, n.d., MA 9-0043av, Box 30.1, Rei-

fel Papers; Donald L. Fixico, *Termination and Relocation: Federal Indian Policy, 1945–1960* (Albuquerque: University of New Mexico Press, 1986), p. 134.

20. Meyer, "Fort Berthold and the Garrison Dam," p. 285.

21. Philp, *Termination Revisited*, pp. 98–99; Fixico, *Termination and Relocation*, p. 135.

22. Philp, *Termination Revisited*, p. 99; Joseph Cash and Herbert T. Hoover, "Relocation; Past and Present: A History of Moving Indians," in *Rosebud to Dallas: The Reservation Indian Relocates to the Urban Environment* (Dallas: Southern Resource Center, 1978), pp. 6–8; Fixico, *Termination and Relocation*, pp. 135, 142–43.

23. Fixico, *Termination and Relocation*, pp. 142–43.

24. Ben Reifel to John M. Cooper, 28 Jan. 1953, Folder 8, Box 5, Chronological Correspondence Relating to Schools, 1890–1955, Fort Berthold Agency, Aberdeen Area Office, RG 75 NARA.

25. Ibid.

26. Meyer, "Fort Berthold and the Garrison Dam," pp. 285–87; Meyer, *The Village Indians of the Upper Missouri*, p. 226.

27. Quoted in Meyer, "Fort Berthold and the Garrison Dam," p. 286.

28. Ibid., pp. 295–300; Meyer, *The Village Tribes of the Upper Missouri*, pp. 229–31.

29. *Fort Berthold Agency News Bulletin*, 17 Aug. 1953.

30. Ibid., 30 Oct. 1953.

31. Ibid.

32. Meyer, *The Village Indians of the Upper Missouri*, p. 232.

33. Minutes of the Oglala Sioux Tribal Council, 13–16 July 1954, Folder 1, Box 180A, Main Decimal File, General Records, Pine Ridge Agency, RG 75 NARA.

34. Ben Reifel to Members of the Fort Berthold Inter-Agency Committee and others, 12 Jan. 1954 (copy), Folder 12, Box 3, MA 9, Reifel Papers.

35. J. W. Robinson to Ben Reifel, 13 Jan. 1954, Folder 6, Box 8, MA 9, Reifel Papers; *Fort Berthold Agency News Bulletin*, 14 Jan. 1954.

36. John S. Painter, "Transitional Sioux Leader: Benjamin Reifel," in *South Dakota Leaders: From Pierre Chouteau, Jr., to Oscar Howe*, ed. Herbert T. Hoover and Larry J. Zimmerman (Vermillion: University of South Dakota Press, 1989), p. 346; *Deadwood* (S.Dak.) *Pioneer Times*, 10 Feb. 1955.

37. Robert E. Daniels, "Cultural Identities among the Oglala Sioux," in *The Modern Sioux: Social Systems and Reservation Culture*, ed. Ethel Nurge (Lincoln: University of Nebraska Press, 1970), pp. 198–99; Frank Lovrich, "The Assimilation of the Indian in Rapid City" (master's thesis, University of South Dakota, 1951), p. 18; Hal Boyle, "Problem of Indian—Assimilate or Die," clipping in Folder 1, Box 6, MA 9, Reifel Papers.

38. Edward Charles Valandra, *Not without Our Consent: Lakota Resistance to Ter-*

mination, 1950–59 (Urbana: University of Illinois Press, 2006), pp. 82, 209; Boyle, "Problem of Indian"; Daniels, "Cultural Identities," pp. 202–3; Painter, "Transitional Sioux Leader," pp. 346–48.

39. Bob Lee, "New Indian Agent Sees Sioux Future in Educated Youth," *Rapid City Daily Journal*, 11 Apr. 1954; Painter, "Transitional Sioux Leader," p. 346.

40. Calendars of Appointments for Ben Reifel for Feb., May, and June 1954, Folder 1, Box 4; Ben Reifel to the People of the Wanblee District, 8 Apr. 1954, Folder 12, Box 3, MA 9, Reifel Papers; Area Staff Officer's Report, 2–3 Mar. 1954, 13–14 Apr. 1954, 15–16 Sep. 1954, and 7 Oct. 1954, Area Staff Officer's Reports 1954 Folder, Box 1; Assistant Area Director to various BIA superintendents, 25 Mar. 1955, Folder 1, Box 5, Unnumbered Memorandums, 1950–1956, Aberdeen Area Office, RG 75 NARA.

41. *Daily News Sheet*, 29 July 1955; *The Pine Ridge*, Feb. and May 1955, Folder 15, Box 3, MA 9, Reifel Papers; Painter, "Transitional Sioux Leader," p. 347.

42. *The Pine Ridge*, Feb. and May 1955.

43. Lee, "New Indian Agent"; untitled clipping, n.d., in Ben Reifel Biography File, South Dakota State Historical Society Archives, Pierre.

44. *The Pine Ridge*, May 1955.

45. Ibid.

46. Minutes of the Oglala Sioux Tribal Council, 13–16 July 1954; Lee, "New Indian Agent."

47. Warren Morrell, "Thru the Hills," n.d., clipping in Folder 1, Box 6, MA 9, Reifel Papers.

48. Minutes of the Oglala Sioux Tribal Council, 11–14 Jan. 1955, Folder 1, Box 180A, Main Decimal File, General Records, Pine Ridge Agency, RG 75 NARA.

49. Minutes of the Oglala Sioux Tribal Council, 13–16 July 1954.

50. Lee, "New Indian Agent."

51. Valandra, *Not without Our Consent*, p. 82; Lee, "New Indian Agent"; Painter, "Transitional Sioux Leader," p. 348.

52. Bill Stokes, "U.S. to Move Reservation Indians to Oakland Homes," *Oakland Tribune*, 26 May 1954.

53. Ibid.; W. O. Roberts to Aberdeen Area Superintendents, 7 May 1954, Folder 2, Box 4, Unnumbered Memorandums 1950–1956, Aberdeen Area Office; Reinhold Brust to Ben Reifel and others, 5 Oct. 1954, Folder 1-54, Box 2, Correspondence Files, RG 75 NARA.

54. *The Pine Ridge*, Feb. 1955.

55. "The Relocation of the Indian in the Los Angeles Area," Folder 4, Box 5, Unnumbered Memorandums 1950–1956, Aberdeen Area Office, RG 75 NARA.

56. Fixico, *Termination and Relocation*, pp. 156–57, 174, 190.

57. Ibid., p. 143; Prucha, *The Great Father*, 2:1079–84; Stokes, "U.S. to Move Reservation Indians."

58. Lovrich, "The Assimilation of the Indian," pp. 2, 14–17, 21, 34; Fixico, *Termination and Relocation*, p. 175.

59. Hal Boyle, "Birth Rate Hurries Task of Redmen," clipping in Folder 1, Box 6, MA 9, Reifel Papers.

60. Bernie Hunhoff, "Ben Reifel's Search," *South Dakota Magazine*, Jan./Feb. 1989: 13.

61. "S.D.'s Reifel Keeps Fighting Tradition," *Minneapolis Sunday Tribune*, 20 Nov. 1960.

62. Boyle, "Birth Rate Hurries Task of Redmen."

63. Morrell, "Thru the Hills."

64. *The Pine Ridge*, Apr. 1955.

65. Morrell, "Thru the Hills."

66. *The Pine Ridge*, Apr. 1955.

67. Ibid.

68. Ben Reifel, "Cultural Factors in Social Adjustment," *Indian Education*, 15 Apr. 1957: 1.

69. Hunhoff, "Ben Reifel's Search," pp. 12–13.

70. Philp, *Termination Revisited*, pp. 84–85; William H. Kelly to Dr. Benjamin Reifel, 26 July 1955, Folder 12, Box 3, MA 9, Reifel Papers.

71. *The Seattle Times*, 21 Nov. 1954.

72. *The Pine Ridge*, Mar. 1955.

73. Will Spindler, "New Agent Sees Education as Only Salvation of Sioux," *Rapid City Daily Journal*, 3 Oct. 1954; Class Record for Ben Reifel, Teacher; Calendar of Appointments for Feb., May, and June 1954; numerous newspaper clippings reporting on Reifel's speaking engagements are also located in Folder 1, Box 4, MA 9, Reifel Papers.

74. "New Agent See Education as Only Salvation of Sioux," *Rapid City Daily Journal*, 3 Oct. 1954.

75. United States Civil Service Commission Position Description for Ben Reifel, Folder 7, Box 8, MA 9.6, Reifel Papers.

76. Ibid.

CHAPTER 5

1. Karl E. Mundt to Ben Reifel, 19 July 1955; William H. Kelly to Ben Reifel, 26 July 1955; John Cooper to Ben Reifel, 28 July 1955; Oliver La Farge to Ben Reifel, 9 Sep. 1955, Folder 6, Folder 12, Box 3, MA 9.3, Benjamin Reifel Papers, South Dakota State University Archives, South Dakota State University, Brookings.

2. Robert L. Bennett to Benjamin Reifel, 18 Aug. 1955, Folder 12, Box 3, MA 9.3, Reifel Papers.

3. Ralph H. Case to Benjamin Reifel, 29 Aug. 1955, Folder 12, Box 3, MA 9.3, Reifel Papers.

4. *Rapid City Daily Journal*, 10 Sep. 1955.

5. "Federal Agencies: Indian Bureau," *Aberdeen American-News*, 25 Mar. 1959.

6. *Aberdeen Area Office Bulletin*, 19 Mar. 1957, Folder 15, Box 3, MA 9, Reifel Papers; Ben Reifel, "Cultural Factors in Social Adjustment," *Indian Education*, 15 Apr. 1957: 1–10; Ben Reifel to Graham Holmes, 3 May 1957, Rosebud Agency Folder, Box 1, Correspondence with other Agencies 1949–1960, Cheyenne River Agency–Sisseton Agency, Aberdeen Area Office, Record Group 75, Records of the Bureau of Indian Affairs, National Archives and Records Administration, Kansas City, Mo., hereafter cited as RG 75 NARA; *Aberdeen American-News*, 16 Nov. 1958; John S. Painter, "Transitional Sioux Leader: Benjamin Reifel," in *South Dakota Leaders: From Pierre Chouteau, Jr., to Oscar Howe*, ed. Herbert T. Hoover and Larry J. Zimmerman (Vermillion: University of South Dakota Press, 1989), pp. 350–51.

7. *Aberdeen American-News*, 31 May 1957.

8. Ibid., 2 Feb. 1959.

9. Ibid., 26 Feb. 1957.

10. Ibid., 16 June 1957.

11. Anson Yeager, "Sioux Caught between Two Ideas: White Man's World of Thrift; And Indian's World of Sharing," *Aberdeen American-News*, 4 Aug. 1957.

12. *Aberdeen American-News*, 20 July 1958.

13. *Aberdeen American-News*, 4 Aug. 1957.

14. *Aberdeen Area Office Bulletin*, 19 Mar. 1957; Edward Charles Valandra, *Not without Our Consent: Lakota Resistance to Termination, 1950–59* (Urbana: University of Illinois Press, 2006), pp. 171–72; *Aberdeen American-News*, 13 Feb. 1959.

15. *Aberdeen Area Office Bulletin*, 19 Mar. 1957; Valandra, *Not without Our Consent*, pp. 265–66; Francis Paul Prucha, *The Great Father: The United States Government and the American Indian*, vol. 2 (Lincoln: University of Nebraska Press, 1984), pp. 1045–46; Nicholas Christos Zaferatos, *Planning the American Indian Reservation: From Theory to Empowerment* (Syracuse, N.Y.: Syracuse University Press, 2015), pp. 30–31; David H. Getches, Daniel M. Rosenfelt, and Charles F. Wilkinson, eds., *Cases and Materials on Federal Indian Law* (Saint Paul: West Publishing, 1979), pp. 466–67.

16. *Aberdeen Area Office Bulletin*, 19 Mar. 1957.

17. Ben Reifel to Walter E. Blomgren, 11 Dec. 1956, Folder 1; Glenn R. Landbloom to Don Huff, 6 July 1956, Folder 1; unknown author to BIA Commissioner, 7 Feb. 1957, Folder 5, Box 1, Correspondence Files 1950–1957, Aberdeen Area Office, RG 75 NARA; "Subcommittee Arrives for Indian Hearings," clipping in Folder 1, Box 6, MA 9, Reifel Papers; *Aberdeen American-News*, 9 Apr. 1957, 26 Mar. 1958, 14 Sep. 1958, 10 Dec. 1958.

18. "Once Indians Held America, Now They Fear the Future," *Minneapolis Sunday Tribune*, 18 Mar. 1956.

19. Official Proceedings of the Pine Ridge Conference on Community Organiza-

tion and Development, Folder 3, Box 167, Pine Ridge Agency General Records, RG 75 NARA. Comments by Reifel appear on pp. 61–74 and elsewhere.

20. Sally Ross, "BIA's Area Director Is Sioux Version of John Foster Dulles," *Aberdeen American-News*, 27 July 1958.

21. *Aberdeen American-News*, 13 Apr. 1958.

22. 1956 All-American Indian Days Program, Folder 10, Box 5, MA 9.5, Reifel Papers.

23. "Dr. Benjamin Reifel, of South Dakota—American Indian of the Year," Extension of Remarks of Hon. Francis Case, Cong. Rec., 84th Cong., 2nd sess., 1956, 102, pt. 11: A5909.

24. 1960 Silver Antelope Awards program, Folder 11, Box 3, MA 9; Ray W. Sweazey to Ben Reifel, 25 May 1960, Folder 12, Box 8, MA 9.6, Reifel Papers.

25. "Sioux Wins Achievement Award," *The Amerindian American Indian Review* 9 (Sept.–Oct. 1960): 1–2.

26. Robert J. Artz to Wesley G. Pippert, 16 May 1960, Folder 12, Box 8, MA 9.6, Reifel Papers.

27. Alan L. Clem, *Prairie State Politics: Popular Democracy in South Dakota* (Washington, D.C.: Public Affairs Press, 1967), p. 41; Herbert S. Schell, *History of South Dakota* (Lincoln: University of Nebraska Press, 1961), pp. 312–13.

28. Clem, *Prairie State Politics*, p. 41; Schell, *History of South Dakota*, p. 313.

29. Stephen E. Ambrose, *Nixon*, vol. 1, *The Education of a Politician, 1913–1962* (New York: Simon and Schuster, 1987), pp. 502–3; Lewis H. Gould, *Grand Old Party: A History of the Republicans* (New York: Random House, 2003), pp. 342–43; Herbert S. Parmet, *Richard Nixon and His America* (New York: Konecky and Konecky, 1990), p. 344.

30. James Denny, "South Dakota's Ben Reifel: That 'Poor Indian Boy' in Congress," *Sunday Omaha World-Herald Magazine of the Midlands*, 5 Apr. 1970, p. 7; Sam Gailmard and John W. Patty, *Learning while Governing: Expertise and Accountability in the Executive Branch* (Chicago: University of Chicago Press, 2013), p. 120.

31. Michael T. Smith, "The History of Indian Citizenship," in *The American Indian: Past and Present*, 3rd ed., ed. Roger L. Nichols (New York: Alfred A. Knopf, 1986), pp. 240–41; Daniel McCool, "Indian Voting," in *American Indian Policy in the Twentieth Century*, ed. Vine Deloria Jr. (Norman: University of Oklahoma Press, 1985), pp. 106–7.

32. "First Lakota in U.S. House Gave Boost to S.D.," *Sioux Falls Argus Leader*, 21 Sep. 2011.

33. Denny, "South Dakota's Ben Reifel," p. 7.

34. Ibid.; "Congress Contests of Special Interest," *Aberdeen American-News*, 5 June 1960; untitled and undated clipping in Ben Reifel Biography File, South Dakota State Historical Society Archive, Pierre; Robert J. Artz to Wesley G. Pippert, 16 May 1960, Folder 12, Box 8, MA 9.6, Reifel Papers.

35. *Aberdeen American-News*, 8 Mar. 1960.

36. Ibid., 16 Mar. 1960; Denny, "South Dakota's Ben Reifel," p. 7.

37. *Aberdeen American-News*, 16 Mar. 1960.

38. From an answer to a questionnaire sent by Harry Jones to the Office of Representative Ben Reifel, 27 June 1964, Folder 10, Box 9, MA 9.6, Reifel Papers.

39. *Aberdeen American-News*, 8 June 1960.

40. Telegraph from Glenn L. Emmons to Robert L. Bennett, 18 Apr. 1960 (copy), Folder 11, Box 8, MA 9.6, Reifel Papers.

41. "Citation for Distinguished Service, Benjamin Reifel," 19 Apr. 1961, Folder 3, Box 3, MA 9, Reifel Papers.

42. Martin N. B. Holm et al., to Ben Reifel, 18 Apr. 1961, Folder 7, Box 9, MA 9.6, Reifel Papers.

43. "Reifel Puts Pole Aside to Fish for S.D. Votes," clipping, n.d., Ben Reifel Biography File, South Dakota State Historical Society Archive, Pierre; E.Y. Berry to Ben Reifel, 6 Apr. 1960, Folder 11, Box 8, MA 9.6, Reifel Papers; *Aberdeen American-News*, 8 June 1960.

44. "First Lakota in U.S. House Gave Boost to S.D."

45. Souvenir program for "Northeastern South Dakota Banquet Honoring Congressman Ben Reifel," 19 Oct. 1965, Ben Reifel Biography File, South Dakota State Historical Society Archive, Pierre.

46. *Aberdeen American-News*, 8 June 1960.

47. Theodore H. White, *The Making of the President, 1968* (New York: Pocket Books, 1970), pp. 39–40.

48. "Indian's Nomination Makes S.D. Proud," *Minneapolis Sunday Tribune*, 12 June 1960.

49. "First Lakota in U.S. House Gave Boost to S.D."; Robert J. Artz to Wesley G. Pippert, 16 May 1960, File 10, Box 8, MA 9.6, Reifel Papers; Jason A. Heppler, "The American Indian Movement and South Dakota Politics," in *The Plains Political Tradition: Essays on South Dakota Political Culture*, vol. 1, ed. Jon K. Lauck, John E. Miller, and Donald C. Simmons Jr. (Pierre: South Dakota Historical Society Press, 2014), pp. 267–68; South Dakota Secretary of State, "Election History," sdsos.gov; Helen L. Peterson, "American Indian Political Participation," *Annals of the American Academy of Political and Social Science* 311 (May 1957): 124–26.

50. *Aberdeen American-News*, 1 Nov. 1960.

51. South Dakota Secretary of State, "Election History."

52. Ben Reifel to Donald E. Messer, 17 May 1967 (copy), Folder 2, Box 10, MA 9.6, Reifel Papers.

53. Sam Stands to Ben Reifel, 10 Mar. 1960, Folder 10, Box 8, MA 9.6, Reifel Papers.

54. J. W. Thompson to Ben Reifel, 8 Apr. 1960, Folder 11, Box 8, MA 9.6, Reifel Papers.

55. Oscar Howe to Ben Reifel, 18 Apr. 1960, Folder 11, Box 8, MA 9.6, Reifel Papers.

56. Ella Deloria to Ben Reifel, 27 May 1960; Jim Blue Bird to Ben Reifel, 13 May 1960, Folder 12, Box 8, MA 9.6, Reifel Papers.

57. "First Lakota in U.S. House Gave Boost to S.D."

58. *Aberdeen American-News*, 8 June 1960.

59. Calendar of television appearances and radio and newspaper ads for Ben Reifel, 17 May to 6 June 1960; E. C. Pieplow to Ben Reifel, 18 May 1960, Folder 12, Box 8, MA 9.6, Reifel Papers.

60. Taped recordings of Reifel campaign ads for June 1960 primary, Box 30.1, MA 9-0042av, Reifel Papers.

61. *Aberdeen American-News*, 8 June 1960.

62. Robert J. Artz to Wesley G. Pippert, 16 May 1960, Folder 12, Box 8, MA 9.6, Reifel Papers.

63. Francis Case to Ben Reifel, 11 Apr. 1960, Folder 11, Box 8, MA 9.6, Reifel Papers.

64. *South Dakota Republican News*, July 1960, Folder 1, Box 9, MA 9.6, Reifel Papers; *Mitchell Daily Republic*, 8 June 1960.

65. *Deseret News*, 11 June 1960; *Washington Post*, 8 June 1960; *San Francisco Chronicle*, 8 June 1960; *Knoxville News-Sentinel*, 10 June 1960; Carroll H. Lockhart to Ben Reifel, 13 June 1960, Folder 1, Box 9, MA 9.6, Reifel Papers.

66. William Burning Breast to Ben Reifel, 22 June 1960, Folder 1, Box 9, MA 9.6, Reifel Papers.

67. Vernon C. Loen, interview by John S. Painter, 13 Aug. 1980, Folder Loen Vernon C., Box 67, John S. Painter Papers, Richardson Collections, Archives and Special Collections, University of South Dakota, Vermillion.

68. Ibid.

69. *Washington Post*, 8 June 1960; *Aberdeen American-News*, 6 July 1960, 12 Oct. 1960, 13 Oct. 1960, and 6 Nov. 1960.

70. Schell, *History of South Dakota*, p. 350.

71. Alan Clem, "South Dakota," in *Explaining the Vote: Presidential Choices in the Nation and the States, 1968*, pt. 2: *Presidential Choices in Individual States*, ed. David M. Kovenock and James W. Prothro (Chapel Hill: University of North Carolina Press, 1973), pp. 253–58.

72. A. James Reichley, *Conservatives in an Age of Change: The Nixon and Ford Administrations* (Washington, D.C.: Brookings Institution, 1981), pp. 22–37.

73. Parmet, *Richard Nixon and His America*, pp. vii, ix.

74. Tom Wicker, *One of Us: Richard Nixon and the American Dream* (New York: Random House, 1991), pp. 19–23, 50, 70, 81–85; Robert Mason, *Richard Nixon and the Quest for a New Majority* (Chapel Hill: University of North Carolina Press, 2004), pp. 2–3.

75. Mason, *Richard Nixon*, p. 6.

76. Parmet, *Richard Nixon and His America*, p. viii.

77. Text of Reifel speech, n.d., Folder 4, Box 5, MA 9.4, Reifel Papers; *South Dakota Republican News*, July 1960.

78. Ben Reifel to Richard Nixon, 7 Mar. 1961 (copy), Folder 7, Box 9, MA 9.6, Reifel Papers.

79. Ben Reifel, response to "Argus Leader Questionnaire" (copy), Folder 3, Box 9, MA 9.6, Reifel Papers. The questionnaire provided the *Sioux Falls Argus Leader* editorial staff with a written record of Reifel's positions on the main issues of the 1960 campaign.

80. Candidate questionnaire for 1960 campaign from an undated and untitled source, Folder 4, Box 5, MA 9.4, Reifel Papers.

81. Jeffrey Frank, *Ike and Dick: Portrait of a Strange Political Marriage* (New York: Simon and Schuster, 2013), pp. 196–97, 201.

82. "First Lakota in U.S. House Gave Boost to S.D."

83. "Argus Leader Questionnaire."

84. *Aberdeen American-News*, 5 Feb. 1960.

85. Theodore H. White, *The Making of the President, 1960* (New York: Atheneum Publishers, 1961), p. 28.

86. "Fitzgerald For Congress" campaign bill, Folder 6, Box 9, MA 9.6, Reifel Papers.

87. Ben Reifel to L. E. Whiteside, 30 Sep. 1960 (copy), Folder 4, Box 9, MA 9.6, Reifel Papers.

88. Questionnaire on federal aid to education, 1960 campaign, Folder 4, Box 5, MA 9.4, Reifel Papers.

89. Ben Reifel to L. E. Whiteside, 30 Sep. 1960.

90. *Aberdeen American-News*, 9 Nov. 1960.

91. Ibid., 18 Mar. 1960.

92. For examinations of Eisenhower-era farm policies, see Jon K. Lauck, "George S. McGovern and the Farmer: South Dakota Politics, 1953–1962," *South Dakota History* 32 (Winter 2002): 333, 337–41, 345–46; Steven Wagner, *Eisenhower Republicanism: Pursuing the Middle Way* (DeKalb: Northern Illinois University Press, 2006), pp. 43–57; Stephen E. Ambrose, *Eisenhower*, vol. 2, *The President* (New York: Simon and Schuster, 1984), pp. 159–60, 460–61; Merlo J. Pusey, *Eisenhower the President* (New York: Macmillan, 1956), pp. 223–25; and Dwight D. Eisenhower, *Mandate for Change*, vol. 1, *The White House Years, 1953–1956* (Garden City, N.Y.: Doubleday, 1963), pp. 557–61.

93. *Mitchell Daily Republic*, 18 Oct. 1960.

94. "S.D.'s Reifel Keeps Fighting Tradition," *Minneapolis Sunday Tribune*, 20 Nov. 1960.

95. "Argus Leader Questionnaire"; questionnaire for 1960 campaign from an undated and untitled source, Folder 4, Box 5, MA 9.4, Reifel Papers.

96. *The Speeches of Vice President Richard M. Nixon Presidential Campaign of 1960* (Washington, D.C.: U.S. Government Printing Office, 1961), pp. 1226–29; "Nixon's Farm Program," Folder 4, Box 5, MA 9.4, Reifel Papers.

97. "Nixon's Farm Program."

98. *Aberdeen American-News*, 7 Oct. 1960.

99. Ibid., 16 Oct. 1960; *Mitchell Daily Republic*, 19 Oct. 1960.

100. *Mitchell Daily Republic*, 20 Oct. 1960.

101. *Aberdeen American-News*, 25 Oct. 1960.

102. *Mitchell Daily Republic*, 20 Oct. 1960.

103. Rolly Samp, telephone interview by author, 27 June 2012.

104. Questionnaire for 1960 campaign from an undated and untitled source, Folder 4, Box 5, MA 9.4, Reifel Papers.

105. "Indian's Nomination Makes S.D. Proud."

106. Vernon C. Loen, interview by John S. Painter, 13 Aug. 1980, Painter Papers.

107. *Aberdeen American-News*, 4 Nov. 1960.

108. South Dakota Secretary of State, "Election History"; *Aberdeen American-News*, 9 Nov. 1960; *Sisseton Courier*, 6 Nov. 1958, 10 Nov. 1960, 8 Nov. 1962, 5 Nov. 1964, 10 Nov. 1966, 7 Nov. 1968.

CHAPTER 6

1. Vernon C. Loen, interview by John S. Painter, 13 Aug. 1980, John S. Painter Papers, Richardson Collections, Archives and Special Collections, University of South Dakota, Vermillion.

2. Charles B. Hoven to Ben Reifel, 10 Feb. 1961 and Ben Reifel to Charles A. Halleck, 4 Jan. 1961 (copy), Folder 1, Box 2, MA 9.1, Benjamin Reifel Papers, South Dakota State University Archives, South Dakota State University, Brookings; souvenir program for the Northwestern South Dakota Banquet Honoring Ben Reifel, 19 Oct. 1965, Ben Reifel Biography File, South Dakota State Historical Society Archives, Pierre.

3. Republican Assignments, Committee on Agriculture, Folder 1, Box 2, MA 9.1, Reifel Papers; Charles B. Brownson, comp. and ed., *Congressional Staff Directory, 1962: Staff Biographies* (Washington: Congressional Staff Directory, 1962), pp. 183–84.

4. Ben Reifel to Orville Freeman, 31 Mar. 1961 (copy), Folder 3, Box 346, Record Group III, Karl E. Mundt Archives, Dakota State University, Madison, S.Dak.

5. Ben Reifel on Farm Bill, n.d., Box 30.2, MA 9–0051av, Reifel Papers; *Mitchell Daily Republic*, 12 May 1961; *Huron Daily Plainsman*, 22 June 1961.

6. Cong. Rec., 87th Cong., 1st sess., 1961, 107, pt. 10: 13488.

7. *Mitchell Daily Republic*, 12 May 1961; *Huron Daily Plainsman*, 22 June 1961 and 18(?) May 1962(?); Vernon Loen to George H. Phillips, 23 Apr. 1964, Folder 10; Reifel for Congress Committee Letter, 15 Oct. 1962, Folder 8, Box 9, MA 9.6, Reifel Papers;

Reifel Shots, 9 May 1963, Reifel Folder, Box 74, Archie M. Gubbrud Papers, Richardson Collection, Archives and Special Collections, University of South Dakota, Vermillion, hereafter cited as *Reifel Shots*; Vernon C. Loen, interview by John S. Painter, 13 Aug. 1980, Painter Papers.

8. Ben Reifel to James B. Utt, 8 Jan. 1962 (copy), Folder 1, Box 2, MA 9.1, Reifel Papers.

9. Vernon C. Loen, interview by John S. Painter, 13 Aug. 1980, Painter Papers.

10. Ben Reifel to James B. Utt, 8 Jan. 1962.

11. Ben Reifel to Ben F. Jensen, 8 June 1962 (copy), Folder 1, Box 2, MA 9.1, Reifel Papers.

12. Alan C. Clem, *The Nomination of Joe Bottum: Analysis of a Committee Decision to Nominate a United States Senator* (Vermillion, S.Dak.: Government Research Bureau, 1963), pp. 13–16.

13. Ibid., pp. 15–20; Ben Reifel to E. R. Doering, 19 July 1962, Reifel Folder, Box 74, Archie M. Gubbrud Papers.

14. Clem, *The Nomination of Joe Bottum*, pp. 20, 23, 27–28, 44.

15. Ben Reifel to Ben Jensen, 9 Nov. 1962 (copy) and Ben Reifel to R.A. Devereaux, 1 Feb. 1963 (copy), Folder 1, Box 2, MA 9.1, Reifel Papers.

16. Vernon C. Loen, interview by John S. Painter, 13 Aug. 1980, Painter Papers.

17. Karl Mundt, *Your Washington and You!*, 10 Dec. 1963, Digital Library of South Dakota, dlsd.sdln.net/cdm/landingpage/collection/mundt.

18. *Huron Daily Plainsman*, 21 May 1963 and 12 July 1963.

19. *Mitchell Daily Republic*, 1 Apr. 1968.

20. "Reifel Asks Retraction on 'Small Farm' Policy," n.d., clipping in Folder 15, Box 5, MA 9.5, Reifel Papers.

21. *South Dakota Union Farmer*, 13 Apr. 1964; *Reifel Shots*, 19 Dec. 1963.

22. "Reifel's Strength," clipping in Box 28, MA 9, Reifel Papers.

23. *Reifel Shots*, 19 Dec. 1963.

24. *Mitchell Daily Republic*, 14 Apr. 1967.

25. Ben Reifel to L. H. Folsland, 11 Sep. 1967 (copy), Folder 9, Box 437, Record Group III, Mundt Archives.

26. Rebecca L. Johnson, *What It Took: A History of the USGS EROS Data Center* (Sioux Falls: Center for Western Studies at Augustana College, 1998), pp. v, 1–11; *Mitchell Daily Republic*, 15 Oct. 1969.

27. Vernon C. Loen, interview by John S. Painter, 13 Aug. 1980, Painter Papers.

28. Ibid.

29. Gordon Gunderson to Karl Mundt, 16 Jan. 1969, and Gordon Gunderson to Ben Reifel, 31 Jan. 1969 (copy), Folder 6, Box 450, Record Group III, Mundt Archives.

30. William H. Smith to Ben Reifel, 7 Feb. 1969 (copy) and Karl E. Mundt to John Ehrlichman, 7 Feb. 1969, Folder 6, Box 450, Record Group III, Mundt Archives.

31. News release from the office of U.S. Senator Karl E. Mundt, 20 Feb. 1969, Folder 6, Box 450, Record Group III, Mundt Archives.

32. Herbert S. Schell, *History of South Dakota* (Lincoln: University of Nebraska Press, 1961), p. 336.

33. *Reifel Shots*, 19 Dec. 1963.

34. Cong. Rec., 89th Cong., 2nd sess., 1966, 112, pt. 4: 4584–85.

35. Cong. Rec., 89th Cong., 1st sess., 1965, 111, pt. 10: 13811; Ben Reifel, "Water Development Essential to Growth"; "$50,000 Given to Irrigation Study," clipping from *Aberdeen American-News*, n.d., Box 28, MA 9, Reifel Papers; Loen to Phillips, 23 Apr. 1964; J. W. Grimes to Ben Reifel, 10 Oct. 1969, Folder 15, Box 1438, Record Group XIII, Mundt Archives.

36. *Mitchell Daily Republic*, 5 June 1969.

37. Ibid.

38. Michael L. Lawson, *Dammed Indians Revisited: The Continuing History of the Pick-Sloan Plan and the Missouri River Sioux* (Pierre: South Dakota State Historical Society Press, 2009), pp. 216–17.

39. Dean Bangsund and F. Larry Leistritz, *Economic Contributions of the Sugarbeet Industry in Minnesota, North Dakota, and Eastern Montana* (Fargo: North Dakota State University, 2004), p. 5; Schell, *History of South Dakota*, p. 354.

40. *Phreno Cosmian*, 10 Apr. 1962.

41. Copy of press release from the Office of U.S. Representative Ben Reifel, 1 Mar. 1962, Reifel Folder, Box 74, Archie M. Gubbrud Papers.

42. Cong. Rec., 87th Cong., 1st sess., 1961, 107, pt. 13: 17810.

43. Ibid.

44. Ibid.

45. *Huron Daily Plainsman*, 22 Jan. 1963; *Aberdeen American-News*, 27 Jan. 1963.

46. *Aberdeen American-News*, 18 Oct. and 31 Oct. 1963.

47. Joon Kim, "The Political Economy of the Mexican Farm Labor Program, 1942–1964," *Aztlán* 29 (Fall 2004): 13–15, 40–41.

48. Cong. Rec., 88th Cong., 1st sess., 1963, 109, pt. 15: 20709.

49. Ibid.

50. Ibid.

51. Kim, "Mexican Farm Labor Program," p. 41.

52. Karl E. Mundt to Nils Boe, 31 Dec. 1964 (copy), Folder 2, Box 13a, Record Group 1, Mundt Archives.

53. "First Lakota in U.S. House Gave Boost to S.D.," *Sioux Falls Argus Leader*, 21 Sep. 2011.

54. Ben Reifel, "What It Means to Be a Republican," entered into the *Congressional Record* as an extension of remarks by Karl E. Mundt, Cong. Rec., 87th Cong., 1st sess., 1961, 107, pt. 13: 17300.

55. From answers to a questionnaire from Harry Jones, 27 June 1964, Folder 10, Box 9, MA 9.6, Reifel Papers.

56. *South Dakota Union Farmer*, 13 Apr. 1964, Box 28, MA 9, Reifel Papers.

57. *Pierre Capital Journal*, 23 Dec. 1963.

58. *Aberdeen American-News*, 17 Oct. 1963; Cong. Rec., 87th Cong., 1st sess., 1961, 107, pt. 15: 19535–36.

59. "Reifel Says Peace Corps to S.D. a Waste of Funds," *Sioux Falls Argus Leader*, 17 Feb. 1963.

60. Ibid.; Richard Nixon to Ben Reifel, 28 Jan. 1970, Folder 14, Box 11, MA 9.6, Reifel Papers.

61. *Huron Daily Plainsman*, 2 May 1968.

62. Bruce Bartlett, "50 Years after the House Vote for the Kennedy Tax Cut," *New York Times*, 24 Sep. 2013, http://economix.blogs.nytimes.com/2013/09/24/50-years-after-the-house-vote-for-the-kennedy-tax-cut/?_r=0.

63. "The Common Sense of Rep. Reifel," *Aberdeen American-News*, 28 Oct. 1963.

64. Allen J. Matusow, *The Unraveling of America: A History of Liberalism in the 1960s* (New York: Harper and Row, 1984), pp. 53–55.

65. Richard Nixon to Ben Reifel, 1 July 1969, Folder 14; Gerald R. Ford to Ben Reifel, 1 July 1969, Folder 9, Box 11, MA 9.6, Reifel Papers.

66. Vernon C. Loen, interview by John S. Painter, 13 Aug. 1980, Painter Papers.

67. *Sioux Falls Argus Leader*, 14 Feb. 1968.

68. Richard Nixon to Ben Reifel, 14 Nov. 1969, Folder 14, Box 11, MA 9.6, Reifel Papers.

69. *Mitchell Daily Republic*, 1 May 1970.

70. Ben Reifel to Gerald Ford, 10 Jan. 1967 (copy); Gerald R. Ford to Ben Reifel, 30 Jan. 1967, Folder 7, Box 1, MA 9.1, Reifel Papers.

71. *Mitchell Daily Republic*, 18 Oct. 1961.

72. *Reifel Shots*, 9 Mar. 1963.

73. Ibid., 23 Oct. 1963.

74. Vernon C. Loen, interview by John S. Painter, 13 Aug. 1980, Painter Papers.

75. Ben Reifel, interview, 1 Nov. [year unknown], Oral Histories, Box 9, Oscar Howe Papers, Richardson Collection, Archives and Special Collections, University of South Dakota, Vermillion.

76. Vernon C. Loen, interview by John S. Painter, 13 Aug. 1980, Painter Papers; Wesley G. Pippert, "Ex-Congressman Ben Reifel: 'Turn Your Back on the Past; Adapt,'" *Omaha World-Herald*, 10 Feb. 1971.

77. Ben Reifel to Warren M. Lee, 14 Feb. 1968, Ben Reifel Folder, Box 12, Wayne S. Knutson Papers, Richardson Collection, Archives and Special Collections, University of South Dakota, Vermillion.

78. Vernon C. Loen, interview by John S. Painter, 13 Aug. 1980, Painter Papers.

79. "S.D. Solons Laud, Criticize Message," clipping in Box 28, MA 9, Reifel Papers.

80. Audio recordings of Ben Reifel, MA 9-0050av and MA 9-0046av, Box 30.2, Reifel Papers; Vernon Loen, interview by John S. Painter, 13 Aug. 1980, Painter Papers.

CHAPTER 7

1. Vernon Loen, interview by John S. Painter, 13 Aug. 1980, John S. Painter Papers, Richardson Collections, Archives and Special Collections, University of South Dakota, Vermillion.

2. Ibid.

3. Michael L. Lawson, *Dammed Indians Revisited: The Continuing History of the Pick-Sloan Plan and the Missouri River Sioux* (Pierre: South Dakota State Historical Society Press, 2009), pp. 78, 150–67.

4. Ibid., p. 167.

5. Cong. Rec., 87th Cong., 1st sess., 1961, 107, pt. 11: 14771–72.

6. Ben Reifel to Malvina Shields, 6 Aug. 1962 (copy), Folder 56, Box 585, Record Group III, Karl E. Mundt Archives, Dakota State University, Madison, S.Dak.

7. Lawson, *Dammed Indians Revisited*, p. 171. All of the tribes dispossessed by the Pick-Sloan Plan, none of whom believed their original settlements to be fair assessments of land values and personal claims, were eventually awarded large reparations from the federal government. By 1996, for example, the Crow Creek Sioux Tribe had received a total of $33,437,614 in compensations. For a thorough discussion on the reparation negotiations, see Lawson, *Dammed Indians Revisited*, chs. 17 and 18.

8. House Committee on Appropriations, Department of the Interior and Related Agencies Appropriations for 1964: Hearings before the Subcommittee on Department of the Interior and Related Agencies, 88th Cong., 1st sess., 1963, p. 36.

9. Philleo Nash to Ben Reifel, 20 Nov. 1964, Folder 10, Box 9, MA 9.6, Benjamin Reifel Papers, South Dakota State University Archives, South Dakota State University, Brookings.

10. Ben Reifel, from a statement provided to Vine Deloria, Jr., for a special issue of the National Congress of American Indians *Sentinel*, 10 May 1967 (copy), Folder 2, Box 10, MA 9.6, Reifel Papers.

11. *Sioux Falls Argus Leader*, 5 Mar. 1964.

12. Karl Mundt, *Your Washington and You!*, 7 July 1964, Digital Library of South Dakota, dlsd.sdln.net/cdm/landingpage/collection/mundt.

13. Vernon Loen, interview by John S. Painter, 13 Aug. 1980, Painter Papers.

14. Untitled press release, 2 June 1964, Folder 7, Box 389, Record Group III, Mundt Archives.

15. Ibid.

16. Vernon Loen, interview by John S. Painter, 13 Aug. 1980, Painter Papers.

17. *Sisseton Courier*, 25 Mar. 1965 and 18 Aug. 1966; Ben Reifel, interview by John S. Painter, 9 Oct. 1988, Painter Papers.

18. *Huron Daily Plainsman*, 18 Aug. 1966; *Mitchell Daily Republic*, 12 June 1967.

19. "Statement of Rep. Ben Reifel, 1st District, South Dakota," n.d., Folder 2, Box 10, MA 9.6, Reifel Papers.

20. Harlan Hammer to Ben Reifel, 17 Nov. 1964, Folder 10, Box 9, Reifel Papers.

21. "$4 Million System May Replace Old Indian School of Ben Reifel," *Aberdeen American-News*, 8 Apr. 1963.

22. Ben Reifel, interview by John S. Painter, 9 Oct. 1988, Painter Papers.

23. Ibid.

24. "$4.9 Million Mission School Unit Dedicated," *Mitchell Daily Republic*, 9 May 1966.

25. *Sioux Falls Argus Leader*, 18 Feb. 1968.

26. Brenda Wade, "Congressman Chipped Away at Racial Barriers," *Sioux Fall Argus Leader*, 1 May 1988.

27. "Statement of Rep. Ben Reifel, 1st District, South Dakota."

28. Cong. Rec., 89th Cong., 1st sess., 1965, 111, pt. 5: 6303.

29. Ibid.

30. Ibid., pp. 6303–4.

31. Ibid., p. 6304.

32. Ibid., pp. 6304–5, 6312.

33. Ben Reifel, from an article submitted to *The Optimist Magazine*, 28 June 1966, Folder 1, Box 10, MA 9.6, Reifel Papers.

34. Francis Paul Prucha, *The Great Father: The United States Government and the American Indian*, vol. 2 (Lincoln: University of Nebraska Press, 1984), pp. 1087–91.

35. Ibid., pp. 1091–95; Alan L. Sorkin, *American Indians and Federal Aid* (Washington, D.C.: Brookings Institution, 1971), pp. 166–67.

36. Sorkin, *American Indians and Federal Aid*, pp. 168–69.

37. Ben Reifel to Marian E. Gridley, 18 Aug. 1966 (copy), Folder 1, Box 10, MA 9.6, Reifel Papers.

38. Senate Committee on Interior and Insular Affairs, Hearing on the Nomination of Robert LaFollette Bennett, of Alaska, to be Commissioner of Indian Affairs, 89th Congress, 2nd sess., 1966, pp. 6–7.

39. Ibid., p. 7.

40. "'Hero' Reifel buried," *Sioux Falls Argus Leader*, 7 Jan. 1990.

41. *Toledo Blade*, 9 Mar. 1964; "Ben Reifel Opposes Special Indian Day," clipping from unidentified newspaper, n.d., Box 28, MA 9, Reifel Papers.

42. "Ben Reifel Opposes Special Indian Day."

43. *Rosebud Sioux Herald*, 1 Mar. 1965.

44. U.S. Department of Agriculture Extension Service, "A Report on the National

Seminar of American Indian Women, Aug. 2–8, 1970, Colorado State University, Fort Collins, Colorado" (1970), p. 4.

45. Ben Reifel to James W. Howden, 17 Aug. 1967 (copy), Folder 2, Box 10, MA 9.6, Reifel Papers.

46. Ben Reifel to Leta James, 14 Sep. 1965 (copy), Folder 11, Box 9, MA 9.6, Reifel Papers.

47. Ben Reifel, interview by Barbara Fitzgerald, n.d., Box 30.1, MA 9-0043av, Reifel Papers.

48. U.S. Commission on Civil Rights, The National Conference and the Reports of the State Advisory Committees to the U.S. Commission on Civil Rights, 1959 (Washington, D.C.: Government Printing Office, 1960), pp. 352–54.

49. Reifel for Congress 1960 press release, 6 May 1960, Folder 12, Box 8, MA 9.6, Reifel Papers.

50. *Aberdeen American-News*, 9 Oct. 1963.

51. Roger W. Kelley to Karl Mundt, 21 Feb. 1964, Folder 8, Box 615, Record Group III, Mundt Archives.

52. "South Dakota GOP Faces Fight on Pledging Convention Slate," clipping from unidentified newspaper, n.d., Box 28, MA 9, Reifel Papers; *Aberdeen American-News*, 29 Feb. 1964.

53. Allen J. Matusow, *The Unraveling of America: A History of Liberalism in the 1960s* (New York: Harper and Row, 1984), p. 136.

54. Clipping from unidentified newspaper, n.d., Box 28, MA 9, Reifel Papers; Alan L. Clem, *Prairie State Politics: Popular Democracy in South Dakota* (Washington, D.C.: Public Affairs Press, 1967), p. 42.

55. Alan L. Clem, "National Convention Impact on Small State Politics: South Dakota Republicans in San Francisco, 1964," *South Dakota History* 2 (Spring 1971): 110. On the issue of civil rights, the Republican Party platform called for the "full implementation and faithful execution of the Civil Rights Act of 1964." See J. William Middendorf II, *A Glorious Disaster: Barry Goldwater's Presidential Campaign and the Origins of the Conservative Movement* (New York: Basic Books, 2006), p. 115.

56. South Dakota Secretary of State, "Election History," sdsos.gov.

57. Dennis R. Holmes, "Political Rights under the Indian Civil Rights Act," *South Dakota Law Review* 24 (Spring 1979): 419–25; Vine Deloria Jr. and Clifford M. Lytle, *American Indians, American Justice* (Austin: University of Texas Press, 1983), pp. 126–30; Thomas Clarkin, *Federal Indian Policy in the Kennedy and Johnson Administrations, 1961–1969* (Albuquerque: University of New Mexico Press, 2001), pp. 262–63; Frank Pommersheim, *Broken Landscape: Indians, Indian Tribes, and the Constitution* (New York: Oxford University Press, 2009), p. 238.

58. Lyndon Baines Johnson, *The Vantage Point: Perspectives of the Presidency, 1963–1969* (New York: Holt, Rinehart and Winston, 1971), pp. 176–78.

59. House Committee on Rules, To Prescribe Penalties for Certain Acts of Violence or Intimidation: Hearings before the Committee on Rules on H. Res. 1100, pt. 2, 90th Cong., 2nd sess., 1968, pp. 34–35, hereafter cited as ICRA Hearings.

60. Ibid., pp. 35–36.

61. Ibid.; Steven C. Schulte, "Removing the Yoke of Government: E.Y. Berry and the Origins of Indian Termination Policy," *South Dakota History* 14 (Spring 1984): 64; Richmond L. Clow, "State Jurisdiction on Sioux Reservations: Indian and Non-Indian Responses, 1952–1964," *South Dakota History* 11 (Summer 1981): 176–79.

62. ICRA Hearings, pp. 35–36; Clow, "State Jurisdiction on Sioux Reservations," pp. 179–83; Charles Wilkinson, *Blood Struggle: The Rise of Modern Indian Nations* (New York: Norton, 2005), pp. 123–25.

63. ICRA Hearings, p. 36.

64. Ibid., pp. 36–38.

65. Ben Reifel, interview by Tom Biolsi, Aug. 1984, Folder Reifel Ben AIH 84-155, Box 67, Painter Papers.

66. ICRA Hearings, pp. 36–37.

67. Ibid., pp. 37–38, 49.

68. Ibid., pp. 48–50.

69. Pommersheim, *Broken Landscape*, p. 238.

70. ICRA Hearings, 48; George Pierre Castille, *To Show Heart: Native American Self-Determination and Federal Indian Policy, 1960–1975* (Tucson: University of Arizona Press, 1998), pp. 65–66; Clarkin, *Federal Indian Policy*, p. 268; Prucha, *Great Father*, 2:1108.

71. ICRA Hearings, pp. 49, 52.

72. Holmes, "Political Rights under the Indian Civil Rights Act," pp. 421, 445–46; Pommersheim, *Broken Landscape*, p. 240.

73. Rolly Samp, telephone interview by author, 27 June 2012.

74. Ben Reifel to Ida B. Alseth, 24 Mar. 1967 (copy), Folder 2, Box 10, MA 9.6, Reifel Papers.

75. "Statement of Rep. Ben Reifel, R-S.D., Before Republican State Central Committee, Marvin Hughitt Hotel, Huron, South Dakota, Wednesday Morning, 6 Sep. 1967," Folder 2, Box 10, MA 9.6, Reifel Papers.

76. Ben Reifel to Genevieve Fish, 14 Aug. 1967 (copy), Folder 2, Box 10, MA 9.6, Reifel Papers.

77. Mildred Fielder, *Sioux Indian Leaders* (New York: Bonanza Books, 1975), pp. 140–42.

CHAPTER 8

1. Matt Schudel, "George B. Hartzog Jr.," p. 88; "Expanded Nation's Park System," *Washington Post*, 6 July 2008.

2. "Reifel Named Indian Advisor," *National Park Courier* 16 (Jan. 1971): n.p., copy in Folder 1, Box 6, MA 9, Benjamin Reifel Papers, South Dakota State University Archives, South Dakota State University, Brookings.

3. Ben Reifel, interview by John S. Painter, 9 Oct. 1988, John S. Painter Papers, Richardson Collections, Archives and Special Collections, University of South Dakota, Vermillion.

4. Ben Reifel, interview, 1 Nov. 19??, Oscar Howe Transcripts, Oral Histories, Oscar Howe Papers, Richardson Collection, Archives and Special Collections, University of South Dakota, Vermillion; Rolly Samp, telephone interview with author, 27 June 2012.

5. Ben Reifel, interview by John S. Painter, 9 Oct. 1988, Painter Papers.

6. Larry Pressler to Rollyn H. Samp, 24 Oct. 1990, Folder 11, Box 3, MA 9, Reifel Papers.

7. National Capital Planning Commission, "About Us—National Capital Planning Commission," http://www.ncpc.gov/ncpc/Main(T2)/About_Us(tr2)/AboutUs.html; Mildred Fielder, *Sioux Indian Leaders* (New York: Bonanza Books, 1975), p. 142.

8. *Rapid City Journal*, 9 Feb. 1972; Fielder, *Sioux Indian Leaders*, p. 143.

9. "Reifel Enters Senate Race," press release, 15 Mar. 1972, Folder 12, Box 5, MA 9.5, Reifel Papers.

10. *Rapid City Journal*, 25 Feb. and 10 Mar. 1972.

11. "Reifel Enters Senate Race."

12. *Rapid City Journal*, 23 Mar. 1972.

13. *Sioux Falls Argus Leader*, 3 Aug. 1983.

14. Ibid.; Fielder, *Sioux Indian Leaders*, pp. 146–47; "Ben Reifel to Be Back in Aberdeen"; "Ben Reifel Will Reside in S. F.," clippings in Folder 15, Box 5, MA 9.5, Reifel Papers; Bernie Hunhoff, "Ben Reifel's Search," *South Dakota Magazine*, Jan./Feb. 1989: 14.

15. *Aberdeen American-News*, 24 Feb. 1971.

16. Ibid., 26 Nov. 1972.

17. *Washington Post*, 31 July 1973.

18. Sean J. Flynn, "Bicultural Conservatism: Native American Congressman Ben Reifel and the GOP," in *The Plains Political Tradition: Essays on South Dakota Political Culture*, vol. 2, ed. Jon K. Lauck, John E. Miller, and Donald C. Simmons Jr. (Pierre: South Dakota Historical Society Press, 2014), pp. 199–200; certificate of appointment of Ben Reifel, Freedom Foundation at Valley Forge, 31 Dec. 1976, Folder 11, Box 3, MA 9, Reifel Papers; "Ben Reifel Named Commissioner of Indian Affairs," Department of the Interior news release, 7 Dec. 1976, Folder 15, Box 3, MA 9, Reifel Papers.

19. "Ben Reifel Named Commissioner of Indian Affairs"; Michael T. Smith, "Benjamin Reifel, 1976–1977," in *The Commissioners of Indian Affairs, 1824–1877*, ed. Robert M. Kvasnicka and Herman J. Viola (Lincoln: University of Nebraska Press,

1979), p. 347; Mark Trahant, "Reifel Proved Indian, White Cultures Can Come Together, Find Harmony," *Sioux Falls Argus Leader*, 28 Jan. 1990.

20. Michael T. Smith, "Morris Thompson, 1973–1976," in *The Commissioners of Indian Affairs*, pp. 341–45.

21. Smith, "Benjamin Reifel," pp. 347–48.

22. Ben Reifel, interview by John Painter, 31 May 1979, Folder Reifel Ben AIH 79-51, Box 67, Painter Papers.

23. Smith, "Benjamin Reifel," pp. 347–48.

24. Trahant, "Reifel Proved Indian, White Cultures."

25. Mark Edwin Miller, *Forgotten Tribes: Unrecognized Indians and the Federal Acknowledgment Process* (Lincoln: University of Nebraska Press, 2004), p. 32.

26. Charles Wilkinson, *Blood Struggle: The Rise of Modern Indian Nations* (New York: W. W. Norton, 2006), pp. 129–37; Francis Paul Prucha, *The Great Father: The United States Government and the American Indian*, vol. 2 (Lincoln: University of Nebraska Press, 1984), pp. 1116–17.

27. Wilkinson, *Blood Struggle*, pp. 137–42.

28. Ibid., pp. 142–43; Prucha, *The Great Father*, 2:1117–19.

29. Leonard Garment, *Crazy Rhythm: My Journey from Brooklyn, Jazz, and Wall Street to Nixon's White House, Watergate, and Beyond* (New York: Times Books, 1997), p. 235.

30. Wilkinson, *Blood Struggle*, pp. 143–45.

31. Ibid., p. 144.

32. Prucha, *The Great Father*, 2:1120.

33. Wilkinson, *Blood Struggle*, pp. 147–49.

34. Brenda Wade, "Congressman Chipped Away at Racial Barriers," *Sioux Falls Argus Leader*, 1 May 1988.

35. Quoted in Wilkinson, *Blood Struggle*, p. 109.

36. Quoted in Peter Nabokov, ed., *Native American Testimony: A Chronicle of Indian-White Relations from Prophecy to the Present, 1492–1992* (New York: Viking Press, 1991), p. 383.

37. Ben Reifel, interview by John Painter, 30 May 1979, Box 67, Painter Papers.

38. Quoted in Nabokov, *Native American Testimony*, p. 383.

39. Wesley G. Pippert, "Ex-Congressman Ben Reifel: 'Turn Your Back on the Past; Adapt,'" *Omaha World-Herald*, 10 Feb. 1971.

40. Ibid.

41. Raasch, "Reifel: He Has the Best of Both Cultures."

42. "Reifel Stresses Need for Better Relations," clipping in Folder 12, Box 5, MA 9.5, Reifel Papers.

43. Raasch, "Reifel: He Has the Best of Both Cultures."

44. "Ben Reifel Addresses," clipping in Folder 15, Box 5, MA 9.5, Reifel Papers.

45. Ibid.

46. *Asheville Citizen*, 19 June and 26 June 1979.

47. *Sioux Falls Argus Leader*, 31 May 1981.

48. *Ikhana Newsletter of the National Committee on Indian Work of the Episcopal Church*, Spring 1987, Folder 4, Box 1, Object ID 40006.09, National Committee on Indian Work, Center for Western Studies Archives.

49. Ben Reifel, interview by ?, 1 Nov. 19??, Box 9, Oscar Howe Transcripts, Oral Histories, Oscar Howe Papers.

50. *South Dakota Art Museum News*, Winter 1989–1990, Ben Reifel Biography File, South Dakota State Historical Society Archives.

51. Doris Giago, "Reifel's Service Boosted State's Progress in '60s," *Sioux Falls Argus Leader*, 3 Jan. 1990.

52. Wade, "Congressman Chipped Away at Racial Barriers."

53. Program from the 1984 National Council Meeting of the Boy Scouts of America, Silver Buffalo Awards ceremony, Folder 11, Box 3, MA 9, Reifel Papers.

54. South Dakota Board of Regents press release, 19 Oct. 19??, Folder 15, Box 5, MA 9, Reifel Papers.

55. Harold Shunk to Ben Reifel, 8 Aug. 1978, Folder 11, Box 3, MA 9, Reifel Papers.

56. "Reifel Honored with First Award," *Humanities* 5 (Oct. 1976): p. 3.

57. Chuck Raasch, "Reifel Says He'll Back Anderson," *Sioux Falls Argus Leader*, 15 July 1980.

58. "Fat Pensions Reflect U.S. Money Problems," *Sioux Falls Argus Leader*, 8 Sep. 1988.

59. Steve Young, "'Hero' Reifel Buried," *Sioux Falls Argus Leader*, 7 Jan. 1990.

60. "Former S.D. Congressman Reifel Dead," 3 Jan. 1990, copy of clipping (possibly from the *Pierre Capital Journal*) in the possession of the author.

61. Doris Giago, "Reifel's Service Boosted State's Progress in '60s," *Sioux Falls Argus Leader*, 3 Jan. 1990.

62. Young, "'Hero' Reifel Buried."

63. "Former S.D. Congressman Reifel Dead."

64. Doris Giago and Janet Lively, "Friends Recall His Sense of Humor," *Sioux Falls Argus Leader*, 3 Jan. 1990.

65. Giago, "Reifel's Service Boosted State's Progress in '60s."

66. "Former S.D. Congressman Reifel Dead."

67. Giago and Lively, "Friends Recall His Sense of Humor."

68. "Straight Shooter Reifel's Mark in History Will Grow," *Sioux Falls Argus Leader*, 6 Jan. 1990.

69. Naomi Schaefer Riley, review of *Indian Spectacle* by Jennifer Guiliano, *Wall Street Journal*, 1–2 Aug. 2015.

70. Naomi Schaefer Riley, "Changing an NFL Team's Name Won't Fix Indian Schools," *Wall Street Journal*, 21 May 2016.

71. Tom Lutey, "Schools on Montana Indian Reservations Face Teacher Shortages," *Missoulian*, 5 July 2014, http://missoulian.com/news/local/schools-on-montana-indian-reservations-face-teacher-shortages/article_79623044-03c6-11e4-b8a7-0019bb2963f4.html.

72. Riley, "Changing an NFL Team's Name Won't Fix Indian Schools."

73. Christopher Doering, "Thune Legislation Targets Suicide by Young Native Americans," *Sioux Falls Argus Leader*, 19 July 2015.

74. Donald L. Fixico, *American Indians in a Modern World* (Lanham, Md.: AltaMira Press, 2008), pp. 32, 35–36.

75. Bette Burg, "Heritage Cost Indians Country, Reifel Tells H.C. History Class," clipping (possibly from *Huron Daily Plainsman*), Folder 1, Box 6, MA 9, Reifel Papers.

76. Young, "'Hero' Reifel Buried."

77. Trahant, "Reifel Proved Indian, White Cultures."

78. Young, "'Hero' Reifel Buried."

79. Patty Beutler, "Indians Advised Think Success," *Lincoln* (Neb.) *Star*, 9 Apr. 1982.

80. Raasch, "Reifel: He Has the Best of Both Cultures."

BIBLIOGRAPHY

MANUSCRIPT COLLECTIONS AND GOVERNMENT DOCUMENTS

Archives of the State Historical Society of North Dakota, Bismarck.
  Ben Reifel Papers.
  Oral Histories, Garrison Dam Relocation.
Center for Western Studies, Augustana University, Sioux Falls, S.Dak.
  Episcopal Diocese of South Dakota Archives.
Dakota Wesleyan University Archives, Mitchell, S.Dak.
  Jennewein Files.
Karl E. Mundt Archives, Dakota State University, Madison, S.Dak.
  Record Group I.
  Record Group III.
  Record Group XIII.
National Archives and Records Administration, Kansas City, Mo.
  Record Group 75, Records of the Bureau of Indian Affairs.
    Aberdeen Area Office.
      Area Staff Officers Reports.
      Cheyenne River Agency–Sisseton Agency.
      Correspondence Files, 1950–1957.
      Fort Berthold Agency.
      Unnumbered Memorandums, 1950–1956.
    Legislation, Wheeler-Howard Act.
    Pine Ridge Agency General Records.
North Dakota State Library, Bismarck.
  Fort Berthold Agency News Bulletin Collection.
South Dakota State Historical Society Archives, Pierre.
  Ben Reifel Biography File.
South Dakota State University Archives, Brookings.
  Benjamin Reifel Papers.
University of South Dakota Archives and Special Collections, Vermillion.
  Archie M. Gubbrud Papers.
  John S. Painter Papers.
    Ben Reifel Interviews.
  Oscar Howe Papers.
  Wayne S. Knutson Papers.

U.S. Commission on Civil Rights. The National Conference and the Reports of the State Advisory Committees to the U.S. Commission on Civil Rights, 1959. Washington, D.C.: U.S. Government Printing Office, 1960.

U.S. Congress. Congressional Record, 1956, 1961–1966.

———. House of Representatives. Committee on Appropriations. Department of the Interior and Related Agencies Appropriations for 1964: Hearings before the Subcommittee on Department of the Interior and Related Agencies. 88th Cong., 1st sess., 1963.

———. House of Representatives. Committee on Rules. To Prescribe Penalties for Certain Acts of Violence or Intimidation: Hearings before the Committee on Rules on H. Res. 1100. 90th Cong., 2nd sess., 1968.

———. Senate. Committee on Interior and Insular Affairs. Hearing on the Nomination of Robert LaFollette Bennett, of Alaska, to be Commissioner of Indian Affairs. 89th Cong., 2nd sess., 1966.

U.S. Department of Agriculture. Extension Service. A Report on the National Seminar of American Indian Women, Aug. 2–8, 1970, Colorado State University, Fort Collins, Colorado. 1970.

U.S. Department of the Interior. Bureau of Indian Affairs. The Resources, People and Administration of Fort Berthold Reservation North Dakota. Missouri River Basin Investigations Report No. 60, 24 Aug. 1948.

———. Attitudes of the Fort Berthold Indians Regarding Removal From the Garrison Reservoir Site and Future Administration of Their Reservation. Missouri River Basin Investigations Report No. 69, 30 Nov. 1948.

U.S. Reports, 1903.

U.S. Statutes at Large, 1887.

NEWSPAPERS, NEWS BULLETINS, AND NEWS SHEETS

Aberdeen American-News, 1957–72

Aberdeen Area Office Bulletin (Bureau of Indian Affairs), 1957

Asheville (NC) *Citizen*, 1979

Bismarck Tribune, 1953

Deadwood Pioneer Times, 1955

Deseret News (Salt Lake City), 1960

Fargo Forum, 1953

Fort Berthold Agency (N.Dak.) *News Bulletin*, 1953–54

Huron (S.Dak.) *Daily Plainsman*, 1961–68

Ikhana Newsletter (National Committee on Indian Work of the Episcopal Church), 1987

Indians at Work (Bureau of Indian Affairs), 1933–42

Knoxville News-Sentinel, 1960

Lincoln (Neb.) *Star*, 1982
Minneapolis Sunday Tribune, 1956, 1960
Minot (N.Dak.) *News*, 1954
Mitchell (S.Dak.) *Daily Republic*, 1960–70
Moody County (S.Dak.) *Enterprise*, 1935
National Park Courier, 1971
Norfolk (Neb.) *Daily News*, 1957
Oakland Tribune, 1954
Omaha World-Herald, 1970–71
Phreno Cosmian (Dakota Wesleyan University), 1962, 1965
Pierre Capital Journal, 1963, 1990
Pine Ridge, 1955
Rapid City Journal, 1954–55, 1972
Reifel Shots (Office of U.S. Representative Ben Reifel), 1963
Rosebud Sioux Herald, 1965
San Francisco Chronicle, 1960
Seattle Times, 1954
Sioux Falls Argus Leader, 1963–2015
Sisseton (S.Dak.) *Courier*, 1958–68
South Dakota Art Museum News, 1989–90
South Dakota Republican News, 1960
South Dakota Union Farmer, 1964
Toledo Blade, 1964
Wall Street Journal, 2015–16
Washington Post, 1960, 1973, 2008
Your Washington and You! (Office of U.S. Senator Karl Mundt), 1963–64

PUBLISHED SOURCES, THESES, AND DISSERTATIONS

Ambrose, Stephen E. *Eisenhower*. Vol. 2, *The President*. New York: Simon and Schuster, 1984.

———. *Nixon*. Vol. 1, *The Education of a Politician, 1913–1962*. New York: Simon and Schuster, 1987.

Anderson, John A., Henry W. Hamilton, and Jean Tyree Hamilton. *The Sioux of the Rosebud: A History in Pictures*. Norman: University of Oklahoma Press, 1971.

Andersson, Rani-Henrik. *The Lakota Ghost Dance of 1890*. Lincoln: University of Nebraska Press, 2008.

Bangsund, Dean, and F. Larry Leistritz. *Economic Contributions of the Sugarbeet Industry in Minnesota, North Dakota, and Eastern Montana*. Fargo: North Dakota State University, 2004.

Bartlett, Bruce. "50 Years After the House Vote for the Kennedy Tax Cut." *New York Times*, 24 Sep. 2013. http://www.economix.blogs.nytimes.com/2013/09/24/50-years-after-the-house-vote-for-the-kennedy-tax-cut/?_r=0.

Biolsi, Thomas. *Organizing the Lakota: The Political Economy of the New Deal on the Pine Ridge and Rosebud Reservations*. Tucson: University of Arizona Press, 1992.

Black, John D. "Higher Education for Farm Counselors: Need to 'Keep on Learning' Urged on the People of Today." *Christian Science Monitor*, 15 July 1950.

Brownson, Charles B., comp. and ed. *Congressional Staff Directory, 1962: Staff Biographies*. Washington, D.C.: Congressional Staff Directory, 1962.

Carlson, Paul H. *The Plains Indians*. College Station: Texas A&M University Press, 1998.

Cash, Joseph H. *The Sioux People*. Phoenix: Indian Tribal Series, 1971.

Cash, Joseph H., and Herbert T. Hoover. "Relocation, Past and Present: A History of Moving Indians." In *Rosebud to Dallas: The Reservation Indian Relocates to the Urban Environment*. Dallas: Southern Resource Center, 1978.

Castille, George Pierre. *To Show Heart: Native American Self-Determination and Federal Indian Policy, 1960–1975*. Tucson: University of Arizona Press, 1998.

Clarkin, Thomas. *Federal Indian Policy in the Kennedy and Johnson Administrations, 1961–1969*. Albuquerque: University of New Mexico Press, 2001.

Clem, Alan C. "National Convention Impact on Small State Politics: South Dakota Republicans in San Francisco, 1964." *South Dakota History* 2 (Spring 1971): 101–18.

———. *The Nomination of Joe Bottum: Analysis of a Committee Decision to Nominate a United States Senator*. Vermillion, S.Dak.: Government Research Bureau, 1963.

———. *Prairie State Politics: Popular Democracy in South Dakota*. Washington, D.C.: Public Affairs Press, 1967.

———. "South Dakota." In *Explaining the Vote: Presidential Choices in the Nation and the States, 1968*. Part 2, *Presidential Choices in Individual States*, edited by David M. Kovenock and James W. Prothro. Chapel Hill: University of North Carolina Press, 1973.

Clow, Richmond L. "State Jurisdiction on Sioux Reservations: Indian and Non-Indian Responses, 1952–1964." *South Dakota History* 11 (Summer 1981): 171–84.

Connell Szasz, Margaret. *Education and the American Indian: The Road to Self-Determination Since 1928*. 3rd ed. Albuquerque: University of New Mexico Press, 1999.

Daniels, Robert E. "Cultural Identities among the Oglala Sioux." In *The Modern Sioux: Social Systems and Reservation Culture*, edited by Ethel Nurge, pp. 198–245. Lincoln: University of Nebraska Press, 1970.

Deloria, Vine, Jr., and Clifford M. Lytle. *American Indians, American Justice*. Austin: University of Texas Press, 1983.

Denney, James. "South Dakota's Ben Reifel: That 'Poor Indian Boy' in Congress." *Sunday Omaha World-Herald Magazine of the Midlands*, 5 Apr. 1970: 6–7.

Eisenhower, Dwight D. *Mandate for Change*. Vol. 1, *The White House Years, 1953–1956*. Garden City, N.Y.: Doubleday, 1963.

Fielder, Mildred. *Sioux Indian Leaders*. New York: Bonanza Books, 1975.

545th Military Police Company Association. "Fort Chaffee." http://www.545thmpassn.com/FtChaffey.htm.

Fixico, Donald L. *American Indians in a Modern World*. Lanham, Md.: AltaMira Press, 2008.

———. *Termination and Relocation: Federal Indian Policy, 1945–1960*. Albuquerque: University of New Mexico Press, 1986.

Flynn, Sean J. "Bicultural Conservatism: Native American Congressman Ben Reifel and the GOP." In *The Plains Political Tradition: Essays on South Dakota Political Culture*, vol. 2, edited by Jon K. Lauck, John E. Miller, and Donald C. Simmons Jr., pp. 179–208. Pierre: South Dakota Historical Society Press, 2014.

———. "Western Assimilationist: Charles H. Burke and the Burke Act." Master's thesis, Texas Tech University, 1988.

Frank, Jeffrey. *Ike and Dick: Portrait of a Strange Political Marriage*. New York: Simon and Schuster, 2013.

Fuchs, Estelle, and Robert J. Havighurst. *To Live on This Earth: American Indian Education*. Garden City, N.Y.: Anchor Books, 1973.

Gailmard, Sam, and John W. Patty. *Learning while Governing: Expertise and Accountability in the Executive Branch*. Chicago: University of Chicago Press, 2013.

Garment, Leonard. *Crazy Rhythm: My Journey from Brooklyn, Jazz, and Wall Street to Nixon's White House, Watergate, and Beyond*. New York: Times Books, 1997.

Getches, David H., Daniel M. Rosenfelt, and Charles F. Wilkinson. *Cases and Materials on Federal Indian Law*. Saint Paul, Minn.: West Publishing, 1979.

Gibbon, Guy. *The Sioux: The Dakota and Lakota Nations*. Malden, Mass.: Blackwell, 2003.

Glover, John Henry. *Tribal Sovereigns of South Dakota: A Description of Contemporary Sioux Governments*. Rapid City, S.Dak.: Chiesman Foundation for Democracy, 2005.

Gould, Lewis H. *Grand Old Party: A History of the Republicans*. New York: Random House, 2003.

Hedren, Paul L. *After Custer: Loss and Transformation in Sioux Country*. Norman: University of Oklahoma Press, 2011.

Heppler, Jason A. "The American Indian Movement and South Dakota Politics." In *The Plains Political Tradition: Essays on South Dakota Political Culture*, vol. 1, edited by Jon K. Lauck, John E. Miller, and Donald C. Simmons Jr., pp. 267–87. Pierre: South Dakota Historical Society Press, 2011.

Holmes, Dennis R. "Political Rights under the Indian Civil Rights Act." *South Dakota Law Review* 24 (Spring 1979): 419–46.

Hoover, Herbert T., and Carol Goss Hoover. *Sioux Country: A History of Indian-White Relations*. Sioux Falls, S.Dak.: Center for Western Studies, Augustana College, 2000.

Hoxie, Frederick E. "From Prison to Homeland: The Cheyenne River Indian Reservation before WW I." *South Dakota History* 10 (Winter 1979): 1–24.

Hunhoff, Bernie. "Ben Reifel on Bridging the Cultural Gap." *South Dakota Magazine*, Jan.–Feb. 1989: 10–14.

Hyde, George E. *A Sioux Chronicle*. Norman: University of Oklahoma Press, 1956.

———. *Spotted Tail's Folk: A History of the Brulé Sioux*. Norman: University of Oklahoma Press, 1961.

Iverson, Peter, ed. *The Plains Indians of the Twentieth Century*. Norman: University of Oklahoma Press, 1985.

Johnson, Lyndon Baines. *The Vantage Point: Perspectives of the Presidency, 1963–1969*. New York: Holt, Rinehart and Winston, 1971.

Johnson, Rebecca L. *What It Took: A History of the USGS EROS Data Center*. Sioux Falls, S.Dak.: Center for Western Studies, Augustana College, 1998.

Karolevitz, Robert J. *With Faith, Hope and Tenacity: The First One Hundred Years of the Catholic Diocese of Sioux Falls, 1889–1989*. Mission Hill, S.Dak.: Dakota Homesteaders Publishers, 1989.

Kelly, Lawrence C. *The Assault on Assimilation: John Collier and the Origins of Indian Policy Reform*. Albuquerque: University of New Mexico Press, 1983.

———. *The Navajo Indians and Federal Indian Policy, 1900–1935*. Tucson: University of Arizona Press, 1968.

Kim, Joon. "The Political Economy of the Mexican Farm Labor Program, 1942–1964." *Aztlán* 29 (Fall 2004): 13–53.

Lauck, Jon K. "George S. McGovern and the Farmer: South Dakota Politics, 1953–1962." *South Dakota History* 32 (Winter 2002): 331–53.

Lawson, Michael L. *Dammed Indians Revisited: The Continuing History of the Pick-Sloan Plan and the Missouri River Sioux*. Pierre: South Dakota State Historical Society Press, 2009.

Lovrich, Frank. "The Assimilation of the Indian in Rapid City." Master's thesis, University of South Dakota, 1951.

Lutey, Tom. "Schools on Montana Indian Reservations Face Teacher Shortages." *Missoulian*, 5 July 2014. http://missoulian.com/news/local/schools-on-montana-indian-reservations-face-teachers-shortages/article_79623044-03c6-11a4-b8a7-0019bb2963f4.html.

Malinowski, Sharon, ed. *Notable Native Americans*. New York: Gale Research, 1999.

Mason, Robert. *Richard Nixon and the Quest for a New Majority*. Chapel Hill: University of North Carolina Press, 2004.

Matusow, Allen J. *The Unraveling of America: A History of Liberalism in the 1960s*. New York: Harper and Row, 1984.

McCool, Daniel. “Indian Voting.” In *American Indian Policy in the Twentieth Century*, edited by Vine Deloria Jr., pp. 105–33. Norman: University of Oklahoma Press, 1985.

Meriam, Lewis. “Indian Education Moves Ahead.” *The Survey* 66 (1 June 1931): 254–55.

Meyer, Roy W. “Fort Berthold and the Garrison Dam.” *North Dakota History* 35 (Summer/Fall 1968): 217–355.

———. *The Village Indians of the Upper Missouri: The Mandans, Hidatsas, and Arikaras*. Lincoln: University of Nebraska Press, 1977.

Middendorf, J. William, II. *A Glorious Disaster: Barry Goldwater's Presidential Campaign and the Origins of the Conservative Movement*. New York: Basic Books, 2006.

Miller, John E. *South Dakota State University: A Pictorial History, 1881–2006*. Virginia Beach, Va.: Donning, 2005.

Miller, Mark Edwin. *Forgotten Tribes: Unrecognized Indians and the Federal Acknowledgment Process*. Lincoln: University of Nebraska Press, 2004.

Minutes of the Plains Congress. Lawrence, Kans.: Haskell Institute, 1934.

Nabokov, Peter, ed. *Native American Testimony: A Chronicle of Indian-White Relations from Prophecy to the Present, 1492–1992*. New York: Viking, 1991.

Nash, Gerald D. *The American West Transformed: The Impact of the Second World War*. Lincoln: University of Nebraska Press, 1985.

National Capital Planning Commission. “About Us—National Capital Planning Commission.” http://www.ncpc.gov/ncpc/Main(T2)/About_Us(tr2)/AboutUs.html.

Otis, D. S. *The Dawes Act and the Allotment of Indian Lands*. Edited by Francis Paul Prucha. Norman: University of Oklahoma Press, 1973.

Painter, John S. “Congressional Conservatism and Federal Indian Policy, 1928–1950.” Paper presented at the annual meeting of the Organization of American Historians, Detroit, 2 Apr. 1981.

———. “Transitional Sioux Leader: Benjamin Reifel.” In *South Dakota Leaders, From Pierre Chouteau, Jr., to Oscar Howe*, edited by Herbert T. Hoover and Larry J. Zimmerman, pp. 331–54. Vermillion: University of South Dakota Press, 1989.

Parmet, Herbert S. *Richard Nixon and His America*. New York: Konecky and Konecky, 1990.

Perrett, Geoffrey. *America in the Twenties: A History*. New York: Simon and Schuster, 1982.

Peterson, Helen L. "American Indian Political Participation." *Annals of the American Academy of Political and Social Science* 311 (May 1957): 116–26.

Philp, Kenneth R., ed. *Indian Self-Rule: First-Hand Accounts of Indian-White Relations from Roosevelt to Reagan*. Logan: Utah State University Press, 1995.

———. "John Collier, 1933–1945." In *The Commissioners of Indian Affairs, 1824–1977*, edited by Robert M. Kvasnicka and Herman J. Viola, pp. 273–82. Lincoln: University of Nebraska Press, 1979.

———. *John Collier's Crusade for Indian Reform, 1920–1954*. Tucson: University of Arizona Press, 1977.

———. *Termination Revisited: American Indians on the Trail of Self-Determination, 1933–1953*. Lincoln: University of Nebraska Press, 1999.

Pommersheim, Frank. *Broken Landscape: Indians, Indian Tribes, and the Constitution*. New York: Oxford University Press, 2009.

Prucha, Francis Paul. *The Great Father: The United States Government and the American Indian*. Vol. 2. Lincoln: University of Nebraska Press, 1984.

Pusey, Merlo J. *Eisenhower the President*. New York: Macmillan, 1956.

Reichley, A. James. *Conservatives in an Age of Change: The Nixon and Ford Administrations*. Washington, D.C.: Brookings Institute, 1981.

Reifel, Ben. "Cultural Factors in Social Adjustment." *Indian Education*, 15 Apr. 1957: 1–10.

———. "The Problem of Relocating Families on the Fort Berthold Reservation." *Journal of Farm Economics* 32 (Nov. 1950): 644–46.

———. "Relocation on the Fort Berthold Indian Reservation: Problems and Programs." Ph.D. dissertation, Harvard University, 1952.

"Reifel Honored with First Award." *Humanities* 5 (Oct. 1976): 3.

Reinhardt, Akim D. *Ruling Pine Ridge: Oglala Lakota Politics from the IRA to Wounded Knee*. Lubbock: Texas Tech University Press, 2007.

Ryan, W. Carson, Jr. "Federal-State Cooperation in Indian Education." *School and Society* 34 (26 Sep. 1931): 418–23.

Schell, Herbert S. *History of South Dakota*. Lincoln: University of Nebraska Press, 1961.

Schulte, Steven C. "Removing the Yoke of Government: E. Y. Berry and the Origins of Indian Termination Policy." *South Dakota History* 14 (Spring 1984): 48–67.

Schusky, Ernest L. *The Forgotten Sioux: An Ethnohistory of the Lower Brule Reservation*. Chicago: Nelson-Hall, 1975.

"Sioux Wins Achievement Award." *Amerindian American Indian Review* 9 (Sep.–Oct. 1960): 1–2.

Smith, Michael T. "Benjamin Reifel, 1976–1977." In *The Commissioners of Indian*

Affairs, 1824–1977, edited by Robert M. Kvasnicka and Herman J. Viola, pp. 347–48. Lincoln: University of Nebraska Press, 1979.
———. "The History of Indian Citizenship." In *The American Indian: Past and Present*, 3rd ed., edited by Roger L. Nichols, pp. 232–41. New York: Alfred A. Knopf, 1986.
———. "Morris Thompson, 1973–1976." In *The Commissioners of Indian Affairs, 1824–1977*, edited by Robert M. Kvasnicka and Herman J. Viola, pp. 341–46. Lincoln: University of Nebraska Press, 1979.
"Societies and Meetings: Educational Conference of Indian Service Superintendents." *School and Society* 34 (5 Dec. 1931): 764–65.
Sorkin, Alan L. *American Indians and Federal Aid*. Washington, D.C.: Brookings Institution, 1971.
South Dakota Secretary of State. "Election History." https://sdsos.gov/elections-voting.
Speeches of Vice President Richard M. Nixon Presidential Campaign of 1960. Washington, D.C.: U.S. Government Printing Office, 1961.
Standing Bear, Luther. *Land of the Spotted Eagle*. Boston: Houghton Mifflin, 1933.
Tanner, Daniel, and Laurel N. Tanner. *Curriculum Development: Theory into Practice*. New York: Macmillan, 1975.
Taylor, Graham D. *The New Deal and American Indian Tribalism: The Administration of the Indian Reorganization Act, 1934–45*. Lincoln: University of Nebraska Press, 1980.
Thompson, Harry F., ed. *A New South Dakota History*. Sioux Falls, S.Dak.: Center for Western Studies, Augustana College, 2005.
Tyler, S. Lyman. *A History of Indian Policy*. Washington, D.C.: U.S. Department of the Interior, Bureau of Indian Affairs, 1973.
Utley, Robert M. *The Indian Frontier of the American West, 1846–1890*. Albuquerque: University of New Mexico Press, 1984.
———. *The Lance and the Shield: The Life and Times of Sitting Bull*. New York: Ballantine Books, 1993.
———. *The Last Days of the Sioux Nation*. New Haven: Yale University Press, 1963.
Valandra, Edward Charles. *Not without Our Consent: Lakota Resistance to Termination, 1950–59*. Urbana: University of Illinois Press, 2006.
VanDevelder, Paul. *Coyote Warrior: One Man, Three Tribes, and the Trial that Forged a Nation*. Lincoln: University of Nebraska Press, 2004.
Wagner, Steven. *Eisenhower Republicanism: Pursuing the Middle Way*. DeKalb: Northern Illinois University Press, 2006.
Waterbuster, DVD film. Directed by J. Carlos Peinado. New York: Brave Boat Productions, 2006.
White, Theodore H. *The Making of the President, 1960*. New York: Atheneum, 1961.

———. *The Making of the President, 1968*. New York: Pocket Books, 1970.

Wicker, Tom. *One of Us: Richard Nixon and the American Dream*. New York: Random House, 1991.

Wilkinson, Charles. *Blood Struggle: The Rise of Modern Indian Nations*. New York: Norton, 2005.

Will, George F. "On the Road to Civilization: A Visit to the Fort Berthold Reservation." *North Dakota History* 15 (Jan. 1948): 5–13.

Wright, Robert K., Jr. *Military Police*. Washington, D.C.: United States Army Center of Military History, 1992.

Zaferatos, Nicholas Christos. *Planning the American Indian Reservation: From Theory to Empowerment*. Syracuse: Syracuse University Press, 2015.

INDEX

Abbreviations "BIA," "BR," and "IRA" stand for Bureau of Indian Affairs, Benjamin Reifel, and Indian Reorganization Act, respectively. Page numbers for photographs are identified by the suffix "p" (e.g. 176p).